WHO SAVED THE REDWOODS?

WHO SAVED
THE REDWOODS?

THE UNSUNG HEROINES OF THE 1920s
WHO FOUGHT FOR OUR REDWOOD FORESTS

by Laura and James Wasserman

To our friend Terri and to the redwoods. Thank you for your interest and support.

Best Wishes

Laura Wasserman

James Wasserman

Algora Publishing
New York

Library of Congress Cataloging in Publication Control Number: 2018055728

Names: Wasserman, Laura, 1950- author. | Wasserman, James, 1952- author.
Title: Who saved the redwoods?: the unsung heroines of the 1920s who fought
    for our redwood forests / by Laura and James Wasserman.
Description: New York: Algora Publishing, [2019] | Includes bibliographical
    references and index.
Identifiers: LCCN 2018061466 (print) | LCCN 2019002131 (ebook) | ISBN
    9781628943757 (pdf) | ISBN 9781628943740 (soft cover: alk. paper)
Subjects: LCSH: Redwoods—California—Humboldt   County—History—20th
century.
    | Women in forestry—California—History—20th century. | Forest
    conservation—California—History—20th century.
Classification: LCC SD397.R3 (ebook) | LCC SD397.R3 W37 2019 (print) | DDC
    634.9/7580979412—dc23
LC record available at https://lccn.loc.gov/2018061466

Printed in the United States

To the great women and men, most long forgotten, who saved the redwoods

Table of Contents

PROLOGUE   1

INTRODUCTION: 160 MILLION YEARS AND COUNTING   3

CHAPTER ONE: THE LOSS OF CARSON WOODS, 1913–1918   9
     A Noble Idea Takes Form   13
     The Nation Should Not Permit This Destruction   18
     The Prickly Congressional Politics of No   23
     Keeping Faith in Themselves   25
     An Avenue Opens   27
     Lost Forever to the World   29

CHAPTER TWO: FIRST ENCOUNTERS WITH SUCCESS, 1919–1921   31
     To Save 20,000 Acres   35
     "Joan of Arc" of the Redwoods   38
     Initial Donations of Land and Money   39
     The Pen Is Mightier Than the Ax   41
     A Turn Toward the State of California   46
     In Honor Of The Dearly Departed   51

CHAPTER THREE: THE ULTIMATE PRIZE, 1922–1923   55
     The Timber Industry's Public Relations Problem   60
     An Awakening of Spirit   65
     Conservation, The Hope of Civilization   67
     In Memory of the Humboldt Pioneers   71
     Enter the Garden Club of America   74

MAPS AND ILLUSTRATIONS   77

CHAPTER FOUR: SHOWDOWN IN THE FOREST, 1924–1925   87
> *Monument to a Founder*   92
> *A Profound Act of Civil Disobedience*   94
> *Preserve the Redwoods to Preserve Our Prosperity*   99
> *One Million Dollars from the Rockefeller Fortune*   103
> *One Hundred Dollars Buys a Tree*   109

CHAPTER FIVE: OUTSIDE INFLUENCES, 1926–1930   113
> *The State Parks Movement Opens a Door*   116
> *A Free Inheritance from Past Ages*   121
> *The New Problem of Tourism*   123
> *A Who's Who of the Social Register Fortunes*   125
> *The Garden Club of America Redwoods*   132

CHAPTER SIX: CELEBRATING SUCCESS, 1931–1934   137
> *The World's Greatest Redwood Forests Are Saved*   139
> *Silence in the Children's Forest*   145
> *A Retrospective*   147
> *To the Women of California*   149
> *Fortunes of the Gold Rush*   152
> *The Grandest of All Wonders*   155

AFTERWORD   161

EPILOGUE   167

ACKNOWLEDGEMENTS   171

APPENDIX A: CHARTER MEMBER CLUBS OF THE HUMBOLDT COUNTY
   FEDERATION OF WOMEN'S CLUBS   173

APPENDIX B: PRESERVE AN AMERICA WORTH FIGHTING FOR   175

APPENDIX C: THE GARDEN CLUB OF AMERICA'S REDWOOD GROVE   179

APPENDIX D: WILD FLOWERS IN THE GARDEN CLUB OF AMERICA GROVE   185

ENDNOTES   189
> Introduction: 160 Million Years and Counting   189
> Chapter One: The Loss of Carson Woods, 1913–1918   190
> Chapter Two: First Encounters With Success, 1919–1921   194
> Chapter Three: The Ultimate Prize, 1922–1923   197
> Chapter Four: Showdown In The Forest, 1924–1925   200
> Chapter Five: Outside Influences, 1926–1930   202
> Chapter Six: Celebrating Success, 1931–1934   205
> Afterword   208
> Epilogue   210

Appendix A 211
Appendix B 211

BIBLIOGRAPHY 213
Books 213
Academic Works and Papers 215
Oral Histories 216
Periodicals 216
Government Documents 217
California Federation of Women's Clubs Documents 217
Humboldt County Women's Save the Redwoods League Documents 217
Save the Redwoods League Documents 217

INDEX 219

PROLOGUE

For countless millions of years before the rise of human beings, the redwoods inhabited large swaths of the earth. In our own time, when they had retreated to 2 million acres on the coast of California, it took barely more than a century for American lumbermen to eliminate nearly all the incomparable old forests.

Yet as the logging crews raced ever faster throughout Northern California, and especially through Humboldt County's great redwood belt, there came a moment, a few breathtaking years beginning in 1919, when people with vision in California and the nation, mostly the unheralded women and men you are about to meet, said, simply, and forcefully, "Enough."

History would show that they were not able to stop the destruction of these magnificent redwoods. Today only five percent of the original California redwood forest remains. Yet in their time, they did save millions of the old-growth giants which still beckon visitors throughout the world. This is how a great environmental movement began.

Introduction: 160 Million Years And Counting

"Nothing can exaggerate the wild beauties of this coast. Its mountains rising and magnificent amphitheaters covered with evergreen forests, with here and there verdant plain near the shore and a snowcapped mountain in the background, offered a view grand and sublime in the highest degree. Here nature reigned undisturbed."

— American Sea Captain William Shaler, offshore Humboldt County, California, in the *Delia Byrd*. May 1804.

Rising in majestic cathedral groves to soaring heights over Northern California and Southwest Oregon, earth's last great coastal redwoods stand as survivors of ancient climate changes, ice ages, fires, and modern industrial lumbering. Descendants of ancestor redwood species that covered North America and much of the world 160 million years ago, their family history impressively surpasses the brief 2.5-million-year story of humankind. Yet as human species vanished and *homo sapiens* alone triumphed to inhabit the earth, so did many redwood species fail to survive prolonged ages of global cooling and drying. As the ancient redwood belts slowly retreated from their bold advances upon the earth, their dwindling species drifted imperceptibly through eons toward cool, moist air on the west coast of North America.[1]

Ceaseless evolution provided the coastal redwood with an outer bark resistant to fire, as well as an inner wood resistant to disease. Redwoods consequently live up to 2,000 years as one of earth's fastest-growing plants. Secure now for 20 million years on a rugged, isolated, and indelibly beautiful sliver of coastal shelf five to twenty-five miles wide and 450 miles long, accustomed to altitudes of 2,000 to 5,000 feet that protect them from heat and provide the cool temperatures of fog, the noble coast redwood flourishes, among the last of its kind.[2]

Native Americans are the first recorded people to enter the 2 million acres of California redwoods that begin in river canyons of the Santa Lucia Mountains in Monterey County and grow larger in height and diameter as groves edge northward through the Santa Cruz Mountains and San Francisco Bay, then the counties of Mendocino, Humboldt, and Del Norte.

At least twelve Native American groups lived in proximity to these California forests and seven groups held ancestral land in the northern redwoods that included Humboldt and Del Norte counties. Among them were Athabascan groups that had lived there for centuries.[3] Collectively, they experienced one of the planet's oldest forests, treading lightly as the first caretakers of fir, hemlock, spruce, and redwoods that rose 300 feet from bases twenty feet thick. Trails leading into or through these wild coastal forests were few. Travel was slow through a thick understory of berries, brushes, ferns, and fallen trees, and few game animals lived inside. The Native Americans occasionally ventured into the forests, but they did not live in them and kept their visits short.

Native Americans in Northern California tapped the forests for limited personal needs, building canoes and lodges from fallen redwoods. They also felled redwoods when necessary, using burning stones to cut through the tall trees. Using a burn-and-scrape technique with hot stones and elk horns, they split the logs into sections and then planks.[4] Across the range of 2 million acres, the impacts of these limited uses would have been unnoticeable. The redwoods' first human caretakers left the forest much as they found it.

By the 1700s a newly aggressive and advancing global civilization discovered the tall trees. In 1769, Spanish explorer Gaspar de Portolá recorded sightings of "Palo Colorado" (red trees) in the Santa Cruz Mountains during a futile overland search for Monterey Bay. Soon after in 1775, the Spanish ships *Santiago and Sonora*, piloted by Captain Bruno de Heceta and Lieutenant Juan Francisco de la Bodega y Quadra, discovered and claimed for Spain a redwood-lined Northern California bay they named "Puerto de la Trinidad" (Humboldt County's Trinidad Bay). Next came the English, in 1793. Captain George Vancouver, sailing from the Hawaiian Islands on a mission to chart the Pacific West Coast, also sailed his ship *Discovery* into forested Trinidad Bay. The Americans followed. Connecticut's Captain William Shaler sailed the redwood coast in 1804 with Vancouver's maps and provided a captivating description to a young nation consumed with expanding to the Pacific:

> Nothing can exaggerate the wild beauties of this coast. Its mountains rising and magnificent amphitheaters covered with evergreen forests, with here and there verdant plain near the shore and a snowcapped

mountain in the background, offered a view grand and sublime in the highest degree. Here nature reigned undisturbed.[5]

The Europeans and Americans initially viewed the redwoods as a species of juniper, cypress, pine, fir, or perhaps giant cedar. Czech botanist Tadeas Haenke, a member of royal Spain's five-year global Malaspina scientific exploration, formally collected the first redwood specimen near Monterey during the expedition's 1791 Survey of the Pacific. Not until 1824 did Scottish botanist David Don give the coastal redwoods the name *Taxodium sempervirens* (evergreens). Austrian botanist and philosopher Stephen Endlicke in 1847 added the genus name of *Sequoia*, a likely reference to the Eastern United States Cherokee Chief Sequoyah.[6]

For countless centuries the only humans to have any impact on the great forests were the Native American tribes, small trading colonies, and explorers. But the quiet of the redwood forests was on the eve of dramatic change. As the pace of Western exploration and settlement accelerated, Jedediah Strong Smith, the first American to visit the redwoods on foot, journeyed through what is now Humboldt and Del Norte counties in 1828 with a party of nineteen men and more than 250 horses and mules.[7] Expedition journals describe a harsh passage through endless "underbrush, hazle, oak, briars, currents, gooseberry, and Scotch cap bushes, together with aldar, and sundry other shrubs too tedious to mention. The soil of the country [is] rich and black, but very mountainous, which renders travelling almost impassible with so many horses as we have got."[8]

Within twenty years of Smith's exploration, the United States gained control of California through the 1848 Treaty of Guadalupe Hidalgo, which ended the Mexican–American War and opened the way for statehood in 1850.[9] Simultaneously in 1848 James Marshall discovered gold near Sacramento. A frenzied global rush of fortune seeking quickly erupted, introducing a devastating plundering mentality to California that would last for decades and instantly gauge the commercial potential of the new state's seemingly inexhaustible redwood forests. Adding to the speculative fever, American sailors in 1850 discovered the location of Humboldt Bay, which opened Northern California's redwood country to settlement and logging.

It was the Americans who brought large-scale commercial logging into the redwoods. They set the stage for the redwoods' rapid destruction with a massive and often-fraudulent transfer of public land to private interests that nearly ruined chances in the future of preserving the forests for public enjoyment. Between 1870 and 1890 2 million acres of California redwoods passed from the federal public domain into private hands, an audacious land grab accomplished by abusing the intent of federal land acquisition laws. A generation later when the national parks movement began to carve magnificent landscapes from the public domain into protected areas the federal government faced an impossible challenge with the privatized redwood forests. It couldn't afford to buy back what it had sold to speculators for so little.

The earliest Californians took immediate advantage of federal land purchase laws upon statehood in 1850, fraudulently logging and abandoning redwood acreage meant to help settlers build a new life in the West. The pattern then ceaselessly repeated itself in five widespread episodes of fraud against the state and federal government until all the redwoods disappeared into the hands of investors.

In the first of these unfortunate chapters, the federal government, through the national Preemption Act of 1841, gifted 500,000 acres of public land to its new state of California. The state, in turn, sold the acreage to finance its earliest infrastructure and internal improvements. Settlers could claim this land by squatting on a parcel for two years, then filing a claim and making a payment to the state. In the redwoods region many simply logged their parcels and left them before making a formal claim. The federal government also gifted the new State of California thousands of acres of swamplands it could sell to finance public improvements. Surveyors then falsely classified the redwood belt's many marshlands and their surrounding redwood forests as swamplands, which transferred more of the giant trees to speculators.[10]

The Federal Act of 1853 provided California still more land grants, the sixteenth and thirty-sixth sections of each township to sell off and finance public schools, as well as seventy-two township sections statewide to finance a public university. Again, in the redwoods region, businessmen made down payments on these sections, logged them, and forfeited their claims to avoid full payment and taxes. The 1862 Homestead Act followed in the interests of settling the Plains and the West, allowing settlers to claim 160 acres at $1.25 per acre on the condition that they first occupy the land for six months. Unscrupulous opportunists twisted the intent of that law, as well, making multiple claims and constructing small buildings on each of their homesteaded parcels to cheaply claim large acreages of redwood forests.[11]

Congress, exasperated by widespread fraud associated with the Homestead Act, passed The Timber and Stone Act in 1878. The Act provided a new legal means for settlers to buy and log up to 160 acres of Western timberlands for $2.50 per acre. But fraud again ruled the day. Investors, who now paid idlers, itinerant sailors, and others known as "dummies" to file individual claims on their behalf and then sign them over for a fee, again consolidated large tracts of forestland.[12]

By 1890 private interests owned nearly all the redwoods in California and among them, monopolies controlled the prime of the redwood belt. The California Redwood Company, largely owned by Scottish investors, held 65,000 acres of redwoods in Humboldt and Del Norte counties. Eventually, public outrage over the company's foreign ownership led the federal courts to pursue fraud convictions and strip the offshore investors of their holdings in the redwoods. But the courts couldn't save the trees. The remaining American investors, before dissolving the company in 1886, logged much of its redwood acreage.[13]

In the years just before 1900 land speculators throughout Northern California's redwood belt finally found the payoffs they had awaited. They transferred the bulk of their often fraudulently-obtained redwood acreage to the nation's newest class of willing buyers, the Eastern-financed timber companies seeking new virgin forests in the West. On the eve of World War I, and repeating a familiar pattern that had decimated the forests of the American East and South, thirty-three owners now held seventy-nine percent of the prime redwood timberland in California.

Although as much as 1.5 million acres of the original old-growth forest remained intact at the time, the worst destruction was just ahead, occurring during and after World War I amid increased demand of redwoods for grape stakes, residential construction, and railroad ties. Improved industrial-scale lumbering later in the century accelerated the pace of logging, as did a policy of California counties taxing standing trees instead of cut lumber. Forest owners had powerful financial incentives to rapidly log the ancient giants for lumber widely then viewed as beautiful, fire resistant, convenient, and cheap. Within eighty years they would nearly log it all, leaving approximately five percent of the original old-growth forest.[14]

Yet amid the powerful industrial-scale destruction of California's redwood treasures a bold conservation movement also took deeper root. As Northern Californians saw their beautiful forest surroundings logged and burned by large outside financial interests, they slowly began to envision an alternate, equally lucrative future of tourism. The sons and daughters of California's pioneer generation increasingly heard the voices of John Muir and others calling them toward reverence and preservation of natural beauty. Beyond California, a new conservation-minded president, Theodore Roosevelt, began to protect vulnerable landscapes in national forests and monuments, and set the stage for a new system of national parks.

Within this environmental awakening there also emerged a significant women's movement to preserve the redwoods. The Sempervirens Club, nurtured by a pair of women writers in the San Francisco Bay Area, formed in 1900 to protect significant redwood acreage in the Santa Cruz Mountains from lumbering. The California Federation of Women's Clubs also established itself in 1900 as a powerful grassroots political force sporting an agenda of forest conservation. Humboldt County women's club affiliates of the statewide federation soon launched their own campaign for a national redwood park. In the East, The Garden Club of America was on the verge of joining the fight after its 1913 formation. The national women's club would soon become a significant player in the movement to protect natural landscapes, and in the 1920s turn its attention to preserving the redwoods of California.[15]

Amidst such promptings, the nation's elite naturalists and scientists banded together in 1918 to form the San Francisco-based Save the Redwoods League to counter the powerful lumber industry. An organization linked to influential women's clubs and wealthy donors, the new national league took its name from the Sempervirens Club motto "Save the Redwoods." Collectively, a powerful network of local, state, and national citizens working with the Save the Redwoods League, prevented the total annihilation of California's redwood forests. The state and national redwood parks we visit today are monuments to their perseverance and vision.

Throughout, they believed that they saved these forests for unborn generations.

We are those unborn generations.

A century after the events described in this book, we drive in late autumn from Sacramento to Humboldt County to visit the last five percent of old-growth redwoods still standing. We are simply tourists like the millions of others who visit these lovely forests, standing spellbound in the cathedral groves of state and national parks. Walking among ferns, sorrel, and ancient redwood giants on a late afternoon, we discover the story of a woman, Laura Mahan, who stopped a Pacific Lumber Company logging crew on a day like this, exactly ninety years earlier, in November 1924.

We have no words for such beauty surrounding us here.

We have learned since, on the enquiry inspired by this visit, that we have many great women and men, most long forgotten now, to thank.

Here's to all of them. This is their inspiring story.

CHAPTER ONE: THE LOSS OF CARSON WOODS, 1913–1918

> "Are we not learning that it is better to conserve these things that we possess than to try and regain them after they are taken from us? Let us hope that the day of ruthless and unnecessary waste is nearing its close. That the California Federation of Women's Clubs shall unite in saying to the destroyers of our natural resources, 'Thus far shalt thou go — and no farther.'"
>
> —Anna L. Royles, State Forestry Chairman, California Federation of Women's Clubs, 1916.

Saturday, September 27, 1913, dawned beautifully across coastal Northern California. In Humboldt County, a cool, early morning grew by noon into a brilliance of blue skies and light ocean winds flowing across the mountainous, forested land. Just as organizers hoped. Picnic weather.

From Eureka, the county seat, a delegation of clubwomen traveled eighteen miles to Fortuna by train. Five men with automobiles then escorted them and others from nearby towns to Carson Woods, a large belt of redwoods on the edge of town. The forest, owned by a prominent Humboldt County timber company, was renowned locally for its location that protected it from high winds and shaped its pleasant open park-like scenery.

"Scarcely a fallen trunk is to be seen throughout the length and breadth of the entire fourteen hundred acres encompassing the tract," a hometown journalist penned in 1910.

Rising to the eloquence that has long stirred writers in the redwoods, the Fortuna reporter described a creek running through Carson Woods, Rohner Creek, "a beautiful little stream at this time of year, winding and twisting its way down to the river from the heights above. Cascades, waterfalls and deep, clear pools are to be seen in abundance, now running along in unabashed nakedness, and again hid by growing ferns and vines, broadening out several yards at some points, and at others, trickling through narrow spaces under logs washed down from above."[16]

At noon, women's club members representing eight Humboldt County towns walked into a forest clearing for coffee, lunch, and the purpose of their gathering, to advance local civic and business efforts to establish the nation's first redwood national park. It is pleasing a century later, when few remnants remain of the original great redwood forests of California, to imagine rows of picnic tables set among the beautiful green ferns, the informal elegance of clubwomen below the tall trees, and the loveliness of an early autumn afternoon near the Pacific Ocean.[17]

Today, ancient, primeval Carson Woods is no more than two words on old maps of Fortuna. The only suggestion of a vanished, logged, 1,400-acre redwood forest is a narrow, paved road bearing its name. Carson Woods Road meanders northeast out of Fortuna past the town's high school baseball fields, through a neighborhood where sheep graze behind fences and massive old redwood stumps still rise in back yards. There is no sense of what was lost, no marker honoring a local campaign that once envisioned a national park for the ages. Only the high, dark walls of second-growth redwoods offer their nod to memory, when a picnic in a forest soon to be destroyed demonstrated the foundational roles of women in the opening acts of a century-long fight to save the redwoods.

In introductory remarks, Mary Loveland of Ferndale, representing the host Ferndale Village Club, welcomed fellow county women's club members into the forest. Loveland, wife of a well-to-do businessman in the prosperous dairy community distinguished by its Victorian homes and architecture, undoubtedly reflected on rising distress locally over the fate of Humboldt County's redwoods.[18] Already, a voracious corporate lumber industry, meeting strong market demand for finished redwood products to build the state's growing cities, had leveled the great forests of the Santa Cruz mountains, San Francisco Bay Area, and Marin, Sonoma, and Mendocino counties. Now a lumber industry financed with Eastern capital and headquartered for the most part in Midwestern or Eastern states was reaching deep into the northernmost end of the California redwood belt. Of Humboldt County's stunning 500,000 acres of old-growth redwoods, the biggest and grandest of the giants growing in California, more than fifteen percent were already gone.[19]

It is easy to assume how these clubwomen, the cornerstones of their communities, may have felt and how it looked as they saw the waste and devastation so quickly widen around them. They had reasons to fear for the aesthetics of their towns and their businesses, and for the values of their properties, even if the economy rested so heavily on mills and logging. Similar, earlier rounds of redwoods clear-cutting in the Santa Cruz Mountains 350 miles to the south offered an awful vision of what might happen. A dozen years earlier, *The Boulder Creek Mountain Echo* had expressed local horror at the ruinous new state of the once-forested San Lorenzo Valley:

> Throughout its entire length of about ten miles the timber has been cut out and for the most part the denuded country presents a scene of utter desolation. Where only a few years ago stood a beautiful and almost unbroken primeval forest, the joy of the camper and the sportsman, there is now only a waste of brush land, fast becoming an almost impenetrable jungle. Private roads are being discontinued because there is no longer material to pass over them, and even the county roads are becoming impassable because the land has been rendered almost worthless for taxation, and there can be, as an inevitable consequence, but little public moneys available to repair them. In so far as business is concerned this valley is fast becoming a solitude and a cipher.[20]

Vida Lane of Ferndale, daughter of a prominent Humboldt County pioneer family and wife of the town doctor, rose from her table as Loveland finished her welcoming address. She set a mood of sentimental defiance to a lumber industry rapidly erasing her county's redwoods, reciting aloud a favorite old poem of forest conservationists at the time, George Pope Morris' *Woodman, Spare That Tree.*[21]

> Woodman, spare that tree.
> Touch not a single bough.
> In youth, it sheltered me.
> And I'll protect it now.
> 'Twas my forefather's hand
> That placed it near his cot
> There, woodman, let it stand,
> Thy axe shall harm it not!

On through the second, third, and final stanza Lane read, likely with the reverence of a prayer amidst the faint rustling of ocean breezes through the dark redwood canopy above.

> My heart-strings round thee cling
> Close as thy bark, old friend.
> Here shall the wild-bird sing
> And still thy branches bend.
> Old tree! The storm still brave!
> And, woodman leave the spot;

> While I've a hand to save,
> Thy axe shall harm it not.

This 1913 gathering of county clubwomen at Carson Woods, seen handily now through history's lens as a groundbreaking opening act to "a success that stands alone in the annals of conservation history," introduced local personalities who would become familiar in coming years as the fight to save Northern California redwoods grew ever more confrontational, then expanded into a statewide and national movement.[22]

In an isolated, mostly rural county of 34,000 people, they were wives of lawyers, landowners, judges, newspaper publishers, businessmen, even of redwood mill owners. Typically, they were the grown children of Gold Rush pioneers who came in ships or drove covered wagons to California and made good, often by assembling and clearing large tracts of land for dairies, farms, and lumbering operations.

They also belonged to a generation redefining ideals of progress and values beyond the plundering that had mostly befallen California since the Gold Rush.

Sixteen of them then from this generation, one by one, gave short talks about how a collective effort might spur the federal government to create its first redwood national park. Several men attending also spoke, among them two clergymen, a professor of agriculture, and a local authority on apple trees.

They all had ideas. Almost certainly the speakers agreed the endangered trees were too rare and important to let their fates be determined alone by local attitudes and finances. The redwoods were a national resource, an earthly treasure, and required higher authority and deeper pockets to save them. After hearing them all out, club members approved a resolution to appoint two women from each of the county's seventeen women's clubs to a redwood national park committee. In the words of the resolution the committee would "decide upon action to be taken to procure a redwood park in Humboldt County."

The next morning's *Humboldt Times* described the event for local readers, and eventually for historians examining the roots of creating Redwood National Park five decades later, under the headline, "Club Women Discuss Park in Redwoods." *The Humboldt Standard* followed a day later with its own story announcing that "Women's Clubs Are for Redwood Park." The Oregon-based *Timberman*, voice of the corporate lumber industry, and surprisingly, an early editorial supporter of redwoods preservation, also reported on the event. Some of the first national exposure for the Humboldt redwoods campaign came when the *Timberman* cited Carson Woods as the favored site for a redwood national park.

"Plans are being made to have John Muir, the naturalist, pay a visit to the county for the purpose of enlisting his support in the redwood park campaign," the industry journal reported.[23]

The encouragement was surely exhilarating.

A Noble Idea Takes Form

The women who gathered in their distant redwoods country in 1913, fresh from winning voting rights in California two years earlier, had every reason to believe they could work in the political arena and interact effectively with men's power structures to save the redwoods.

They had a background for the fight. During the earliest years of the 1900s, the cause of preserving forests to protect sources of fresh water ranked at the top of women's club agendas throughout California. Women could also see victories elsewhere in the state, where other communities had saved patches of their redwoods. And finally, it was an era when a conservation ethic rose to the forefront of American life, when presidents of the United States, particularly Theodore Roosevelt, aggressively preserved millions of acres of wild landscapes in national forests, parks, and monuments.

Among inspirational models beckoning Humboldt County women's clubs to save their redwoods was the powerhouse California Club of San Francisco, founded as a women's organization in 1897 and led by "brilliant, dynamic founder and president" Laura Lyon White.[24]

White's California Club won passage of a Congressional resolution in 1900, later signed by President William McKinley, to negotiate a federal purchase of 8,000 acres of Sierra Nevada Giant Sequoias known as the Calaveras Big Trees. For years afterward White and 500 members of her prestigious club repeatedly pressed Republican House Speaker "Uncle Joe" Joseph Cannon to allocate the agreed-upon $200,000 to buy the grove, a persistence that finally prompted a 1905 outburst from the speaker that the ladies could "go to hell."

White fired back at the "dour, thrice-vigilant Watchdog of the Treasury" with withering commentary in *The San Francisco Chronicle*:

"He laughed at all the influence we could bring to bear, including the personal visits of several of our ladies. For six years, he as chairman of the Claims Committee, has treated the matter as a joke ... These are twenty-two hundred acres of the most majestic trees in the world, lying in constant danger of being taken from us. Uncle Joe is the sole obstacle in the way of the efforts of the clubwomen of California to perpetuate these objects of beauty."[25]

The same Congressional reluctance would also confound the earliest efforts of women's clubs to save the Humboldt redwoods. White once remarked on the simplicity of women's lofty conservation and beautification goals in comparison to the complex, grandiose aims of men, saying, "The great problems of the world are so bewildering, the theories of great men are so puzzling ... I'd much rather confine myself to making the world more beautiful. The creation of a park or playground does as much good to the world as the study of a difficult problem."[26]

The California Club's campaign to win public ownership of the Calaveras groves remained unfulfilled at White's death in 1916. But the 3,000-year-old giants for which she provided the earliest institutional support eventually became in 1931, the 1,951-acre North Grove of Calaveras Big Trees State Park.[27]

More inspirational were Santa Cruz Mountains writers Carrie Stevens Walter and Josephine Clifford McCrackin, first to use the phrase, "Save the Redwoods." Through their newly formed Sempervirens Club, called later by historians "a rare instance for the time of a mixed association of men and women," they organized a movement to save the redwoods of the Santa Cruz Mountains in alliances with other prominent figures, including the presidents of Stanford University and Santa Clara College.[28]

Walter and McCrackin stand out in the history of redwoods preservation as California's first major media voices to rouse popular support for the old trees. Walter, in *The San Francisco Chronicle* in May 1900, offered the long view, writing prophetically, "Imagine a time in the not very remote future when the whole peninsula from San Francisco to San Jose shall become one great city; then picture at its very doorway, this magnificent domain of redwood forest and running streams, the breathing place of millions of cramped and crowded denizens of the city."

McCrackin followed with a fierce sense of urgency in the August 1900 *Overland Monthly*, a magazine published in California. "There are four sawmills at work over there now, eating their way into the heart of the timber — grinding, grinding, grinding, not slowly as do the mills of the gods, but swiftly and surely, as demons and destruction always work."[29]

Backed by public sentiment aroused by Walter, McCrackin, San Jose photographer Andrew P. Hill, and others, the Sempervirens Club won within a year a victory without precedent in the history of protecting the redwoods: $250,000 from the legislature and Governor Henry Gage to save

2,500 acres of Santa Cruz Mountain redwoods from what Walter called "criminally extravagant" lumbering practices.[30]

President Roosevelt himself marveled at the accomplishment. In a speech at Stanford University on May 12, 1903, he told students:

> "Yesterday, I saw for the first time a grove of your trees, a grove which it has taken the ages several thousands of years to build up; and I feel most emphatically that we should not turn into shingles a tree which was old when the first Egyptian conqueror penetrated to the Valley of the Euphrates and which can be put to better use. That, you may say, is not looking at the matter from the practical standpoint. But there is nothing more practical in the end than the preservation of beauty, than the preservation of anything that appeals to the higher emotions in mankind."[31]

A final inspiration, 260 miles south of Eureka, was Marin County's new 294-acre Muir Woods National Monument established in 1908.

The redwood park at the northern edge of the San Francisco Bay Area owed its existence to President Roosevelt's signing and use of the 1906 Antiquities Act, and to land subsequently provided for a national monument by wealthy California businessman and future congressman William Kent, and his wife, Elizabeth Thatcher Kent, a prominent women's voting rights activist.[32] Kent asked of Roosevelt that the redwood park be named for their old acquaintance, John Muir, whose travels and writings from his farmhouse in Martinez spurred a preservationist impulse across the West. Kent later gained additional renown among conservationists in carrying 1916 legislation to create the National Park Service.

Yet it was the changing roles of women that offered club members in Humboldt County the most hope and made the greatest difference. Across the United States, women were moving beyond the restrictive caretaking roles assigned them for centuries in the family, garden, and local parks. In the turbulent decades following the Civil War, women organized public campaigns for their rights to vote and be educated, for their equality and economic survival. The Progressive Era that followed, a time of great social and political reforms that began to regulate industries, help the immigrant poor, expand voting rights to women, and preserve millions of acres of natural wilderness, provided women social platforms and release to adopt a larger view of the world beyond their homes and local communities. Women by the thousands suddenly gravitated toward conservation of forests, water, and wildlife, "on grounds that these resources were essential to the human household and needed to be saved for use by future generations."[33]

Gone in a new generation of women's clubs were traditional, older visions of simply nurturing natural environments in their gardens. As efforts to save the redwoods began to unfold in California, women were now at the center of national wilderness preservation campaigns and widely engaged in politics to protect nature. Women's clubs became especially adept at educating and recruiting their members to support environmental causes; once educated and recruited, club members excelled in the necessary fund-raising.[34]

Overall, women were moving beyond simple moralist attitudes about caretaking the natural world to more practical activities in environmental conservation, politics and science. In the words of historian Shana Miriam Cohen:

> Women's clubs working collectively on behalf of land, water and wildlife led them to seek out partnerships with government agencies such as the U.S. Forest Service's Division of Women's Activities and various state highway departments. Garden clubs became recognized leaders in the fields of conservation education; agencies often looked to these clubs to spread public awareness.[35]

In California, these confident new voices revived and gave fresh urgency to earlier, long forgotten, and ignored appeals by men in government to save the redwood giants from extinction.

In 1852, California Assemblyman Henry Crabb of San Joaquin County had introduced a resolution to ban commercial lumbering in the vast redwood belt. Crabb had seen the Gold Rush ravages of the Sierra Nevada foothills and feared the same fate for the state's abundant timberlands. The state lawmaker employed an ancient Roman and English concept of common law, viewing the redwoods the same way the California Constitution viewed the state's magnificent ocean shoreline: a natural landscape owned by the people, a public trust not available for private ownership.

The resolution had asked simply that California's congressional delegation introduce a bill declaring the redwood forests "the common property of the citizens of California for their private use and benefit" and prohibiting "the settlement and occupation of all public lands upon which Red Wood is growing."

It proved, unfortunately, an idea ahead of its time. Crabb's proposal, introduced twelve years before President Abraham Lincoln banned lumbering and commercial development in Yosemite Valley and its nearby Mariposa Grove of Giant Sequoias, found itself weakened in the state Assembly, defeated in the state Senate, and cited ever since, amid the near-annihilation of the state's 2 million acres of old-growth redwoods, as opportunity lost.

Years later, in 1879, German-born forester and United States Secretary of the Interior Carl Schurz, then serving under President Rutherford B. Hayes, recommended that Congress remove 92,000 acres of federally owned California redwoods from sale to private interests. Schurz, with plentiful foresight, argued, "These species of trees, the noblest and oldest in the world, will entirely disappear unless some be taken to preserve at least a portion of them."

His recommendation, while "milder and much more intelligent" than the Crabb proposal twenty-seven years earlier, also disappeared into history.[36]

Finally, these old appeals to the better nature of humanity found a new audience. In 1900, Los Angeles women's club leader Clara Burdette made the fate of the redwoods a rallying cry in organizing a new California Federation of Women's Clubs (CFWC) under the motto, "Strength United Is Stronger."

Burdette, a wealthy heiress, socialite, and Progressive Republican who contributed heavily to health care causes in Southern California, believed the redwood forests had value not only for "their matchless grandeur" but because "under their shadows live the springs of water that give vitality to the time and glory to the harvest — life unto themselves and little ones — wealth to the state."[37] During an address to 95 local women's clubs at the federation's first statewide conference in Los Angeles, Burdette roused her audience with a soaring appeal to match the deeds of women elsewhere in the United States:

> "The preservation of the forests in this state is a matter that should appeal to women. While the women of New Jersey are saving the Palisades of the Hudson from utter destruction by men to whose greedy souls Mount Sinai is only a stone quarry, and the women of Colorado are saving the cliff dwellings and pueblo ruins of their state from vandal destruction, the word comes to the women of California that men whose souls are gang-saws are meditating the turning of our world-class Sequoias into planks and fencing worth so many dollars."

Burdette called defiantly for an alternate future. "Better one living tree in California than fifty acres of lumberyard," she proclaimed. "Preserve and replant them and the state will be blessed a thousand-fold in the development of its natural resources.[38]

Burdette's federation of California women would provide formidable new statewide energy for the redwoods campaigns to come, engaging in fundraising, publicity, and government lobbying, as well as recruiting public support. The California federation also brought powerful, new national allies to its redwoods campaign by joining (as its thirty-seventh member) the larger General Federation of Women's Clubs founded in 1890.[39]

In the East another women's club was soon to carve out a leading role in the 1920s redwoods preservation movement, The Garden Club of America, established during a May 1, 1913, gathering of society women in Philadelphia. Garden clubs at the time typically brought together friends for mutual assistance in creating grand flower gardens at their estates. Local clubs, up from their historic roots as horticultural societies of the 1880s, often had evolved into elegant gatherings in beautiful homes and gardens among the highest levels of society.

In Philadelphia, twenty-four representatives of a dozen garden clubs in the Eastern and central United States met for the first time inside a majestic colonial-era home preserved by the National Society of the Colonial Dames of America in the city's historic Germantown section. The invitations had arrived from a pair of wealthy Philadelphia society women, Elizabeth Price Martin and Ernestine Abercrombie Goodman, founders a decade earlier of the Garden Club of Philadelphia. On the day of the national club's founding, its inaugural members named Martin as their first president, and soon announced in The Garden Club of America's *Bulletin* of July 1913 the purpose of the new club: "The objects of this association shall be to stimulate the knowledge and love of gardening among amateurs, to share the advantage of association, to aid in the protection of native plants and birds, and to encourage civic planting."

Within a decade of its founding The Garden Club of America would turn to the redwoods. Eventually, it would declare its efforts there the club's greatest accomplishment.[40]

The Nation Should Not Permit This Destruction

But first came that long, lonely incubation period for any new idea to take hold in the popular imagination. In California's Humboldt County, named after Nineteenth Century German naturalist and explorer Alexander von Humboldt, the concept of saving redwoods in public parks would have an especially long wait for results.

The idealists and aesthetic-minded locals with their idea to protect the redwoods for future generations, had little money to buy land from rough and tumble, practical-minded timber companies. And timber companies held absolute power in a Northern California economy of raw materials and natural resources.

The start of the long, hard journey to save Humboldt County's redwood giants might be traced to 1902, when Burdette's California Federation of Women's Clubs invited women from Eureka's Monday Club, a forerunner to the Eureka Women's Club, to its annual convention in San Francisco. There they would hear how women's clubs elsewhere had protected redwoods.

In 1902 there were no paved roads out of Humboldt County and no trains to San Francisco. The Eureka women boarded a southbound ocean steamer to the booming Pacific Coast city of nearly 350,000 people. There they experienced for the first time the federation's spirited annual debates over such social issues as child labor, civil service reform, and unrestricted logging in the state's forests. Conversations with other members showed the federation's particular interest in protecting Humboldt's redwoods.

But it was too much so soon. After hearing out the returning delegates, Monday Club leaders decided to avoid controversy sure to arise with a campaign to preserve old-growth local redwoods. Historian Cameron Binkley, in a 2002 written analysis of women's roles in the earliest save the redwoods movement, offered a perspective for their decision:

"There are several reasons for the group's hesitation. The first of these was simply that one-third of Monday Club members belonged to families involved in the lumber industry. The mills of Eureka and nearby Arcata furnished a tremendous volume of timber cut from Humboldt County's rich stands of redwood and Douglas fir. Since the frenetic Gold Rush years, logging had been the county's major economic activity, as it remains today. Club women from families involved in logging included Mary Bell Carson, whose father-in-law was William Carson, co-owner of Dolbeer & Carson, one of the most prominent Pacific Coast lumber companies. Lumbermen were likely to fear public discussion of their trade as inimical to the industry's interests. If so, the Monday Club gave the fear due regard."[41]

By October 1913, however, many clubwomen in Humboldt County were leading the fledgling new save-the-redwoods movement alongside the Eureka Chamber of Commerce. They were no longer afraid. Since the late September women's club picnic in Carson Woods, sixty county businessmen had also toured Carson Woods and named it their preferred site for a redwood national park.[42]

An emboldened new women's Redwood Park Committee formed in the wake of the Carson Woods picnic moved quickly, headed by Annie Zane Murray, prominent women's club activist and wife of a county superior court judge. In 1908, Murray hosted clubwomen throughout the county at her home to found the Humboldt County Federation of Women's Clubs, which began with seven member clubs and later admitted a Native American Women's Club.[43]

On Saturday, October 18, 1913, Murray's small Redwood Committee convened at Eureka's Carnegie Library. Inside, these few women living in a remote county in the far north of California, produced a remarkable formal resolution in support of redwoods preservation generally, and specifically for congressional legislation proposing investigation of possibilities for a redwood national park in Humboldt County. [44] The soaring sentiment of their ground-breaking declaration still resonates after a century, rising eloquently above the hard, industrial lumbering ethic that defined their region and people in the early 1900s:

"Civilization demands that the natural wonders of the world be preserved for future generations to study and enjoy. The grandest of all the natural wonders that make our country interesting and attractive are the giant redwood trees of California, the greatest natural monuments of the Creator's handiwork. These greatest natural monuments of the forest have stood sentinel over this enchanted land from the dawn of civilization. With their majestic beauty towering to the skies with outstretched arms they have welcomed the coming of civilization. Nowhere else can such wonderful products of the earth be found." [45]

Wielding their pens, committee members appealed nobly to the ideal of civilization itself and remarkably for their time, considered people not yet born, the millions who have since hiked a state or national redwood park trail and quietly absorbed the otherworldly spell of an old-growth forest. In identifying the unnamed authors of this bold declaration challenging the forest-ravaging mentality surrounding them, it is fair to speculate on Murray, an early Humboldt redwoods activist who also advocated for the trees within the California Federation of Women's Clubs.

Another likely writer was Minnie Ryan, the women's Redwood Park Committee secretary. She briefly attended Stanford University in 1896 and married a Humboldt County Justice of the Peace who was also a prominent timber claims specialist with the Pacific Lumber Company in the county town of Scotia. Also likely was Eureka landscape and still life painter Laura Mahan, a graduate of Mills College for women in Oakland, a one-time art student at the Mark Hopkins Institute in San Francisco, and wife of a prominent Eureka attorney. [46]

"The nation should not permit this destruction of all our great redwoods," resolved Murray's Redwood Park Committee. The federal government, it continued, "should save and protect a few of these natural wonderful monuments from the devastating hand of commercialism." [47] The resolution, which stands among the founding documents of the great redwoods campaigns of the 1920s, envisioned a new national park for the redwoods, preferably at Carson Woods, to stand among the handful of national parks already in existence: Yosemite, Yellowstone, Crater Lake, Glacier, Mount Rainier, and Muir Woods National Monument.[48]

Within days of the Saturday gathering, the Federated Women's Clubs of the San Francisco District of the statewide federation, adopted the Humboldt County resolution as its own. Club members forwarded it to Congress with a dire warning: "The woodman's ax is busy and unless action is taken at once it will be too late."

The woodsmen of California were undeniably busy, as they had long been in a booming new state that needed wood for its physical development. By the 1860s five square miles of San Francisco Bay redwoods stretching from Oakland to Moraga disappeared to build Gold Rush-era San Francisco and Sacramento. The redwood giants of the Santa Cruz Mountains were largely obliterated by the 1880s and 1890s. Over decades the mill owners steadily consolidated their operations and grew ever more financially sophisticated and powerful.[49] Humboldt County press reports of the early 1900s show a community wondering if the timber industry now on its doorstep would cut down its every last local redwood forest.

The Humboldt Times, on February 26, 1907, published an impassioned editorial, "Work for Eureka's Women," summoning local women to the fight known now as environmentalism. "The warm hand of man scars and gashes the beautiful face of nature in Humboldt, oft-times, but the smooth and gentle hand of woman can touch the wounds and heal them."

The *Times* appealed to women's clubs to beautify Eureka and preserve "those natural beauty spots in and around the city that have been spared by the woodman." The editorial marked another historic turning point in the slowly rising consciousness of a new movement. Women took the Eureka newspaper's admonition to heart. Soon locally, stirred a redwoods campaign managed by women, yet aligned with local businesses aiming to jump start a tourist economy for a new generation of motorists. The partnership would sustain itself for twenty-five years, at first in vain, then with rising momentum and outside help to save thousands of acres of redwoods in state parks.

Within a year of the editorial, the crusade for a redwood park opened with a national publicity sensation involving local school children. More than 2,000 students studying forestry in Eureka's public schools petitioned President Roosevelt in February 1908 to establish a redwood national forest in Humboldt County:[50]

"We the children of the Eureka schools have been studying about our redwood forests and along with the rest of the people of our country we feel that representative groves of these trees should be preserved for ourselves and coming generations of children. We respectfully petition the United States government to take some action toward establishing a national forest of redwoods."

Though there are no recorded fingerprints on origins or coordination of the petition, some historians see a hidden hand of Eureka women's clubs and the Eureka Chamber of Commerce.[51] Another view holds that while the petition's origins are vague, "a committee of club women and members of the chamber of commerce lost little time in conveying the petition" to the new U.S. Forest Service established by Roosevelt three years earlier.[52]

Newspapers played up the story. It was irresistible. *The San Francisco Call* hailed the children's crusade under a February 23, 1908, headline, "Children Plead for Redwood Park." Boston's *Journal of Education* declared it "one of the most unique petitions ever sent to Uncle Sam," and "unlike any other which has ever been sent to a government department to ask for the preservation of forests."[53] The *Journal*, citing sympathies of government foresters with the children, stated, "It has been only a few years since the redwood trees stood thick on the land around the larger towns of Humboldt County. But now all the readily accessible timber has been removed and the people see the time when the redwoods groves will have disappeared."

President Roosevelt was quick with a reply, telling the children he was "exceedingly anxious to assist in preserving representative bodies" of the redwoods.[54] But despite the president's promising words, prospects to save some of the nation's greatest redwood forests changed not at all. The roadblock was Congress, still Congress, unwilling, as during Laura Lyon White's campaign to save the Calaveras Big Trees, to budget any funds for redwood parks. This continuing failure to win federal funding would become the running storyline of the earliest Humboldt redwoods campaigns.

Nonetheless, a budding save-the-redwoods sentiment continued to ferment publicly. Soon after the children's petition, Edith Woodridge, one of the 800 residents of Fortuna near Carson Woods, penned a public letter that would have been at home during the Northern California redwood wars of the 1960s, 1970s, and 1990s.

"Every acre destroyed is a national loss which future generations will feel," she warned her fellow inhabitants of the threatened landscapes in Fortuna's weekly *Humboldt Beacon*. Woodridge reminded the newspaper's readers that Humboldt County had already lost 90,000 acres of its original 500,000 acres of redwood forests since settlers arrived in the 1850s. Nearly twenty percent of the original old-growth redwoods were gone, she said, the county's once-pristine scenery deteriorating daily for all to see.

"Today, the hills are no longer covered with redwood forests, but with charred stumps and fallen monarchs," Woodridge wrote. "There is a grave danger threatening the younger portion of the nation unless these things are recognized and prompt action taken. There is a reckless, selfish use of natural resources which if unchecked, will lead to blighting poverty."

Woodridge noted that "these gigantic trees hold a weird fascination for anyone who beholds them," and challenged the customary justifications of harvesting redwoods for jobs, taxes, and the economy. She blamed the visible devastation of Humboldt County and the "short-sighted destroying of its resources" on personal ambitions "to make money quickly, to roll up fortunes for quick success."[55]

Her words were no match for the ax, however. The forests continued to fall.

The Prickly Congressional Politics of No

Of every problem confronting Humboldt County businessmen and women's club members as they campaigned through the teens of the Twentieth Century for a redwood national park one was worst: the smothering indifference of locals and of Washington, D.C. In Humboldt County, thousands of residents owed their livelihoods to lumber camps and sawmills and paid the redwoods campaigns little mind. In Washington, Congress showed little interest in buying back redwoods its government so carelessly sold to land speculators a generation earlier in settling the West with newcomers. Private timber companies now owned nearly all the redwood belt of California. It was impossible for Washington to establish a national park in the traditional way, roping off wilderness already owned by the federal government.

It might take hundreds of thousands of dollars, even millions of dollars, to buy private land for a sizable redwood park system.

In the Santa Cruz Mountains, Californians had shown that fierce, raw politics could win state taxpayer dollars to save redwoods. Humboldt County would take its fight to a bigger arena. On March 29, 1912, Democratic Congressman John Raker, representing much of Northern California, including Humboldt County, introduced House Joint Resolution 284. It proposed a national commission to investigate the "advisability and necessity" of establishing a redwood national park in Humboldt County.[56]

In Eureka, an informal redwood park committee of the mayor, three newspaper editors, and a prominent local attorney, suggested with the blessing of local redwood timber owners that the commission include "at least three congressmen, and perhaps more, an official from the forestry service [U.S. Forest Service], a noted forestry authority like John Muir, and the Mayor of Eureka." The aim locally was to win quick passage and "have the Congressional committee visit here this coming summer in order to get early action from Congress."[57]

House leaders assigned the legislation to the Agriculture Committee, which promptly received resolutions of support from the Humboldt County Federation of Women's Clubs and the 20,000-member California Federation of Women's Clubs.[58] The statewide federation came aboard after Humboldt County clubwomen made a grueling 470-mile trip to lobby members at its 1912 convention in Paso Robles in San Luis Obispo County. Months later, federation president Eliza A. Orr of San Francisco returned the gesture, visiting the Humboldt redwoods and launching a years-long trend of presidents making difficult overland or ocean steamer trips to Eureka in support of protecting the giant trees in parks.

"When one is in the midst of the virgin forests of the giant redwoods," Orr wrote in the federation's November 1912 newsletter, *The Clubwoman*, "the importance and necessity of the National Forestry Service is painfully apparent. Each giant stump proclaims the sad fact that this unique forest of magnificent redwoods is doomed to almost complete extirpation in the course of the next generation."[59]

Washington, as usual, could offer no help.

Raker's resolution died without even a hearing. There was no federal money to buy redwood forests, nor for any investigation of possibilities. The county establishment's disappointment would have been total, though likely little noticed by most Humboldt County residents. At the time the idea of "preserving a tract of virgin redwoods timber in the county for future generations" attracted little more than laughs locally. It was an opinion rarely shared in public, recalled then-Eureka Mayor Frederick W. Georgeson in a 1920 letter to Robert G. Sproul, future president of the University of California at Berkeley.[60]

Raker tried again with a new president, Woodrow Wilson, in the White House, introducing House Joint Resolution 4 on April 7, 1913. It contained identical language to the first attempt.[61] The legislation went to the Committee on Rules, which ignored it. After seven months of futility, Raker asked Laura Mahan, the women's redwood activist in Eureka, to help generate local enthusiasm he could muster for more congressional backing. At home Mahan stirred up fresh support through the Eureka Chamber of Commerce and a local "Promotion Club" formed to talk up the legislation locally. Statewide, she again solicited the California Federation of Women's

Clubs, which swiftly asked member clubs throughout the state to petition and write Congress in support of the new resolution.[62]

Mahan also contacted a Washington, D.C., lobbyist with whom she had had a recent chance encounter, Hester Eloise Hosford, author of the 1912 political biography, *Woodrow Wilson and New Jersey Made Over*. Hosford had accompanied Mahan on a 1912 tour of the Humboldt County redwoods, where reportedly the sights of logged-over landscapes caused her to "become tremendously interested in the cause." Hosford agreed to lobby President Wilson and others in Washington to support Raker's redwoods resolution.[63]

Hosford rapidly won support of the American Forestry Association, headed by conservationist Gifford Pinchot, founder and former chief of the U.S. Forest Service under President Roosevelt. But elsewhere it was the familiar Washington story.

"Again, the resolution was not reported out of committee, and the effort was abandoned," wrote California redwoods historian Susan R. Schrepfer in 1971.[64]

It was thoroughly over, an overwhelming disappointment in the earliest history of saving the redwoods. As storm clouds also gathered in Europe and guns then thundered through five years of World War I, any possible momentum in Washington for the Northern California redwoods stopped cold. Humboldt County's fight to save the trees would be long and endure no end of obstacles. Not until 1968 would the federal government budget money for a Redwood National Park in Humboldt County.[65]

Keeping Faith in Themselves

Facing repeated failures in the national arena, Humboldt County women's clubs and Eureka business associations eventually suspended the legislative campaign for a redwood park. But the women's clubs, with unwavering support from their state federation, showed their continued faith in the idea. Again, on August 31, 1915, 200 club members gathered at Carson Woods to host their newest state federation president, Helen M. Knight of San Francisco, and founding federation president Clara Burdette.

"The day was a perfect one, marked by splendid hospitality, ideal weather, touches of philosophy, flashes of wit, and hearty good fellowship," Knight wrote to 30,000 club members in the October 1915 *Clubwoman*. "Prominent among the hostesses were the sixteen members of the 'Grandmother's Club,' that unique organization which demands that one must attain the dignity of grand motherhood before being eligible to membership. Most of the members thereof are pioneers of Humboldt County, having arrived as early as '56, and reminiscences of pioneer days are frequently exchanged at their meetings."

Accompanying her commentary was a full-page picture of Carson Woods, titled, "Save the Carson Woods." *The Clubwoman* also published a full-page photo of Knight in white, posing with three redwood giants, her right hand resting on a wide trunk. It was titled, "Our President Among The Redwoods." Knight recalled for her readers statewide that "nature's magnificent out-of-door theater, Carson Woods near Fortuna" is one of the "splendid tracts which the residents of Humboldt County are endeavoring to have set aside as a national park. One cannot visit this beautiful country of 'Sequoia Sempervirens,'" she wrote, "without feeling a renewed and personal interest in these stately children of nature which reach their highest development here, and which must be saved from the woodman's ax and other destructive agencies."[66]

Carson Woods National Park, however, came no closer to reality, even as President Wilson soon signaled his own commitment to save magnificent Western landscapes. In August 1916, he signed California Congressman Kent's legislation to establish a new National Park Service overseeing fourteen national parks and twenty-one national monuments.[67] It was a breathtaking moment for Progressive Era conservationists, and for a public with cars to visit their country's wildest landmarks.

Yet among redwood park activists in faraway Humboldt County and their allies statewide, there was a growing sense of being left behind as new national parks opened throughout America. Days after President Wilson's August 25 announcement of the new National Park Service *The Clubwoman* responded with a statewide alert from its forestry chair, Anna L. Royles of Woodland, an agricultural town near Sacramento. Royles reminded members to support Humboldt County women in their campaign for a national park at Carson Woods:

> Cannot and will not the California Federation of Women's Clubs stand back of these faithful women and help to create a sentiment that will save the Carson Woods of Humboldt County? A committee of twenty-one women worked earnestly and faithfully, and for a time it seemed their efforts would surely be crowned with success, but alas, politics and personal interests intervened, and proved too strong a foe, and the plans of these patriotic women were frustrated.[68]

It was a fitting description of a failed campaign.

An Avenue Opens

The long continuing lull over Carson Woods surely felt like an endless uncertain journey with no mileposts to ease a growing sense of unease, impatience, and weariness. Yet, November 1916 brought a sudden new victory for redwoods preservation. In Sonoma County, voters created California's first redwood park since Muir Woods in 1908, approving a special tax to bring 400 acres of virgin redwoods into public ownership.

Heirs of a lumbering family that had earlier clear-cut most of the redwoods near the small Russian River town of Guerneville had offered Sonoma County a discounted price of $80,000 for a picturesque family-owned grove known as Armstrong Woods. Lizzie Armstrong, daughter of lumberman Colonel James Armstrong, agreed to contribute $5,000 toward the purchase price, as did an Armstrong family friend who owned half of the grove.

For the next seventeen years Sonoma County managed California's newest and third public redwoods park before ceding it to the state in 1934 in a deal to protect the county's ocean beaches in state parks.[69] A stone monument erected in the park by the California Federation of Women's Clubs in 1929 still acknowledges Lizzie Armstrong's contribution to the state's growing acreage of protected redwood forests.

Then, at last, similar good fortune visited Humboldt County. After years of dashed hopes that defined the redwood campaigns in the northernmost reaches of California, August 1917 delivered the breakthrough that put Humboldt County redwoods on a world stage. A summer road trip by three eminent scientists to visit the giant trees still stands out today as a turning point in the movement to save the redwoods. In the story's well-known retelling, Dr. John C. Merriam, paleontology professor at the University of California in Berkeley; Madison Grant, chairman of the New York Zoological Society; and Henry Fairfield Osborn, president of the American Museum of Natural History, found themselves awed by the great redwood forests of Humboldt County and appalled by their destruction.

The three men, acquaintances of the late naturalist Muir and of former President Roosevelt, held national reputations for their studies and publications about the evolution of life on earth. Grant, in 1877, helped Roosevelt found the outdoors-oriented Boone and Crockett Club, "whose general purpose was to perpetuate the American pioneering instinct and spirit of independence by preserving for public resort and recreation some significant remnants of the great American wilderness and its associated forms of wildlife."[70] Merriam, for his part, learned about the threatened redwoods from the Humboldt County Federation of Women's Clubs, which earlier sought his support and help in saving them.[71]

Touring on August 9, 1917, the threesome penned a letter from Arcata in Humboldt County to California Governor William Stephens. They described the redwoods region as one of the finest they had seen in all their world travels and suggested it would one day "be visited by people from all parts of the United States, as well as from abroad." The scientists urged Stephens to preserve the "incomparably grand" redwood forests alongside a new state highway on the South Fork of the Eel River and culminating in the "superb woods" of Bull Creek Flat.

"I believe that a Redwoods Park of Humboldt County, if practicable, would be one of the most gratefully received and long remembered acts of your administration," the letter stated, "and I trust that the matter may commend itself to your judgement and that the means of making this glorious forest secure for all time with the people may be found."

The road trip would pay enormous dividends in the attention it received and the publicity it generated. The following summer the three scientists established the Save the Redwoods League, bringing national attention to a still largely local cause supported statewide only by the California Federation of Women's Clubs.

The federation, through its presidents and forestry chairs, never wavered as the Carson Woods stalemate stretched through much of 1917, then into 1918. In September 1918, five years after Humboldt County women's club members picnicked in Carson Woods, and six years after the federation's first presidential visit to the Humboldt redwoods, federation Vice President Adella T. Schloss of Los Angeles, made the newest northern pilgrimage.

Writing in *The Clubwoman*, she described a "wonderful all-day trip of a hundred and twenty-five miles through the big redwoods of Humboldt County" and reminded 36,000 federation readers of continuing support among women's clubs statewide for a redwood national park.[72] Schloss, fortunately, would become president of the women's federation nine months later and would preside during a great burst of redwood campaign successes just ahead. By 1921, she also joined the Save the Redwoods League's advisory council, one of three women's club members named to the assembly of national business, scientific, and civic leaders.

As fresh momentum slowly gathered for a redwood park in Humboldt County, *The Timberman*, chronicler of the national timber industry, weighed in with an endorsement of the new Save the Redwoods League and its preservation goals. "The object of this association is to stimulate interest in securing sufficient funds through private subscription to purchase a tract of redwood in Humboldt County, preferably on Bull Creek, now owned by the Pacific Lumber Co., containing some five thousand acres or more. There is no more typical stand of the Sequoia Sempervirens species to be found than on Bull Creek. The location is ideal and the stand of timber is magnificent."

The publication's Oregon-based owners called the league's formation an opportunity for patriotic lumbermen to give back to a nation that had richly rewarded them.

> Other basic industries, such as steel, have contributed the Carnegie libraries; the oil industry, through Rockefeller, institutes; and the meat industry, through the Armours, have each given back to the country in some permanent form something of real and lasting benefit to the country at large. The lumber industry, except through its contribution to the Yale Forest School, has never had a real opportunity to give something of real permanent value to the country.

The editorial expressed optimism that industry leaders would "doubtless be glad to contribute generously to a fund of this nature. They are public-spirited men and proud of the industry. If these men will head the campaign for a National Redwood Park the object can be obtained." *The Timberman* placed itself among leaders to rally the nation's lumbermen:

> Every lumber industry newspaper will help in the movement and every regional lumber association would back the National in its general campaign for raising the necessary funds. *The Timberman* most willingly places itself behind the movement in common with others, believing that the time is ripe for the creation of a sentiment which can be crystallized into a reality. The United States is dear to us at this time. It means more than ever before. Let us preserve its natural forest beauty by the creation of a National Redwood Park which will stand for all time as emblematic of the lumber industry's gift to the world.

It remains tragic to this day that the industry failed to grasp and then missed the opportunity so vividly described in June 1918. It would fall to an often-uncooperative Pacific Lumber Company more than a decade in the future to finally bring *The Timberman's* vision to fruition.

Lost Forever to the World

Meanwhile, time ran out for Carson Woods. Its luck and long life as a locally beloved old-growth forest of stately groves and running waters vanished alongside thousands of acres of redwoods after World War I. A peacetime economy had roared to life and with it extraordinary demand for redwood products. Even the powerful new Save the Redwoods League was little help. From its beginnings, the league favored the preservation of the South Fork of the Eel River forests along the state highway over saving Carson Woods.

On Friday, October 13, 1923, Fortuna's *Humboldt Beacon* reported the impending leveling of the old forest under the headline, "Carson Woods to be Entered by Woodsmen."

In the brief account one still hears the sigh of a long-gone newspaperman as he bids farewell to a community's ancient and cherished local forest: "Surveyors are at work laying out the line along Palmer Creek for a logging railroad for the Holmes-Eureka Lumber Company. A spur is to be constructed to the redwood timber from the Northwestern Pacific Railroad line west of Fortuna."

The Holmes-Eureka company, readers learned, would log Carson Woods in a way to preserve for six to eight more years the portion nearest Fortuna, "which is so dear to nature lovers and pleasure seekers. For a few more years," wrote an unnamed reporter in an eloquent requiem for the national park that might have been, the redwood giants would "afford inspiration and joy to numerous visitors before they crash before the ax and are forever lost to the world."

Chapter Two: First Encounters With Success, 1919–1921

"The preservation of these mighty giants is our rightful duty and its accomplishment would mean not only distinct economic advantages, but also an advancement in civilization. As long as we allow avarice to blind us to the beauties of nature, to influence us to destroy the works of the Creator, we are vandals."

—Ru-Flo Harper Lee. Eureka High School Senior. 1921 Sequoia Yearbook. Eureka, California.

Nothing in the grim early months of 1919 hinted at the breakout year it would become in the history of saving the redwoods. The year opened with the death of former President Theodore Roosevelt on January 6, the Spanish flu stalking the northernmost reaches of California, and not an acre of its redwoods yet saved from the timberman's ax.

Winter that year was unusually wet, the flu frightening and terrible. Public schools and downtown theaters closed, reopened, and closed again during expanding and retreating waves of the flu virus. Eureka's 13,000 residents walked their sidewalks wearing masks while newspapers tallied the dead, more than 200 countywide from October 1918 to February 1919.[73]

Now with the end of the Great War a peacetime economy suddenly returned to life and began to drive renewed commercial and residential demand for Humboldt County's prized lumber. The pace of logging visibly accelerated, especially in southern Humboldt County along a scenic stretch of the state's new north-south Redwood Highway, Highway 101.

The highway, better known in the modern era as the Avenue of the Giants, fronted beautiful, wide expanses of the South Fork of the Eel River as it coursed through thousands of giant redwoods. The new motorway, a government wonder that many locals believed would finally bring mass tourism to the great redwoods, owed its existence to a statewide highway bond of $18 million passed by California voters in 1910.

Yet the region's beloved new highway brought an unexpected and unintended consequence. What made it easy for motorists to visit Humboldt County, and for county residents to visit the rest of California, also made it easy for timbermen to open up nearby logging areas. They moved into roadside forests now easily accessible, set up mill operations by the side of the highway, and handily moved out their finished products.

The sudden, unseemly destruction of stately redwood giants along the region's tourist highway appalled many Humboldt County residents. The outside world became equally horrified as local lumber operators began trashing a scenic wonderland such as existed nowhere else on earth.

The fate of these remote old trees, long of little concern beyond the women's clubs of Humboldt County and their federation colleagues statewide, suddenly took on a kind of national urgency among the wealthy and powerful of San Francisco, Chicago, New York, and Washington, D.C. In that breathless, dramatic year of the redwoods, 1919, numerous Eastern and California elites drove to Humboldt County to personally inspect devastation which the well-traveled among them likened to ruined battlefield landscapes of France. During that historic summer the Save the Redwoods League also engaged as first of the great land trusts that in the coming century would save millions of acres of wildlands in the United States. In the great excitement Humboldt County women's club members, too, restarted their dormant campaign to save redwoods in national or state parks. They could scarcely imagine the scale of their coming accomplishments.

How quickly 1919 became the year when everything changed.

The crucial year marked especially the arrival of men to a movement largely until then populated and steered by California women's club members. Momentum shifted so abruptly in 1919 and so firmly toward saving the redwoods for future generations, that it has cemented in history a story of men, particularly a few influential men, as the chief driving force. Their legends ultimately crowded out other legends present at the beginning, those who gave to the cause their land, their money, their time, and who were more often than not women.

The new and far-sighted Save the Redwoods League began almost entirely as a club of wealthy men. Its leaders were men with power who sought out other men with power, men of capital and finance, men who owned timber mills and large holdings of redwoods, and men who managed the vital local, state, and federal government agencies. League men, for instance, quickly and successfully persuaded the United States Railroad Administration and the Southern Pacific and Northwestern Pacific railroads to stop buying redwood ties produced in Humboldt County forests.[74]

From the beginning a league founder had assured anxious redwood timberland owners that the league aligned itself, loftily, with the "fundamental interests of thinking people." That is, with interests of other successful businessmen, professionals, and men of power and wealth. League men gravitated to others like themselves who held shared views of profits, affluence, and obligations of philanthropy. It was little surprise then, that in the wake of the charitable tax deduction passed by Congress in 1917 to encourage charitable giving by the nation's elites, the deduction became a central plank of league fund-raising strategy.[75]

Such storied men literally leap from the pages of 1919 and the early 1920s as the movement to save the best of the redwoods accelerated into a national cause. They journeyed great distances to Humboldt County to make speeches and rally residents to agitate for national or state redwood parks. They lobbied other powerful men in America and named them to Redwood Committees. They became iconic figures in the redwoods story: National Park Service Director Stephen T. Mather of California, Northern California Congressman William Kent, and Save the Redwoods League founders Henry Fairfield Osborn and Madison Grant of New York, and John C. Merriam of California.

The standout among them all was Save the Redwoods League Executive Director and Secretary Newton B. Drury of California. He coordinated for years a growing web of donors and activists, as well as relations with government officials and corporate timber interests. A prolific letter writer inside a whirlwind of fund-raising and land negotiations, Drury frequently operated steps ahead of axes that aimed to claim the same trees that the league wanted to save. Late in life he recalled that the Save the Redwoods League had started from scratch, just three men driving a car over wagon roads into Humboldt County when not a single tree in the world's finest forest was publicly owned.[76]

But storied American women also rose to match these men in the fight for the redwoods. Advocates always for green spaces, women supported now the preservation of nature well beyond their gardens and neighborhood parks. History would not always recognize their powerful contributions, but empowered by Progressive Era values, women often led the nation's conservation campaigns for wildlands and historical sites.

Iowan Cora Whitley, who chaired the General Federation of Women's Clubs Conservation Committee, explained in 1925 that clubwomen typically saw the larger picture in fights for natural areas due to their comprehensive study and understanding of conservation issues:

> "Women have not shown their interest, as has sometimes been imagined, simply by expressing their love for trees or by planting memorial avenues. They have tried to study the question from the utilitarian, the economic, as well as the aesthetic stand-point; to learn from history what forests mean to the prosperity of a nation."[77]

In the earliest direct work and financial contributions that saved thousands of acres of Northern California redwoods, women frequently stood at the forefront with the men of the Save the Redwoods League. Collectively, they helped pave the way for the modern environmental movement and left millions of visitors stunning places of quiet and beauty in California's redwood parks. Women, it was said, finally got the chance to venture outside their homes and do something they held dear and wanted to do. This was what they could do. They could save the redwoods.

"It is to the women that we owe very largely the success that has thus far attended our efforts to establish the Humboldt Redwoods Park," acknowledged California oil industrialist, financier and Save the Redwoods League Chairman Joseph D. Grant in 1922. Historian Cameron Binkley eighty years later affirmed Grant's assessment of women at the forefront, writing, "Indeed, judging by an impressive volume of correspondence, the national Save the Redwoods League worked more closely with women from 1920 to 1925 than any other entity."[78]

Binkley noted that women's efforts in the redwoods fostered their greater societal ambitions, buying them entrance into men's larger arenas of politics and public policy:

> "Conservation was a defining feature of progressivism — and particularly important in the arid West, where it was simultaneously an instrument of political, social, and economic reform. Such club leaders as Clara Burdette, Laura White, and Laura Mahan recognized the advantages that conservation had in enabling them to garner woman's support for increased involvement in public life. Moreover, by embracing conservation from a domestic perspective, clubwomen gained a voice in debate about major public policy issues — issues of political economy, a man's exclusive domain."[79]

The league in 1921 formally recognized the roles of powerful women in its campaign and named three women to its all-male council of business leaders, politicians, and professors. Adella T. Schloss was president of the California Federation of Women's Clubs and a long-time leader in the feminist and voting rights movement. Anna C. Law was president of the California Civic League of Women Voters. Eleanor Margaret Toll headed the Ebell Club in Los Angeles, one of the largest women's clubs in the nation.[80]

Toll, explaining in April 1921 why her club was in the redwoods fight, said, "If everyone could see the frightful waste and devastation to which these giants of the forest are succumbing, even along the highways, there would be such a protest that the State would ring with the voices. Let Ebell help to the limit of its capacity in this movement."[81]

The beginnings of this special, lasting partnership of local, statewide, and national women with the Save the Redwoods League can be traced to a long-forgotten event in Eureka, the inaugural meeting of the Humboldt County Women's Save the Redwoods League.

Inside a grand public room at Eureka City Hall on a late summer Saturday, August 9, 1919, dozens of Humboldt County women's club members and veterans of the earlier unsuccessful Carson Woods campaign, convened anew. Minnie Ryan, member of the women's Redwood Park Committee formed in 1913, opened the momentous meeting with an account of the electrifying attitude change among elites in California and elsewhere in America regarding their redwoods. The women listening, as will be seen shortly, were about to make history.[82]

To Save 20,000 Acres

This newest phase in the local redwoods campaign, a campaign nearly extinguished following years of failure and lack of action, had opened three weeks earlier in Eureka, during a mid-July visit by United States Agriculture Secretary David Houston, overseer of the U.S. Forest Service, and the nation's Chief Forester Henry Graves.

Houston sounded a patriotic theme during his trip, endorsing the quest for a redwood national memorial park "in recognition of the California boys who gave their lives to the country's service during the war." The Cabinet secretary's visit electrified the local establishment, prompting an immediate Eureka Chamber of Commerce meeting to unify Humboldt County residents behind an idea to preserve 20,000 acres of redwoods.[83]

Never had anyone suggested a number so ambitious.

Houston, addressing reporters a week later in San Francisco, continued to cloak his redwood park proposal as an act of patriotism. "Nature," he said, "has provided in the redwood forests such a monument as no man could ever build. I believe that these forests, preserved and consecrated to the memory of those who died that others might live more happily, would convey better than any other memorial the spirit of our love for these boys and our appreciation of their sacrifice."

Houston also applauded the growing power of tourism as an economic force in the Humboldt region.

> California is building a paved highway through these forests and Oregon is meeting the road from the north," he said. "This highway is the most magnificent in the world with its combination of mountains and ocean. Its forest screen of magnificent trees, ferns and flowers on every hand, from Willits via Eureka and Crescent City to the Oregon line and Grant's Pass, must be protected. No other highway in the world exceeds this in grandeur and beauty.[84]

Another national-level delegation in August raised hopes higher still for a redwood national park in Humboldt County. National Park Service Director Mather and Save the Redwoods League cofounder Madison Grant arrived in the county five days after a league redwoods campaign organizing meeting at San Francisco's beautiful Palace Hotel. (The league did not formally incorporate until October 21, 1920.) Driving toward Eureka they toured threatened redwood forests along the new Redwood Highway, near the South Fork of the Eel River, and also saw the magnificent redwood stands of Bull Creek Flat and Dyerville Flat forty-five miles south of the county seat near the small town of Weott.

Their nighttime speeches at Eureka High School sparked the leadership class of Humboldt County like nothing before. "If you want these redwoods preserved, you will have to keep at it to get anything done," Mather told the crowds. Mather had already pushed the region's new congressman, Clarence Lea, to reintroduce the old Raker bill proposing a national commission, a small group of experts to examine the redwoods and decide whether a national park was feasible, and if so, where.

In response to Mather's call to action, the Eureka Chamber of Commerce named five men to a fund-raising committee for a redwood park. On August 9 *The Humboldt Times* printed an enthusiastic editorial in support of the cause: "Let's Save The Redwoods, We Can Do It." The *Times* calculated that if 60,000 tourists visited Humboldt County's redwoods annually and each spent $20, it would steer an extra $1 million a year into the region's economy. The *Times* cheered, "It is up to the people to get busy. Let's go."[85]

That same afternoon at Eureka City Hall Humboldt County women's club members also revived their campaign begun in earnest six years earlier during the picnic in Carson Woods. The assembled clubwomen passed a formal resolution "that we band ourselves together to form a league for the preservation of redwoods." Annie Zane Murray, chair of the women's previous Redwood Park Committee, produced a constitution, which stated:

> The object of the league shall be to take any and all steps to preserve the magnificent Redwoods along the California State Highway in Humboldt County, and to use anything possible to induce our Government to establish a National Redwood Park along the highway on the lands which these redwoods stand.

The constitution set dues at fifty cents, later reduced to twenty-five cents in the club's bylaws, and admitted men who wanted to work alongside them.[86] The group's new logo was a sensation. It revealed two sides of a highway: one verdant and lined with old-growth giants, the other a jumble of stumps, fire, and piled lumber.

The women elected one of the most determined among them, Laura Mahan of Eureka, to lead what Binkley would call their "unique organization — a woman's club dedicated solely to saving redwoods."[87] Decades later Humboldt redwoods historian John J. Amodio recalled its mighty impact:

> Until 1925, they never lowered their vigilance or their vision. They were increasingly more effective, and they were increasingly the backbone of the local effort. The Humboldt County Women's League was organized and active in every municipality of the county, from Arcata to Garberville. Their strength was in their large membership and steady leadership, with Mrs. Laura Mahan being the steadfast leader of the Humboldt County effort.[88]

The new women's league fought off suggestions that it become an auxiliary of the national Save the Redwoods League, with all its implications for a secondary role. Members chose to retain their independence while helping the national league in every way possible. The strategy would pay off during difficult times ahead when the going got rough and opinions widely diverged between the two leagues.[89]

The women's league also approved an idea that quickly won invaluable local publicity, a barnstorming tour of county towns to find vice-presidents and anchor the new club as a regional power.

By September everyone had seen the "Save the Redwoods Car" driven by Eureka chauffeur Frank Silence with four women riders and a large "Save The Redwoods" banner draped across its side. A photo of the women and the car made its first public appearance in the September 6, 1919, *Humboldt Standard*, and remains to this day a definitive, iconic image of the campaign for the Humboldt redwoods.

All four women riding the highways that summer and fall were pillars of the Humboldt County business and social establishment, and members of the newly formed Humboldt County Women's Save the Redwoods League.

Illinois-born Lucretia Anna Huntington Monroe was a school teacher married to a prominent local attorney.[90]

Kate Harpst, a Northern California native who owned the car and provided the gasoline, was the widow of a pioneer Arcata merchant and lumberman.[91]

Minnesota-born Mary Anne Atkinson was the wife of a wealthy lumber company owner who had prospered in the timber trade in Michigan and Wisconsin and moved his company operations into the California redwoods.[92] Atkinson chaired the Conservation Committee of the Humboldt Federation of Women's Clubs and was known as a generous local philanthropist.

Wisconsin-born Ella Georgeson provided an especially powerful voice in the women's campaign to save the redwoods as co-owner and editorial director of *The Humboldt Standard* through the first three decades of the 1900s. Georgeson was a one-time president of the Humboldt County Federation of Women's Clubs and a prominent redwoods activist. Her publisher husband was a one-time Eureka mayor.[93]

The collective barnstorming strategy proved enormously successful, bringing fourteen vice-presidents, one for each town in the county, to the new women's league and attracting nearly 800 members within three months.[94] Quickly, the Humboldt County Women's Save the Redwoods League ranked among the county's largest and most influential civic organizations.

"At its core were about thirty-five women who met on a regular basis in a member's home," wrote historian Cameron Binkley. "The size of the core group was typical of a traditional women's club. Its officer-heavy structure, however, allowed the club to mobilize a much larger membership."[95]

Much of its success would rely on one woman.

"Joan of Arc" of the Redwoods

Laura Mahan was fifty-one years old when the summer of 1919 ushered in a defining moment in the survival of California's redwood giants. Born Laura Perrott on November 29, 1867, on a prosperous dairy ranch in southern Humboldt County, she was the daughter of pioneer parents who had traveled overland across the great expanses of the United States to reach California. Humboldt County at the time was filled with such stories of distant origins and hardships on the journey West.

Laura's father, William Perrott, who was orphaned at age six when his parents died of typhus a decade before the Civil War, grew up in Buchanan, Michigan, a small town north of South Bend, Indiana. After turning seventeen in 1859 he headed West, providing armed security for a military ammunition wagon train traveling from St. Louis, Missouri, to Salt Lake City, Utah. Perrott later rode another wagon train to California. He worked five years on ranches and dairy farms in Butte and Marin counties before arriving in Humboldt County.

There, in 1864, he merged his future with that of the prospering family of his new wife, Iowa native Sarah Jane Van Duzer. She had also ridden West in a wagon train, in 1848, at the age of three, traveling with her parents from St. Louis to Salt Lake City.[96] The Van Duzer family had wintered near the Great Salt Lake before taking the Oregon Trail to Oregon and then traveling south by ship to Humboldt County.

The newly-married couple homesteaded a ranch next to the Van Duzer's in picturesque dairy country near the present-day towns of Loleta and Ferndale.[97]

Laura was the middle child between an older brother, William, and a younger sister, Luella. She was a rarity for women of her place and time, attending Mills College for women in Oakland, then studying art at the Mark Hopkins Institute in San Francisco. Mahan's oil and watercolor paintings frequently featured landscapes of the redwoods.[98] Upon her return home, she was often seen in the woods and elsewhere with her easel and paints, capturing the region's extraordinary beauty.

Laura, who was hailed in a Eureka newspaper as "one of the most popular members of the social set," married prominent Eureka attorney James P. Mahan on July 15, 1908, at the age of forty. Her new husband, a 1905 law graduate of the University of Michigan and a month shy of forty, was similarly hailed as "one of Eureka's brightest and most promising young attorneys." The pair honeymooned in Yosemite National Park and moved into a two-story house at 819 I Street in a lovely Victorian-dotted neighborhood of Eureka.[99] There for a quarter century Mahan led her campaign to save the Humboldt County redwoods, earning a distinction reported in *The Los Angeles Times* as a "Joan of Arc" of the redwoods movement.[100]

Initial Donations of Land and Money

Humboldt County women's generosity with their family redwood holdings distinguished the national save the redwoods cause from the very beginning.

The first 160 acres of old-growth redwoods contributed for public use in Humboldt County, a historic first that instigated the eventual survival of 89,000 acres of virgin redwoods in Humboldt and Del Norte counties, was a gift from Martha McClellan of Eureka and her daughters Gertrude Fraser and Jeanette Graham during the summer of 1919.[101]

McClellan, born Martha Cook in Henry County, Iowa, also belonged to a generation that moved West in the years following the California Gold Rush. She was the widow of Hugh Webster McClellan, a Massachusetts native and Humboldt County pioneer rancher, businessman, and banker who died in 1911.[102]

McClellan's gift, proclaimed as "the nucleus of the national park" which was then envisioned along the state highway in southern Humboldt County, eventually became a section of The Garden Club of America Grove, which now encompasses more than 5,000 acres in Humboldt Redwoods State Park.

A second gift that summer, thirty acres of redwood forest along the new state highway, came from Laura Mahan's mother, Sarah Jane Perrott. Perrott, like McClellan, had also been widowed by the 1911 death of her husband.

The rush for cash was on, as well. With barely $100 in the Save the Redwoods League treasury during the summer of 1919, Mather, the millionaire Californian who ran the National Park Service, assumed the role of chief fundraiser, tapping both the nation's wealthy elites and residents in the redwood belt. The league arranged informative automobile rides through the South Fork of the Eel River redwood forests with the expected donation being $10,000.

Mather, after taking the tour himself, offered $15,000. Then, he surprised Kent by pledging another $15,000 in his name. Kent good-naturedly agreed to the pledge. The two officials of the federal government surely knew that the only way to get Humboldt County redwoods into a national park was to raise great sums of cash and buy forest tracts directly from timbermen.

News of the $30,000, doubled by a sudden matching donation from the Humboldt County Board of Supervisors, sent spirits soaring. Within a year these first donations paid for 297 acres known as Vance Bottom along the South Fork of the Eel River. The large tract of old-growth redwoods become in 1921 the Stephen T. Mather and William Kent groves along today's Avenue of the Giants.[103]

These earliest cash donations, alongside the substantial McClellan and Perrott land donations, were greeted as a great, hopeful beginning of the save-the-redwoods cause in Humboldt County. All received standing ovations during an enthusiastic September 6, 1919, rally for the redwoods at the Humboldt County courthouse in Eureka.

The local new women's save the redwoods league accounted for a fourth of the audience. Collectively, the town cheered a round of high-level promises to save their forests from Governor William Stephens via telegram, as well as from the State Forestry Board, the State Highway Commission, and the Save the Redwoods League.

Almost overnight, after years of frustration, dead ends, and inaction, it seemed possible, even likely, that a great national park would rise in their midst. Even in a county beholden to timber industry jobs, a confident aura of public spiritedness permeated the rally and grew contagious. Several businessmen offered small cash donations. Some small lumber operators assured the crowd they would cease cutting redwoods along the highway and sell parts of their holdings for park purposes.[104]

Eureka newspapers hailed the county's women for long sustaining and then reinvigorating the redwoods preservation movement. *The Humboldt Standard* printed a picture of the four women and their Save the Redwoods car, praising the barnstorming tactic "used so extensively in arousing the county to an understanding of the true nature of the park movement."[105]

The Pen Is Mightier Than the Ax

Success would require more, however. It would require rousing the nation.

Soon then began a barrage of national magazine stories aimed at the cream of the scientific community and designed to hasten a great awakening regarding the endangered redwoods. Save the Redwoods League founders Grant and Osborn led the way in *Natural History*, *National Geographic*, and a *Special Redwoods Bulletin* of the New York Zoological Society.

California writer Edna Hildebrand Putman, member of the California Federation of Women's Clubs, also toured the devastation of Humboldt County forests during the summer and fall of 1919. Putnam published her account the following summer in the upscale magazine, *Travel*, as well in the California Federation of Women's Clubs monthly *Clubwoman*.

Altogether it was a burst of beautiful, persuasive writing in the flowery language and media of a time before radio and television. Grant in September 1919 published the first of these magazine stories in his New York Zoological Society *Bulletin* only weeks after visiting Humboldt County with Mather.

"The forests are now threatened with annihilation," he warned readers in "Saving the Redwoods, An Account of the Movement During 1919 to Preserve the Redwoods of California." Grant described in detail the stark, rapid deterioration of Humboldt County's massive redwood belt, explaining,

"The writer drove through these same groves two years ago in August 1917 and the change was sickening. This example of human greed and waste can scarcely be described."

Grant, who founded and chaired the zoological society, also in 1916 authored *The Passing of the Great Race*, a book of since-discredited racial theories that promoted Nordic superiority under the science of eugenics.[106] A century later these theories, also espoused by other league founders, have left an unfortunate mark on the earliest legacy of the Save the Redwoods League, but they were not central to the League. Its focus today, as it was in the beginning, is the conservation of California's redwood forests.

Grant was talking about the plant world, for now, in which his expertise excelled. He vividly described an epic defacement of nature occurring within the world's most magnificent forests, writing, "It is scarcely necessary to dwell on the crime involved in the destruction of the oldest and tallest trees on earth. The cutting of a Sequoia for grape stakes or railroad ties is like breaking up one's grandfather's clock for kindling to save the trouble of splitting logs at the woodpile, or lighting one's pipe with a Greek manuscript to save the trouble of reaching for the matches."

Grant continued with the theme of antiquity, adding, "After the fall of the Roman Empire, priceless works of classic art were 'needed' for lime, and statutes by Phidias and Praxiteles were slacked down for this purpose, but the men who did it are today rightly dubbed 'vandals and barbarians.' What then will the next generation call us if we continue to destroy these priceless trees because lumber is 'needed' for grape stakes and railroad ties?"

Grant pointed out that one timber company, unnamed, "having thoroughly devastated large areas of its home state in the East, has recently purchased great tracts of redwoods." He called for governments to get busy and engage in similar feats of land acquisition so future generations could see the great trees:

> It will cost money to preserve the Redwoods — many millions; but California has no choice. Either the amount needed to save the groves must be supplied today, or else a far greater sum will be required ten years hence to purchase a butchered and isolated tenth part of the forests. These are the only alternatives. The protection of these Redwoods must be secured by Humboldt County and by the State of California, but the Federal Government also must do its share by establishing a large National Redwoods Park. The fundamental tragedy of the whole Redwood situation lies in the fact that these great trees are nearly all in the hands of private owners who cannot reasonably be expected to sacrifice their holdings for public benefit.

The state and nation, however foolish they may have been in giving away these lands, must now buy back at least a large portion of them.

Grant paid special homage to tourism as a viable alternative to timber cutting. He called it a loftier use of the redwoods and predicted correctly it would, in the long run, provide a richer source of permanent revenue.

"The inhabitants of Del Norte and Humboldt Counties have scarcely awakened to the possibilities of fabulous wealth in their Redwoods as an attraction for visitors," he wrote. "When Humboldt and Del Norte Counties awaken to a full realization of the revolution effected by automobiles, which will flood the country with tourists as soon as the highways are completed, they will find that a Redwood grove such as Bull Creek Flat is an attraction that is worth to the county many times the full net value of the timber contained within it." [107]

Eighteen black and white photographs accompanied Grant's story, contrasting forest scenes of natural and unspoiled beauty with images of burning redwoods and grape stakes piled along the tourist road. Where Grant's words failed, the photos supplied shock value and showed endless Humboldt landscapes destroyed by roadside lumbering.

Eureka photographer Emma Freeman, renowned for her portraits of Native Americans on the North Coast of California, took many of the stunning and alarming photographs accompanying Grant's story. Little is remembered today of Freeman's black and white photos of serene beauty and lumbering in the Humboldt redwoods, yet they provided great national impact when it was most needed. Freeman, who died in 1928, has since become a folk hero among photographers and feminists.

"She was a renegade woman who defied the constraints of the male-dominated world of the early 1900s," wrote art historian Peter Palmquist in a 1976 Freeman biography, *With Nature's Children: Emma B. Freeman (1880–1928) — Camera and Brush*:

> Schooled as an artist, she became an accidental photographer. A farm girl who pined for the art mecca of San Francisco, she did her most creative work in the unsophisticated backwoods. Her artistic output, like the history of Northern California Indians, was largely ignored until recently. Both remain a basis for legend.

In Washington, D.C., Mather engaged in his own attention-seeking spectacles to dramatize the redwoods. As director of the National Park Service, he ordered that redwoods be planted in front of the White House on November 11, 1919, to celebrate the first anniversary of the Armistice. In a 1970 account Mather biographer Robert Shankland recalled the scene:

General [John J.] Pershing was there representing the Army, and General [George] Barnett representing the Marine Corps, and distinguished people turned out in force. [Northern California Congressman Clarence] Lea delivered the dedicatory address, which gave generous attention to the redwoods in California, and the story went out all over the country. None of the redwoods planted that day, however, came within a thousand years or so of the normal life expectancy of the species; the Washington climate made short work of them.[108]

Within weeks of Mather's spectacle, the Humboldt County Women's Save the Redwoods League pulled off its own publicity coup, receiving approval from U.S. Postmaster Willard Wells to stamp outgoing mail from Humboldt County with the slogan, "Save the Redwoods." The women's league won fresh public funding for the redwoods, as well, after passing a resolution pressing the Humboldt County Board of Supervisors to allocate more money for roadside timber tracts along the South Fork of the Eel River. The board complied within four days, budgeting $34,000 to protect another 234 acres of the river redwoods from the ax and saw.[109]

In December of the auspicious year, 1919, a second and then a third national magazine story arrived to promote the redwoods before mass audiences of readers. "Sequoia — the Auld Lang Syne of Trees" appeared in *Natural History* imploring the nation to save "the greatest forests in the world." The author was Henry Fairfield Osborn, president of the American Museum of Natural History, a Save the Redwoods League founder, and who, like Grant, believed in since-discredited theories of eugenics in the realm of human affairs.[110]

Osborn painted a terrifying picture of the roadside damage being done by lumbermen:

> There are parts of the northwestern highways where for miles the road is narrowed and blocked with piled grape stakes and shingles and on the other hand, the ground is covered with a jumble of treetops, branches, slabs, and bark. Nor would I direct the gaze to the miles of desolate country where everything has been leveled and only charred stumps of giant trees mark the site of the forests destroyed. Instead, I would bring to the imagination the acres of forests still uncut and the potential joy for Americans of today and tomorrow in their possession.

Osborn then vividly described the magnificent untouched old-growth landscapes awaiting motorists in areas not yet visited by the lumbermen:

> There are stretches where the roadway leads from open sunshine and distant views of green, wooded mountain slopes into the giant forest

and on through colonnades of trees where the air is cool and fragrant and long beams of sunlight slant down through the green of redwood foliage.

Osborn offered hope to his elite audience, explaining that preservationists in Humboldt County and the Save the Redwoods League had already saved 800 acres along their state highway and just weeks earlier negotiated a temporary halt to further cutting along the tourist motorway. Yet he railed against the foolishness that made it necessary to buy back redwood tracts only recently publicly owned, and invoked the great land fraud that had put the redwood belt into private ownership:

> Uncle Sam owned all this redwood timber country. Yet Uncle Sam was so desirous of giving every man in the free United States his chance that millions of acres of timber land were sold at [$2.50] an acre when just one individual tree of the wide-stretching forests was worth at the lowest figure one hundred dollars. Thus, the timber went into the hands of private and corporation capital and nothing could be done about the crazy bargain — at least, the sales could not be undone.

Osborn, recalling for his largely Eastern audience the wholesale extermination of forests throughout the East, added, "That all these redwood lands are under the ownership of lumber companies means that saving them from the ax will be done only so fast as money can be found for their purchase."[1111]

Months later, in August 1920, Edna Hildebrand Putnam picked up the theme anew in the magazine, *Travel*. In "The Oldest Living Thing in the World," she wrote of an almost mystical or religious feeling she encountered in the redwoods:

> It came to me that perhaps the All Highest gave the Sequoia the gift of its long life in order that the survivors of those vanished forests might convey to us of today a proper conception of the magnificence of creation as it was when the world was young. I felt an undefined reverence for the patriarchal giants 'round about me.' And then a feeling of revulsion came over me as I remembered the purpose of my visit among them.

Putnam described how the new Redwood Highway to connect San Francisco and Oregon had opened Humboldt County to tourist traffic, and unexpectedly, to the horrors of lumbering on both sides of the highway.

> From spring until late fall, a continuous stream of motorists flooded in and what they saw sent them away sick at heart. At various points along the broad, new highway logging operations had been

commenced. Warning signs of falling timber were posted along the route. Tie camps and sawmills were busy converting the stately colonnade of age-old giants to a scene of indescribable havoc and ruin.

During the morning we had tramped about among the wreckage of the two sawmills and various tie camps. It hadn't been pleasant. The colonnade of stately old trees towering two and three hundred feet toward heaven had given place to piles of grape stakes, telegraph poles, and railroad ties. As if to add to the atmosphere of desolation the piles of brush and debris had been burned over in order that the massive trunks of the fallen monarchs might be managed more easily.

Putnam described the urgency propelling a new generation of leaders in their quest for a redwood national park. She hailed the Humboldt County Women's Save the Redwoods League in Eureka and the Save the Redwoods League in San Francisco. She recalled for her affluent audience of sophisticated travelers that the first outright donations of redwood forests to the preservation cause had been made by women: the two Humboldt County widows, Martha McClellan and Sarah Perrott.

Putnam, appealing to the nation's business and commercial leaders, as well as directly to the timber industry, explained that the new save-the-redwoods campaign did not propose to interfere with the legitimacy of lumbering the great forests. Instead it wanted to "restrict it to necessity, and to save the great trees directly bordering the highway and a representative forest tract to remind future generations of the marvel God wrought in the redwood forests that will then have vanished forever."

Putnam criticized an apparent lack of interest in redwood parks among lumber interests, the mostly out-of-state corporate operators "to whom a redwood tree represents so many thousand feet of lumber at so much per thousand." The work of defending redwood forests against such a mentality would require "the efforts of all who loved the beautiful and marvelous in nature," she wrote, and added, with perhaps too much optimism, "The world would not countenance the demolition of the Pyramids of Egypt to provide paving stones for the streets of Cairo. Neither will it sanction the total destruction of the oldest and greatest living forest in the world."[112]

A Turn Toward the State of California

As the new save-the-redwoods rhetoric soared, the U.S. government at last agreed to study the potential for a redwood national park in Humboldt or Del Norte County. On May 3, 1920, Congress approved Representative Lea's proposed study commission in the redwoods. Analysis of the national redwoods question fell to the U.S. Forest Service. The agency, in turn, appointed to its small commission a member of its own executive ranks, a University of California forestry professor, and a deputy state forester from the State of California.

After six months of study the group filed its so-called Reddington Report in October 1920. The report lamented the immense difficulty of selecting locations for a redwood national park when everywhere the commission member looked the sites were ideal. Ultimately, the commission, financed by the Save the Redwoods League, recommended a national park site in the Klamath River redwoods north of what is now Prairie Creek Redwoods State Park in northern Humboldt County. As customary, and perhaps entirely predictable for a preservationist idea still finding its way in Washington, D.C., little came of the report. Though the decade's economy showed all signs of earning its signature nickname, the "Roaring Twenties," the federal government could muster no action.

It could still spare no money for the redwoods.[113]

A century later, such federal stubbornness appears as profoundly irrational policy. But at the time few understood the national political angle better than former Congressman Kent. He wrote Drury with a realistic explanation of why Congress declined to budget money for redwoods as he explored land swaps with timber companies as an alternative to federal funding:

> This would entirely avoid what we found in Congress, namely that every Congressman would feel that if the government made an appropriation for a California Redwood park, each other state and every other congressional district would want something of the same for itself.[114]

As 1920 neared its end with no prospects for federal funds to buy large, threatened tracts of redwoods, Humboldt County leaders realized they could hardly keep asking timber operators to hold off logging their highway tracts. Told they would need $500,000 to buy out all operators alongside the scenic Redwood Highway, the Save the Redwoods League, which didn't have that kind of money, finally turned to the deeper pockets of the state legislature.

The federal government had failed them.

Now everyone in the triangle of actors working for publicly-owned redwoods, the county women's league, Eureka Chamber of Commerce, and the Save the Redwoods League, hoped the state would be more forthcoming. Humboldt County Superior Court Judge Fletcher A. Cutler drafted legislation to bring the money north. It was introduced in January 1921 as

Assembly Bill 80 by Assemblyman Frank Cummings of Ferndale and Senate Bill 64 by Senator Hans W. Nelson of Eureka, both Republicans.[115]

The identical bills proposed that California taxpayers buy the threatened South Fork of the Eel River roadside timberland in southern Humboldt and northern Mendocino counties. A century later, the legislation in Sacramento, named the Redwoods Preservation Bill, stands as the definitive origin of Avenue of the Giants and Humboldt Redwoods State Park, which would eventually host 53,000 acres of publicly-owned redwoods.[116]

Women's clubs in Humboldt County and statewide wasted no time in getting behind the bills, launching a barrage of letter writing, lobbying, and guided tours of the forests. In February 1921, Mahan and Murray of the Humboldt County Women's Save the Redwoods League joined Assemblyman Cummings and William L. Miller, secretary of the Eureka Chamber of Commerce, to escort powerful Assembly Ways and Means Committee Chairman T.M. Wright of San Jose through the South Fork of the Eel River redwoods. Joining Wright was a member of a state budget oversight board.

The women's league covered expenses for the trip of 290 miles from Sacramento to the Humboldt redwoods. Mahan, in a summary of the women's league activities for 1921, reported to her members that lobbying for the bill's passage constituted its top undertaking that year:

> The Woman's League endeavored to reach the influential people of practically every county in the state through correspondence, urging their support of the matter. Telegrams were dispatched to our representatives in the legislature, and prominent men and women were urged to the personal interview and letter to use their influence for passage of the measure. A direct result was that when the appropriation measure came up for consideration by a joint committee from the Senate and Assembly, Mr. Wright, then presiding officer, spoke in favor of the appropriation, a most unusual measure for the chairman of such committee.[117]

With Wright's support during a critical April 12, 1921, hearing, an allocation of $300,000 to buy Humboldt County redwoods cleared the Assembly and Senate committees responsible for what requests received state funds and what didn't. Before the vote, the bill received convincing, but overpromising testimony from U.S. Assistant National Park Service Director Horace Albright, who assured the committee "that state action on this matter would pave the way for a federal appropriation," and ultimately, a redwood national park in northern Humboldt County.[118]

That was not to be for another forty-seven years.

Mahan testified on behalf of the Humboldt County Women's Save the Redwoods League and 50,000 members of the California Federation of Women's Clubs.[119] Numerous others voiced support during the hearing: Kent, Sierra Club President William Frederic Badè, Save the Redwoods League Secretary Drury and representatives of the State Highway Commission, Humboldt County timber industry, and the State Board of Forestry, which operated as the California version of the U.S. Forest Service.[120]

The bill's backers by then had eliminated a crucial portion of the original proposal, which gave the state authority to condemn privately-owned forest land along the entire Redwood Highway through Humboldt County. The change, negotiated at the insistence of the Pacific Lumber Company and agreed to by the Save the Redwoods League, exempted the company's substantial holdings from potential condemnation.

The company, in the wake of that exemption, provided its support for the bill.[121]

Pacific Lumber's political clout at the time was formidable. It could be expressed in a thinly-populated rural county by its 1,500 employees, two mills, a railroad, and company town, Scotia, in southern Humboldt County. The familiar old company, founded locally in 1869 with 10,000 acres of redwoods, had become by 1905 the property of Michigan and Illinois investors who merged it with other holdings to form the Pacific Lumber Company of Maine. The Eastern-based company owned by 1921 almost 69,000 acres of Humboldt redwoods. It had already leveled 26,000 of those acres.[122]

As California lawmakers considered the Redwoods Preservation Bill in the spring of 1921, the graduating class at Eureka High School reflected the growing spirit in favor of preserving the great forests. The school's 1921 yearbook, the *Sequoia*, contained a poignant plea by graduating senior Ru-Flo Harper Lee not to vandalize, but to protect the big trees. Harper Lee, the teen-age daughter of a prominent Eureka Ford dealer, wrote:

> The current question of saving the redwoods and establishing a national park in this county should be of paramount interest to every resident of Humboldt County. The preservation of these mighty giants is our rightful duty and its accomplishment would mean not only distinct economic advantages, but also an advancement in civilization. As long as we allow avarice to blind us to the beauties of nature, to influence us to destroy the works of the Creator, we are vandals. Such magnificent grandeur as is embodied in the redwoods was not intended to be destroyed in a few generations but to live on and on in its primeval beauty. We being members of an educational institution should do our utmost to support this movement and to prevent the

ruin and the desolation which the woodman's axe is bringing on these — the last of a great forest. Save the Redwoods!¹²³

In adulthood, Harper-Lee would remain a Eureka resident. She became, in her own words, the "little old lady in tennis shoes" who helped lead local advocacy for a Redwood National Park during the 1960s and 1970s.

On April 20, 1921, a day of legislating that opened with a Sacramento pastor's prayer at 9:30 a.m. and ended with the bang of a gavel at two minutes before midnight, the State Assembly passed Assembly Bill 80 with one dissenting vote. Nine days later the Senate also approved the bill and sent it to Governor Stephens for his signature.¹²⁴

Days before the bill reached his desk, sixteen supporters, including Mahan and a representative of numerous Los Angeles women's clubs, had already pressed their case to the governor, a Republican from Los Angeles. Joining them were familiar faces in the fight for the redwoods: Eureka's Judge Fletcher, First National Bank of Eureka President Arthur E. Connick, the state forester, state highway commissioner, state superintendent of banks, a University of California professor, and representatives of two Humboldt County timberland owners, the Pacific Lumber Company and Sage Land and Improvement Co.¹²⁵

While the governor considered his options, President Adella Schloss and her California Federation of Women's Clubs, which earlier urged members "to do all they can" for the bill's passage, also resolved at its twentieth annual convention in Yosemite Valley that Governor Stephens should sign the bill, "that our Redwoods may be saved."

The federation also passed a formal resolution expressing its continued statewide support for a redwood national park in Humboldt County. The women's federation forwarded its resolution to President Warren Harding and the California congressional delegation, expressing intent that "they be urged to do their utmost to save and protect these wonderful trees while a few remain." ¹²⁶

The act of convincing Governor Stephens to finally sign the bill has become legendary in the history of saving Humboldt redwoods. The governor had long assured his support for the Save the Redwoods League and Humboldt County Women's Save the Redwoods League. But he balked suddenly at signing the bill. The state's two-year budget, he complained, was $14 million in the hole.

How could he spare $300,000 to buy trees?

By one popular anecdote, the governor's long-time friend Kent gave him a firm talking to. "Oh, hell, Bill. Shut the schools down," goes the account. "The kids would enjoy it, and it would only take them a year or two to make the work up. If these trees all go, it will take two thousand years to make them up."[127]

Another version of the story reported in Oregon's *Timberman* credited the governor's wife. Flora Stephens was long a member of the Los Angeles Friday Club, one of the most prominent of the city's women's associations and the largest individual member of the California Federation of Women's Clubs. Surely, she was familiar with her federation's long campaign to preserve redwoods in northernmost California.

The *Timberman* reported:

> During the last hours before the time elapsed for the signing of the bill, proponents of the measure gathered at the Capitol, and the anxiety was at fever pitch because no word had come from the governor as to whether he would give his approval to the large appropriation. It was within two hours of the closing time when Mrs. Stephens, wife of the governor, called on the telephone from the state mansion to ask whether the measure had been signed. And almost immediately announcement was made that the governor had given the measure his approval.

The date was June 3, 1921.[128]

Madison Grant, ever blunt, wrote to Merriam in Washington, D.C., exulting over the success and telling him, "Now that we have our teeth into the Treasury, we can bite hard on the taxpayers. Someone should suffer for the reckless squander of public property in the past."[129]

In Honor Of The Dearly Departed

With its first major victory still fresh, the Humboldt County Women's Save the Redwoods League, Save the Redwoods League, and "many leaders in the movement to preserve California's most unique trees" gathered weeks later on August 6, 1921, in southern Humboldt County to dedicate the first memorial grove in the redwoods.

It was a salute to World War I hero Colonel Raynal C. Bolling of Greenwich, Connecticut, a key force in developing a U.S. military air strategy for the war and a former chief counsel of U.S. Steel. Colonel Bolling was the first American officer of high rank to die in the war. The story of his death at the age of forty-one, for which he was posthumously awarded the Distinguished Service Medal Cross and the Cross of the Legion of Honor, is told on a historical marker to Bolling in Washington, D.C.:

> In mid-March 1918, the Germans launched an enormous drive along the Somme. On March 26, driving toward the front lines, Colonel

Bolling and his chauffeur, Private Paul L. Holder, encountered German machine-gun fire from both sides of the road. A German officer shot at Holder; Colonel Bolling shot the German with his sidearm and was killed by return fire of a second officer. Holder was captured and later released after the Armistice.[130]

A donation of $12,000 from Bolling's brother-in-law, Dr. J. C. Phillips of Wenham, Massachusetts, bought the thirty-five-acre redwood grove. Later, the Save the Redwoods League expanded the grove at Elk Creek and the South Fork of the Eel River to 100 acres.

The grand gesture of a redwoods memorial was considered the nation's first natural monument to a fallen soldier of the Great War. Madison Grant, in dedicating the memorial, combined themes of patriotism, country, and conservation in a speech titled, "Preserving an America Worth Fighting For."

Men like Bolling, Grant declared, "did not give their lives for a field of blackened stumps, nor for a river drained dry in summer, nor a raging torrent in winter. They did not give their lives for a mountainside torn open for the minerals and coal within it. They gave theirs for a country that had trees on the hillsides, that had fish in the streams, that had birds in the air, that had feathers and fur in the forest."

Grant suggested to the dignitaries before him, who represented the American Legion, Veterans of Foreign Wars, Native Sons of the Golden West, Sierra Club, Sempervirens Club, State Forestry Board, and State Highway Commission, that the nation could preserve more of California's redwood groves as a tribute to its fallen soldiers.

> "The American Legion and those of us who desire to do honor to the men who fought, should carry on this idea of Dr. Phillips," he said. "Instead of spending vast sums of money in useless monuments, the example of this memorial should be followed."[131]

The historic first of a redwood memorial grove to Colonel Bolling marked more than the beginning of Humboldt Redwoods State Park. In the wake of Grant's suggestion at the dedication ceremony, league promoters launched an enormously successful memorial grove program that would sustain itself for decades to save thousands of acres of redwoods.

Much credit goes to war widow Ethel Lansdale, an influential Garden Club of America member-at-large from San Rafael in California's Marin County. She introduced the idea of memorial groves to the Save the Redwoods League and persuaded many women in the old-money East and in California's new circles of wealth to save redwoods in memory of family members.[132]

Leading by example, Lansdale bought her own eighty acres of Humboldt redwoods in 1921. She christened the grove along the Redwood Highway as a memorial to her father, San Francisco Bay Area businessman Sidney Mason Smith, and her late husband, U.S. Navy Lt. Philip Lansdale, who had been killed in Samoa twenty-two years earlier, shortly after their marriage, during an anti-colonial uprising.[133]

Initially, the memorial grove concept allowed individuals to either help finance a grove or buy the land outright. The next step was to deed the land as a gift to the Save The Redwoods League, which in turn, deeded it to the State of California for inclusion in a state redwood park.

These memorial groves of the 1920s marked the opening acts of an American land trust sector that a century later has become fiercely powerful and connected to the highest levels of wealth and political influence. Current generations might imagine this has always been so. But in 1921, buying redwood groves from timber companies to save them for posterity represented an almost entirely new idea, that California's ancient redwoods had immense, and perhaps their greatest patriotic, spiritual, and economic value in remaining untouched.

The trees were going fast, however. By late 1921, twenty-one percent of Humboldt County's old-growth redwood forests were gone, the U.S. Forest Service and California State Board of Forestry reported.

The timber industry clearly still held the upper hand. Sixty-two percent of Sonoma County's ancient redwoods had already vanished. Likewise, twenty-eight percent of those in Mendocino County were gone. Only Del Norte County remained relatively untouched, according to the government report. Only nine percent of its virgin redwood forest had been leveled.

All told, from the 1850s through the end of 1921, some 90,000 acres of old-growth redwoods had disappeared statewide. Yet that was hardly the most alarming figure. Another 785,000 acres of old-growth redwoods for all practical purposes were also nearly gone. Many of the trees had already been cut "because of the prevailing logging practices which cut the timber two or three years in advance of the yarding of the timber." They were lying on the forest floor to be hauled away and milled.

Approximately one million acres of California's original 2 million acres of redwoods remained untouched.[134] The race for them, as the 1920s began, was on.

Chapter Three: The Ultimate Prize, 1922–1923

Today they are cutting the redwoods,
Cutting the beautiful trees.
I can hear no sound in the world
But the cry of the falling trees.

> —Georgia Russ Williams. Ferndale, California. Dedication ceremony, Humboldt Pioneer Redwood Grove. September 2, 1923.

In Los Angeles in the late spring of 1922, Laura Mahan looked out across the audience seated before her and made an improbable pitch for her hometown.

Everyone present, she said, addressing 1,000 members of the California Federation of Women's Clubs, should come to Eureka next year.

It was an audacious bid for the federation's 1923 convention.

Many in the audience inside the grand clubhouse of the women's Los Angeles Friday Morning Club surely gasped. Eureka? How would they get there and where would they stay, 1,000 of them, in Eureka? Humboldt County was then, as now, distant and remote, "somewhere up there," 270 miles north of San Francisco. In 1922, it belonged to a wild, vast forested region that had never hosted a major statewide convention of any kind.

The other city pursuing the 1923 convention seemed much more sensible, an obvious choice, Santa Cruz, easily accessible in the center of California and long accomplished at hosting large numbers of visitors.

Working alongside Mahan that day, William L. Miller, secretary of the Eureka Chamber of Commerce, assured federation members that Mahan's request was entirely reasonable. He talked up the city's wonderful Victorian charm, its amenities, meeting facilities, and new hotels. He described the growing ease of its transportation links to the rest of California.

Most of those listening to Mahan and Miller had never seen Eureka, nor the country around it. There were many easier, more sophisticated and wonderful cities to visit in their booming state of 3.5 million people. Yet there was a precedent. Many California Federation of Women's Clubs presidents had made the trip to Humboldt County redwoods over the past ten years to visit the federation's affiliate clubs there and all had written flatteringly about their trips in *The Clubwoman.*

Mahan offered a powerful closing argument. She reminded federation members it was their important and collective work, the letter writing, lobbying, publicity, and visits to the powerful, that secured $300,000 for the Humboldt redwoods from state government in 1921. Many groups had assisted at the Capitol in Sacramento, but the federation's lobbying was "most effective," in the words of Save the Redwoods Secretary Newton B. Drury.[135]

"You should come up to that magic God-made spot to see the results of your own action in working for the measure that passed," said Mahan, offering the invitation.

It was a long shot. But to the delight of Eureka's two newspapers, business establishments, and budding tourism industry, the California Federation of Women's Clubs agreed. Its members would meet the following year in Eureka.[136]

It was a pivotal moment in the history of saving the redwoods. Not only would it broaden statewide support for the new movement to preserve them. It would lead to financial backing from many of California's most prominent families and the direct acquisition of a woman's federation grove.

Santa Cruz would get its convention in 1925.

If bringing 1,000 women's club members to Eureka wasn't a big enough accomplishment, hearts stirred that spring and summer in Humboldt County for another reason. The State Board of Forestry, with $300,000 from the Redwood Preservation Bill in hand, was displaying the full power of the state in the fight for the redwoods.

The forestry board, industry-friendly, responsible for regulating forest management practices in California, spent the opening months of 1922 in full swing, negotiating agreements with timber owners for holdings up to a half-mile wide along the Redwood Highway. Leading the effort, Deputy State Forester Solon H. Williams reported the state was paying "commercial value and no more" for the beautiful forest groves along the highway. "All lands were purchased on a stumpage basis. No payments have been made until check cruises had been made by a reputable cruiser of the board's selection," he wrote for the record.

By year's end Williams and the board of forestry had assembled and placed under state jurisdiction, "a continuous strip of land from the township line, between townships One and Two South, on both sides of the highway to Miranda, a distance of approximately twelve miles excepting two pieces for which the owners are asking exorbitant prices."

It was a stunning government accomplishment in only eighteen months.

The board of forestry bought and saved outright 1,654 acres of exceptionally beautiful redwood country along the winding South Fork curves of the Eel River. Humboldt County residents and a handful of other contributors through California and the United States deeded another 675 acres of South Fork of the Eel River redwoods to the state.

What the state had done in the Santa Cruz Mountains twenty-two years earlier, what President Roosevelt had done at Muir Woods in 1908, and what Sonoma County had done near the Russian River in 1917, had now been accomplished among the world's greatest stands of redwoods in Humboldt County. In response to the new question of how to properly maintain more than 2,000 acres of publicly-owned redwoods, wealthy philanthropist Ethel Crocker of Hillsborough, California, daughter-in-law of transcontinental railroad baron Charles Crocker, contributed another $25,000 to assist with upkeep of the properties.[137]

When combined, the 2,319 acres marked the beginning of something extraordinary, the Avenue of the Giants between Weott and Miranda, a first great success in saving the state's northernmost redwoods. And it was only the beginning. Within a decade, the new state park born from these earliest donations and land acquisitions, Humboldt Redwoods State Park, would grow to more than 20,000 acres.[138] That also was just a beginning for the park that now holds the largest contiguous area of old-growth redwoods in the world.[139]

California forestry historian C. Raymond Clar in 1959 praised the supporting role played by the Save the Redwoods League as a "virtual arm of the Board of Forestry in persuading, negotiating, and investigating among landowners and potential donors. This cooperative venture," wrote Clar, "seems to have worked with remarkable smoothness."[140]

Williams formally reported the state's successes in the redwoods in the Ninth Biennial Report of the State Board of Forestry sent to California Governor William Stephens on January 2, 1923. Governor Stephens, in signing the Redwood Preservation Bill in 1921, had clearly now accomplished the legacy foreseen by three Save the Redwoods League founders during their inaugural 1917 trip into the Humboldt redwoods. An impressive scenic and protected redwood drive in southern Humboldt County would be one of the long-remembered acts of his administration. In recognition of the governor's important political contribution to the redwoods movement, the state board soon set aside 317 acres purchased through the Redwood Preservation Bill and named it the Stephens Grove. With additional land purchases through 1950 the Redwood Highway grove paying respects to the former governor of California came to total 347 acres.[141]

Given the significance of this first great government accomplishment in the redwoods, it is useful to read Williams' accounting of the venture precisely as he wrote it nearly a century ago. In describing the public acquisitions along the South Fork of the Eel River, Williams wrote for the record and for posterity,

The following lands have been secured by purchase:

Vance Bottom, 297 acres, price $36,219.16

Sage Land & Improvement Company, 394 acres, price $60,000

Melinda Stoddard et al., 160 acres, price $22,155.66

Standish and Hickey, 40 acres, price $2,000

Logan Estate, 396 acres, price $70,000

Devoy & Gillogly, 120 acres, price $30,000

R.C. Chapman, 47 acres, price $22,000

Baldwin & McKinnon, 200 acres, price $19,991.16

Williams explained that the state's acquisition of nearly 300 acres along the Redwood Highway at Vance Bottom, later subdivided into the Stephen T. Mather and William Kent groves, was eased by Mather and Kent's financial contributions in 1919.

Williams also cited a contribution of $2,000 from wealthy socialite Clara Hinton Gould of Santa Barbara to help purchase the Chapman property and noted it would be called the Gould Memorial Grove. Gould provided the funds in memory of her late husband Frederick Saltonstall Gould, a New York-born naturalist and an 1875 graduate of Harvard University.[142] A year earlier, Gould also contributed $10,000 in her husband's name to Harvard University for a library in its new division of chemistry.[143]

In addition to the list of lands acquired by the state with public funds, Williams reported to Governor Stephens "a list of lands donated to the state":

Mrs. Sarah Perrott et al., 15 acres

Hammond Lumber Company, 30 acres

Humboldt County, 275 acres

Dr. John C. Phillips, 35 acres

Save the Redwoods League, 40 acres

Standish and Hickey, 3 acres

Mrs. J. Hobart (Lora) Moore, Mr. Edward E. Ayer, 160 acres

Standish and Hickey, 40 acres

R.C. Chapman, 7 acres

Three of these land donations on and near the Redwood Highway fit into a new league fund-raising strategy of saving redwoods in dedicated memorial groves. Phillips' thirty-five acres, contributed in memory of his late brother-in-law, became the Colonel Raynal C. Bolling Grove dedicated to the deceased war hero in 1921.

Fifteen acres deeded to the state by Sarah Jane Perrott and Laura Mahan became the Perrott Memorial Grove honoring their late husband and father. The grove site near Weott is marked with a bronze roadside plaque that reads: "In Memory of William Perrott, Pioneer, Kind Husband, Father, Foster Father, and Friend."

Another forty acres contributed by Oakland lumberman Henry B. Hickey and his wife, Emma, at the southern gateway to the redwoods in Mendocino County, became the Edward Ritter Hickey Memorial Grove. The contribution from the Hickeys, co-owners of the San Francisco-based Standish-Hickey Timber Company, paid tribute to their young son who died in 1918 of the Spanish Flu while helping infected residents of Fort Bragg on the Northern California coast. The memorial, now known as the Standish-Hickey State Recreation Area, has since grown to nearly 1,000 acres due to subsequent donations by members of the Standish family and the Save the Redwoods League.[144]

For reasons unknown, Williams did not report the 160 acres of redwoods gifted by Martha McClellan and her daughters, nor the thirty acres contributed by Sarah Jane Perrott during the earliest burst of redwoods park enthusiasm in the summer of 1919. Nonetheless, Williams paid a special, moving tribute to women like them in Humboldt County. The deputy state forester credited county women with sparking both the local movement to save their redwoods and for formation of the national Save the Redwoods League.

Wrote Williams to Governor Stephens:

A few years ago a small company of earnest women of Eureka, Humboldt County, conceived the idea of saving a portion of the redwoods in Humboldt County for future generations. The idea spread all over the United States, and as a result of the propaganda instituted by this band of enthusiastic women, the Save the Redwoods League was formed in 1919. This organization, headed by Dr. John C. Merriam, of the Carnegie Institution of Washington, D.C., has worked untiringly to the end that a portion of these redwoods shall be saved.

Williams likewise paid homage to the Save the Redwoods League for results that could only be described as spectacular given the trials local preservationists had endured, the years of federal inaction, and without public money, their initial slim prospects of success.

"Too much praise cannot be given the Save the Redwoods League for their untiring activity in securing donations for this park," Williams wrote. "Other tracts will no doubt be donated adjoining the main tract and in other sections of the redwood belt in the near future."[145]

Save the Redwoods Secretary Drury, late in his life during the early 1970s, said that timber companies also deserved credit for preserving the beautiful views along the Redwood Highway. "In general, the lumber companies were not antagonistic to the Save the Redwoods program," he said. "In general, also they felt that they should have a quid pro quo, that if this lumber were taken from them, we should pay the going market rate, with which we had no quarrel at all. There's never been any friction on that score."[146]

In the wake of the state acquisitions, the Save the Redwoods League and the Humboldt County Women's Save the Redwoods League dreamed bigger than the South Fork of the Eel River alone. Now they wanted the grandest of all the redwoods in Humboldt County. The Save the Redwoods League had its eyes on the rich alluvial stands of Bull Creek Flat redwoods near Weott. The women's league was intent on saving the nearby lowland forests of Dyerville Flat.

Both stands of world-class redwood timber belonged to the Pacific Lumber Company.

The Timber Industry's Public Relations Problem

In the earliest days of the redwoods preservation campaigns, Drury made repeated assurances of fairness in the league's dealings with lumber companies. Yet most of the corporate mill operators remained wary of these powerful and nationally-connected outsiders eyeing their forest holdings. The remarkable success of the Save the Redwoods League, in partnership with state government and women's clubs throughout California, earned them much anxious attention within the executive suites of the Humboldt redwood products industry. Though most timbermen initially supported redwood preservation along the South Fork of the Eel River, and many found a new revenue source in the league's willingness to pay market prices, the largest companies with the best timberland sensed a dangerous threat in the new public mood regarding their properties.

Humboldt County lumber companies were long accustomed to setting and enforcing their commercial agendas in the redwoods. They did this handily by providing livelihoods for a majority of the local population, paying the most taxes, dominating and controlling the local economy, and subsequently, the politics that protected their agendas.

Suddenly now, despite 7,000 jobs they provided in a county of more than 37,000 residents, these outsiders with state and national agendas were pushing and strengthening a new conservation agenda inside the redwood forests they owned.[147]

Even the Humboldt County Board of Supervisors was now in the conservation game. The board had allocated more than $100,000 in local taxes to buy redwood forests during 1921 and 1922. Those were taxes largely paid by timber companies and their employees, spent now to protect county redwoods along the Redwood Highway from timber companies.

Aiming to defend their forest properties if it became necessary six major companies — the Hammond Lumber Company, Little River Redwood Company, Mendocino Lumber Company, Pacific Lumber Company, Union Lumber Company, and Glen Blair Lumber Company — commissioned a forestry expert from Portland, Oregon, to gauge public attitudes about their forest management practices in the redwoods.

The findings were troubling.

The public attitude was cautious and even skeptical toward the timber industry, respected consulting forester David T. Mason reported. Mason, known widely as the father of sustained-yield forestry in the United States and a champion for sound forest management practices, conveyed an unwanted message to his industry colleagues:

> Whether we like it or not, the public is coming more and more to feel that lumbermen should not remove the old-growth timber and leave an unproductive wasteland behind them. In talking with people outside of the lumber industry in the redwood region it has been found that the rather common feeling is that when the timber has been cut and the lumber industry is through in the region, prosperity will be largely gone. The Save the Redwoods League movement is especially calling attention to the redwoods in a way not felt by any other species.[148]

Mason's warning compelled no dramatic or immediate changes among the lumbermen in cutting their forests. In hindsight, their corporate decisions to stay the course in the redwoods is easily understood given the high regard among Californians for the redwood products they manufactured and sold. While most people enjoyed stories about the stately redwoods from friends who saw them, they were far more familiar with the beautiful, resilient end products of the old giants in their everyday lives.

Renowned California botanist Willis Linn Jepson, raised by Gold Rush-era pioneer parents on a ranch near present-day Vacaville, California, described his easy familiarity with redwood products in his second edition of *The Trees of California*, published in 1923:

> The writer of these lines is a Californian. He was rocked by a pioneer mother in a cradle made of Redwood. The house in which he lived was largely made of Redwoods. His clothing, the books of his juvenile library, the saddle for his riding pony were brought in railway cars chiefly made of Redwood, running on rails laid on Redwood ties, their course controlled by wires strung on Redwood poles. He went to school in a Redwood schoolhouse, sat a desk made of Redwood and wore shoes, the leather of which was tanned in Redwood vats. Everywhere he touched Redwood. Boxes, bins, bats, barns, bridges, bungalows were made of Redwood. Posts, porches, piles, pails, pencils, pillars, paving-blocks, pipelines...were made of Redwood.[149]

Jepson, a University of California professor and a founding executive committee member of the Save the Redwoods League, lived to be ninety years old. During a lifetime that ended in 1946 he saw hundreds of thousands of acres of California's redwood forests fall to the ax. The big redwood timber companies of the 1920s and their successors, each in the business of providing products beloved by the market and meeting its unrelenting demand, largely continued to resist calls to preserve their lucrative redwoods in state or national parks. Consequently, in the brief span of eight decades, an infinitesimal moment measured against the average lifespan of a single old-growth tree, they leveled ninety-five percent of California's redwood inheritance.

The Pacific Lumber Company, still absorbing Mason's assessment of widespread popular support for a new conservation ethic in the redwoods, opted in August 1922 for more than staying the course. It unleashed a blunt strategy of trying to weaken the movement that increasingly coveted its rich forest holdings for uses other than redwood lumber.[150]

The company made its first move with a divisive and diversionary tactic, offering the preservationists a section of its South Dyerville Flat forest on the Redwood Highway for a public redwood park. In exchange for their approximately 300-acre gift company executives added a controversial condition. The Humboldt County Women's Save the Redwoods League, Save the Redwoods League, and the State of California must cease any future requests to buy Pacific Lumber Company land for parks.

The company's generous one-time donation appeared brilliantly conceived to fit with the league's new promotional and fund-raising strategy. The donation would be in the form of a memorial redwood grove to the late founder of Pacific Lumber, Simon J. Murphy.

In a letter to the Save the Redwoods League, Fred Murphy, spokesman for the Detroit-based family that owned the lumber company, declared that its gift:

> .... should appeal to thoughtful people who are interested in preserving redwoods without seriously interfering with the development of the community by so handicapping the lumber companies that they will be unable to operate successfully. In making this park available I am selfish enough to want to feel that in agreeing to the acceptance you and your associates also agree that not only will you cease any agitation for acquiring more redwood timber in the two sections noted (Bull Creek and the main Dyerville flats), but you will use your best efforts to curb any propaganda which may be started by others.

In a definitive account of this early confrontation redwoods historian Susan R. Schrepfer asserts that the offer quickly had its intended effect on the movement. The proposal neatly divided what had been a unified save-the-redwoods campaign along its local and national lines, even as members of both lines uniformly disliked the offer and particularly, its conditions.

Pacific Lumber had cleverly exposed the rifts between the Humboldt County Women's Save the Redwoods League and county residents who wanted to buy the entirety of the company's beautiful Dyerville Flat forest, and the national Save the Redwoods League, which wanted first and above all to buy the company's magnificent Bull Creek Flat holdings.

Members of both groups worried among themselves that there wasn't enough money to buy both of their prized areas, especially from a company that clearly did not want to sell either.

"The local residents saw the league's desire for Bull Creek as standing in the way of the acquisition of the main Dyerville Flat," historian Schrepfer wrote in 1971.

Dyerville Flat, a large forest near Weott on the South Fork of Eel River, consisted of two forests divided by a slight ridge. The southern part being offered by Pacific Lumber was thinly populated with redwood trees and considered inferior to the main northern forest where locals had long enjoyed picnics amid denser stands of the big trees.

Yet an offer was an offer. Eureka's business establishment began to crack under pressure applied by a powerful local employer, landowner, and taxpayer.

The Eureka Chamber of Commerce soon began to tone down its support for Save the Redwoods League ambitions to acquire thousands of acres of Bull Creek Flat and possibly Dyerville Flat for a state park. Ominously, Eureka Banker Arthur E. Connick, who belonged both to the local chamber's Redwoods Committee and the national league's advisory council, also began to soften. As president of Eureka's First National Bank, Connick was familiar with the finances of local lumber companies and had proved an exceptional help in negotiating deals during 1921 and 1922 with timber owners along the Redwood Highway. The Pacific Lumber Company, he began to say to his various audiences, had every right to refuse to consider outside offers for its extensive timber holdings.

But neither Connick nor the Eureka Chamber of Commerce prevailed.

The Humboldt County Women's Save the Redwoods League and the Save the Redwoods League turned Connick's reasoning on its head and defiantly refused to consider the timber company's offer. In a letter to the Pacific Lumber Company, Save the Redwoods League Chairman Joseph D. Grant wrote that the league could in no way "cease agitation and propaganda" for saving the Humboldt redwoods. More importantly, he stated, as a representative of the public in its desire to acquire land for parks, the league would not sign onto "a program which is counter to public opinion or the public interest."

Grant's blunt rejection of the offer, backed by local sentiment, prompted a threat by Pacific Lumber that the company would talk no more about selling any of its forests.

The company had long maintained that it needed Dyerville Flat "for a railroad, logging yards, yards for piling their timber products, and camp sites for their men." In that regard, selling Dyerville Flat was bad for business. The company would need a new site for its railroad and yards, a new site farther from its large timber holdings. That would increase costs. With increased costs the company could not compete on the market.[151] It was an entirely reasonable business position, except that it clashed head on with public sentiment.

All sides were now dug in for a longer battle. The company's opening tactic had failed. Yet neither had the preservationists with their big dreams of public parks saved an acre of redwoods beyond those donated or purchased through the state Redwoods Preservation Bill.

In August 1922 it was impossible to know that this clash of wills and resulting stalemate was simply the opening act in a drama that would consume nine years and tax the patience and resolve of all involved. In the end, somehow, and almost miraculously, the standoff between business and conservation produced a deal for 13,000 acres of exceptional redwoods and gave both the locals and the league what they wanted, the entirety of Dyerville Flat and neighboring Bull Creek Flat for Humboldt Redwoods State Park.

An Awakening of Spirit

Meanwhile, a crescendo of inspirational writing awakening the nation's conscience to the plight of the Northern California redwoods continued. Los Angeles Audubon Society President Carrie F. Bicknell penned the newest love story to the Humboldt redwoods in the California Federation of Women's Clubs' October 1922 *Clubwoman*.

Bicknell, chairman of Birds and Wildlife in the federation's Los Angeles district, described an automobile trip of twenty-eight days with friends and grandson Frederick Bicknell Gombro through thirty-nine counties of California and Oregon. Like anyone who sees the ancient redwood forests of Northern California for the first time, Bicknell enthusiastically described the stunning scenery and a self-described awakening of her spirit:

> A narrow sharply curving mountain road through fire-swept knobcone pines led us across the Oregon line into California, where the drive along the Redwood Highway to Crescent City and Eureka was a revelation to us — that California possessed such a wealth of primeval forest. Majestic redwood groves towering so high that at midday the roadbed seems in twilight. Masses of beautiful ferns bedeck the upturned roots of the fallen monarchs. Vines climb their broken trunks and their moss-embedded bark is studded with young trees while stumps of parent trees, partly gone to decay, are circled by a vigorous growth of slim redwoods.

Bicknell, a lover of nature since her childhood as "the little shepherdess" who mothered stray lambs in her father's Wisconsin flock, declared her new devotion to saving the redwoods:[152]

> Through miles and miles of tree-arched highway we rode entranced, our wonder ever increasing and our enthusiasm never waning. More than ever is our interest aroused and will our efforts be put forth to

help save these giant redwood forests for future generations. Necessity for quick action is apparent as lumbermen already cover every acre of this valuable timber.

Bicknell, who was married to a Los Angeles physician and surgeon, also described her visit to Eureka and chronicled the preparations underway there for the California Federation of Women's Clubs' May 1923 convention. The new Eureka Inn was nearing completion, she advised federation members who would need rooms there. "We had the pleasure of viewing the interior of this hotel and meeting one of the representatives of the Chamber of Commerce who volunteered to mail us any forthcoming literature on the Redwood Forests."[153]

A similar awakening of spirit showed at the state Capitol in Sacramento, as the new 1923 legislative session showed rising public interest in protecting redwoods along the state's new highways. Assembly Member Albert A. Rosenshine, a Republican attorney from San Francisco, introduced Assembly Bill 106 to help wealthy benefactors buy redwood forests from unwilling sellers and deed them to the state for parks. The bill, which applied only to redwood forests, was sponsored by an anonymous wealthy California woman aiming to buy and preserve the Giant Sequoias in the Sierra Nevada known as the Calaveras Big Trees. The grove, championed two decades earlier by Laura Lyon White and her San Francisco-based California Club, remained in private ownership. California publisher William Randolph Hearst had also sponsored the legislation. He similarly aimed to buy and preserve a tract of Santa Cruz Mountain redwoods and deed them to the state.

Both sponsors were immensely frustrated by their experiences in trying to save the Sequoia and Coast Redwood forests. Each was trying to perform a public good. Neither could get owners of the land they coveted to set a price.

Assembly Bill 106 was designed to solve their problem. It specified that when a landowner refused to sell to a buyer who would preserve the property in its natural state for a park, the buyer could have the property condemned. The bill required first that the buyer deposit funds in the state treasury equal to the forest's appraised value. If the owner then refused to sell, condemnation proceedings would begin immediately.[154]

The bill caught perfectly the spirit of conservation then flourishing throughout California and the nation. Prominent backers included National Park Service Director Stephen T. Mather. Locally, the Humboldt County Women's Save the Redwoods League declared itself among supporters of the bill. Members mobilized support with letters and telegrams to state lawmakers, Governor Friend Richardson, and officers of the California Federation of Women's Clubs.

The timber industry mobilized its own support to oppose the bill. Company owners expressed to lawmakers their confusion and anxiety about increasing numbers of well-heeled donors who wanted to buy their prized company redwoods and deed them to the state. Timber lobbyists complained correctly that the state had no organized plan guiding its proposed redwood parks. Timber companies could hardly plan a long-term business strategy when their best holdings could be easily condemned under the proposed bill.

The timber industry eventually arrived en masse in Sacramento with its own severe countermeasures. It proposed to ban eminent domain for park purposes entirely. Industry representatives lobbied for a moratorium on land acquisitions for state parks. The moratorium would remain in place until the state produced an overall vision and plan for state parks.

The industry proposals alarmed redwood park promoters. Such rules, they said, would make it impossible to save treasures of national significance such as Bull Creek Flat.

Compromise between the two forces ultimately toned down demands of the timber industry. But it also weakened the bill's original purpose to ease the purchase of threatened redwoods. The bill ultimately approved by the legislature and signed by the governor cemented the compromise into law. It allowed continued condemnation of redwoods for state parks. But it set conditions that would make condemnation almost impossible. There would be no moratorium on buying redwoods for parks. Instead, the state would produce a parks plan to end the piecemeal approach to protecting redwood forests that so distressed the timber companies.[155]

The central forces in the fight for the redwoods, the timber companies and Save the Redwoods League, were pleased with the compromise. The Humboldt County Women's Save the Redwoods League was much less enthusiastic. In meeting minutes for December 2, 1923, the women's league aptly reported: "The bill was finally passed and signed after its teeth had all been carefully extracted."

Conservation, The Hope of Civilization

On a Tuesday morning in 1923, the first day of May, readers of *The Humboldt Times* awoke to see its welcoming message to 1,000 California Federation of Women's club members beginning at last their convention in Eureka. The newspaper's owners saluted the federation's arrival as "one of the most important gatherings of the kind ever held in Humboldt County" and implored local residents to behave and "favorably impress the delegates."

It was a spectacle in a city that had seen nothing like it. Federation members throughout California filled every hotel in Eureka and Arcata. More stayed in hundreds of private homes throughout the city. At the downtown train station 300 club members arrived at once on a special State Daylight Convention Train from the Ferry Building in San Francisco. Upon arrival, each delegate received a badge with an image of a redwood tree and a program that included photographs of redwoods suitable for framing. Each federation member was also handed a souvenir redwood box filled with cheeses and other Humboldt County products.

Eureka's three major women's clubs had worked months on such welcoming details and the endless other arrangements for the four-day convention. The city's Monday Club, Wednesday Club and Departmental Club performed as one so well in its monumental task that members soon after the convention voted to merge into a single club. That was the new Eureka Women's Club which still meets regularly nearly a century later.[156]

On the convention's opening morning, Annie Zane Murray offered a stirring welcome as a representative of both the Humboldt County Federation of Women's Clubs and the Humboldt County Women's Save the Redwoods League. Additional welcomes followed from William L. Miller, secretary of the Eureka Chamber of Commerce, and Fletcher A. Cutler, who had written the 1921 Redwood Preservation Bill and still served on the chamber's Redwood Committee.[157]

Though the club members gathered in Eureka under a theme to protect the redwoods, their agenda portrayed the wide range of women's interests during the early 1920s. It was a decade already shaping up as one of the most conservative in memory with its prohibition of alcohol, limits on immigration, and preference for business over the activist government of the Progressive Era. Yet for the women deliberating their issues in Eureka in 1923, the decade also embodied a carefree optimism with its new soaring economy, mass production of automobiles and electric appliances, and its booming new American middle class nourished by a rush of factory-building and industrialization.[158]

There were sessions on law and international relations with speakers from England and Mexico. A Stanford University history professor advised club members on American foreign policy. Women attended sessions on educating children, child welfare, criminal justice, and labor laws affecting women and children. They discussed fine arts and music, preserving

California's historic sites, and the newest state legislation being considered in Sacramento.

In days of meetings, the delegates telegrammed California Governor Friend Richardson and thanked him for cooperating with their federation's interests. They sent a telegram to President Warren G. Harding, then in the last three months of his life, requesting support for saving the redwoods. They sent another telegram to the 3-million-member General Federation of Women's Clubs, requesting national support for their California redwoods campaign during its annual meeting soon in Atlanta.

On the convention's fourth and final day federation members fulfilled the primary purpose of their 1923 gathering, to protect the old-growth redwoods of Northern California. Hundreds visited the Bolling Memorial Grove fifty miles south of Eureka on the Redwood Highway. They passed by sawmills converting the big downed trees into lumber products. They picnicked beneath the splendid redwoods of Dyerville Flat on tables decorated with wild flowers.

There they finally saw the beautiful lowland forest so beloved by county residents and the Humboldt County Women's Save the Redwoods League. They heard firsthand about struggles with the Pacific Lumber Company over its future. *Los Angeles Times* writer Myra Nye was there with them and described the incomparably beautiful Dyerville forests for her readers back home:

> Shafts of sunlight fell aslant, like those of dim cathedral interiors. The forest pathways were lined with low-growing trilliums, hepaticas and spring beauties of such fragile and rare beauty as is never elsewhere seen. Gorgeous rhododendron massed itself in crimson walls ten feet high; the orchid and shell tints in their omnipresent loveliness vied with the chaste dogwood blossoms and the sprays of wild syringa.

The sights ultimately inspired one of the great lasting achievements of the federation, its ninety-acre California Federation of Women's Clubs Redwood Grove dedicated a decade later at North Dyerville Flat. Within hours of the May 4 decision by federation members to buy and deed to the state a redwood grove of their own, the grove's acquisition fund swelled with its first $300. Within two years the fund reached to nearly $45,000.[159]

The Humboldt Times, which had enthusiastically welcomed the federation to Eureka days earlier, now saluted its decision with a front-page headline: "Clubs Will Buy Redwoods Tract on Highway. One Dollar Each from 60,000 Members will Purchase Grove of Trees."

Ten years later during dedication ceremonies for the federation grove, Laura Mahan, president of the Humboldt County Women's Save the

Redwoods League, placed the *Times'* May 5, 1923, news story alongside other items in a buried copper time capsule.

The historic decision to save a stand of old-growth redwoods marked one of the final acts of the convention that Mahan had delivered with her impassioned plea the previous year. Afterward, federation women formally concluded their gathering with a poignant changing of the guard. Beneath the tall Dyerville redwoods President Minnie Fitzgerald of Stockton and San Francisco ended her 1921–1923 term and yielded the post to Augusta Urquhart of Los Angeles. Fitzgerald, a long-time women's club activist and writer married to the publisher of *The Stockton Independent*, had notably empowered the federation as a formidable political force in winning $300,000 in state funds to buy redwoods.[160]

Urquhart would make her own mark during the next two years with a major fund-raising campaign for the federation's redwood grove in Humboldt County. The wife of a Los Angeles physician, she had gained her executive experience as president of the federation's Los Angeles district and as former president of the Women's Christian Temperance Union in California.[161]

Nye captured the poignant closing spirit with a personal note in *The Los Angeles Times*:

> Never shall I forget the closing days of this year's convention at Eureka. California's club womanhood had come from San Diego and Sonoma, up and down the middle of the world. They had come from Mendocino across to Mono on the Nevada line. A thousand of them gathered in the forest, and there among the trees, whose boles the sunlight had not touched for a thousand years, in the dim forest at noonday, they clasped their hands and pledged themselves to Conservation — The Hope of Civilization.

Nye reflected further in *The Times* that "of all the resolutions that were passed, the one of conservation will long be remembered and long wield an influence."[162]

The prediction proved both memorable and true. Nearly a century later, the federation's work in the redwoods remains one of its signature identities. Thousands upon thousands of motorists driving the Avenue of the Giants every year discover the existence of the California Federation of Women's Clubs through its redwood grove conceived during its annual convention in Eureka on May 4, 1923.

In Memory of the Humboldt Pioneers

Two months after the excitement of the convention had died down a surprise memorial donation created a fresh stir and marked the important beginning of a new Prairie Creek Redwoods State Park sixty miles north of Eureka. The new park with its gentle creeks, deep forested hillsides, and herds of Roosevelt Elk would prove itself a major tourist draw and decades later, reaching 14,000 acres, become a key component of Redwood National and State Parks.

The donor was Zipporah Russ, eighty-four years old and the matriarch of a Ferndale pioneer family that had prospered mightily on the California frontier. Russ announced, through the Save the Redwoods League, a gift of 166 acres of old-growth redwoods in memory of her late husband, Joseph Russ, and "all the early settlers who helped to build up Humboldt County and the state."[163]

The gift was Russ' second contribution to preserving the Humboldt County wilderness. Three years earlier she had given 105 acres to the City of Ferndale, stipulating that Russ Park in the forested hills above the town would be a bird and wildlife sanctuary with no shooting or hunting allowed.[164]

Her newest gift at Prairie Creek was to be called the Humboldt Pioneer Redwood Grove. *The Humboldt Standard* saluted the gift on July 11, 1923, reporting:

> Some of the largest trees of the Redwood Belt are found on this tract of timber. One enormous Sequoia particularly has been discovered which is believed to be among the largest in existence. Not only redwoods, but also the massive firs, hemlocks, maples, spruce, oaks and other trees found on this tract, together with the giant ferns and other undergrowth, make it an area of unusual beauty. It is still in its primeval state, and many of its acres have probably never been trodden by man.[165]

Russ was a child of the Gold Rush, a fourteen-year-old girl who left Illinois with her parents in a covered wagon on May 6, 1852. They journeyed five months across the Great Plains, the Western deserts, and the Sierra Nevada before arriving in Sacramento on October 26. A Save the Redwoods League program prepared for the grove's dedication ceremonies explained how Zipporah Russ became one of Humboldt County's earliest settlers and described the rough frontier conditions which her young pioneer family faced at the time:

The following spring her father, Nehemiah Patrick, took up a preemption claim of 160 acres in Humboldt County, and thither he took his family. There were no wagon roads, and all their household goods were packed over the trails on horseback. Mr. Patrick immediately cleared his land, and set out the first orchard in his community, and one of the first in Humboldt.

Within two years of her arrival, Zipporah Patrick, sixteen years old, met and married another recent emigrant from the East, Joseph Russ, and in years to come, gave birth to thirteen children. Ever after, she and her husband stood out among thousands of their generation uprooted and attracted to California by the discovery of gold.

Joseph Russ, who had sailed from New England on the *Midas* around the Cape of Good Horn, reached San Francisco on March 15, 1850. Two and a half years later he arrived in Humboldt County driving a herd of cattle from Sacramento. Russ invested in Humboldt County grazing land and before long, owned 50,000 acres of range and forest, 13,000 sheep, and 4,000 head of cattle.

It was the kind of fortune and hard work that became legendary among pioneers of their era. The young couple had risked it all and won big.

In 1870, twenty years after his arrival in California, Joseph Russ entered the redwood lumber business and there, rapidly acquired so many acres of Humboldt timberland that his business associates, and later, Russ himself, caught the eye of a federal investigation. Prosecutors alleged fraud in their sale of thousands of acres of redwood timber to Scottish investors who had banded together as the California Redwood Company Ltd. Though federal charges of violating the 1878 Timber and Stone Act never stuck, and none of the eleven men accused, including Russ, ever spent a day in prison, their names were frequently and publicly linked in newspapers to the investigations.[166]

Russ' popularity was hurt hardly at all. His business successes opened a door into California politics. He represented Humboldt County for nearly a decade as a state lawmaker, serving in both the Assembly and Senate from 1877 until his death at age fifty on October 8, 1886.[167]

Almost four decades afterward it was likely awkward to recall the association of a prosperous businessman and prominent citizen with old and largely forgotten allegations. Zipporah Russ had many noble reasons for making her donation. Without doubt, the gift of a large redwood grove helped polish her husband's name for posterity. The public and the Save the Redwoods League asserted the rule of politeness. Not a word of the Russ legal issues appeared in newspaper accounts or speeches related to the Humboldt Pioneer Redwood Grove.

Dozens of invited peers and pioneers from the earliest days of Humboldt County flocked to a formal dedication ceremony on September 2, 1923. All were greeted with a moving local tribute to a fading generation that had settled a remote, wild region and built the foundations of a new Northern California society. Humboldt County Superior Court Judge George W. Hunter, himself a wagon train emigrant in the earliest days of California statehood, paid special homage to donor Zipporah Russ, and the women of her day, so often overlooked in recollections of the county's earliest pioneer history:

> The women are entitled to as much credit as the men. I say all honor to the brave women who crossed the plains or the Isthmus or possibly made the trip "around the Horn," and in the early days settled in Humboldt County. They shared with their husband all the trials and difficulties of getting here, and after their arrival endured all the dangers and hardships of pioneer life; bearing and rearing children, not within telephone call or reasonable distance of a physician, helping one another, getting along with but few conveniences, often planting the garden and milking the cows, and frequently not near a church or schoolhouse, usually deprived of all the pleasures which now go to make up our social life. There were strong men and women in those days, an adventurous lot of people with a common bond of sympathy, independent, honest and aggressive, all striving to establish for themselves homes in this new land; and the women did their full share nobly and well.[168]

Keynote speaker William F. Badè, professor of Old Testament Literature at the Pacific School of Religion in Berkeley, president of the Sierra Club from 1919 to 1922, and a Save the Redwoods League Councilor, singled out the Russ contribution as the first of its kind by a pioneer family of the redwood belt. As Madison Grant had done two years earlier at the Bolling Grove dedication on the South Fork of the Eel River, Badè called it a principled example for others to follow:

> Since the Sequoias are the nearest approach that nature has ever made to a demonstration of immortality, this memorial area will be a living monument in more senses than one. The aromatic branches of these evergreen trees will wave their tributes to the memory of Joseph Russ and other departed pioneers of Humboldt County far beyond the duration of any monument in bronze or stone. Above all they symbolize the continuing beneficence of the dead to the living. If

I mistake not, this is the first time that one of our California pioneers of the Redwood belt has established such a memorial and the officers of the Save the Redwoods League sincerely hope that others may follow the noble example of Zipporah Russ.[169]

Enter the Garden Club of America

For all its early successes, the redwoods movement needed far more outside help. Near the end of 1923 *The Humboldt Standard* published an uneasy local analysis of a save-the-redwoods movement now in its fifth year. Though 2,500 acres of Humboldt County Redwoods had been saved in a surprisingly short time, reporter Margaret Scott, nonetheless, gave voice to local frustrations over the snail's pace of it all. There was still more appearance of action than any real action in the fight for the redwoods, she wrote:

> Attempts to interest the nation as a whole have resulted principally in the drafting of resolutions, which have sooner or later become dust-laden in cluttered pigeon holes, or in promises which have amounted to very little when their fulfillment was desired.

Scott mourned the continuing, mounting losses as residents waited for results so slow in coming:

> Some of the most beautiful tracts are fast coming within reach of the sharp saws of the lumbermen. Some almost priceless groves have been entirely destroyed and only stumps remain as tombstones of a vast burial ground. About ten years ago the Native Sons of the Golden West advocated a natural redwood park along the railroad at Samoa flats. But the matter was allowed to drop and the trees long ago emerged from the sawmills as grape stakes and railroad ties. A great effort was made also to establish a state redwood park near Fortuna, in Carson Woods, which is now being cut. In much the same way attempts were made to acquire the Stafford and Russ land, which some said were by far the most beautiful in the county. They were located where the Percy Brown mill now stands, between Scotia and Dyerville. And the past tense indicates their fate.

Visitors to the redwoods in 1923 had pumped $1 million into Humboldt County, Scott told readers. She asked the obvious question:

> What would draw the vast number of travelers to this section if the redwoods were not here? The county would surely lose its most distinguishing characteristics, its most valuable asset.[170]

In distant Southern California, days earlier, *The Los Angeles Times* had also worried aloud. It touted the rising importance of redwoods tourism, reporting the remarkable statistic that "More automobiles from Los Angeles County made this trip last season than came from all other states into California." The *Times* also fretted about lumber companies soon eradicating the magnificent redwood forests that drew its readers north to Eureka. It reported concerns expressed by "even the most sanguine citizens" that, at the rate of cutting in 1923, the Humboldt County redwoods, as people then knew them in all their quiet splendor, would be gone in forty years.

It was an extraordinarily accurate estimate. By the late 1950s only ten percent of California's original 2 million acres of old-growth redwoods remained uncut.[171]

As the eventful year, 1923, came to an end, Laura Mahan in Eureka expanded her search for new sources of outside help. She traveled to San Francisco to meet Alice Ames Winter of Minnesota, president of the 3-million-member General Federation of Women's Clubs, and the federation's famed former conservation chair, Mary Belle King Sherman of Colorado. Sherman had guided six national parks into creation in Colorado, Arizona, California, Washington, and Florida. Conservationists throughout the United States knew her as "the national parks lady," stemming from 700 personal letters she had written to government officials before 1916 urging establishment of the National Park Service.

Sherman was due to become president of the national women's federation in 1924.[172]

Mahan invited them both to visit the redwoods.

Newton B. Drury, learning of the invitation, was delighted. The national women's federation held immense respect and political power in conservation matters. He congratulated Mahan for enticing Sherman, "one of America's most prominent women," into the redwoods campaign and offered to cover expenses when they made their trip.[173]

Mahan probed in other directions, as well, writing to Detroit automaker Henry Ford. She sent him materials on the league's new fund-raising concept of memorial redwood groves and requested that Ford consider a contribution in memory of family members or friends. Mahan sent a similar package and request to prominent New York retailer and philanthropist Nathan Strauss. There is no indication either took her up on the idea.[174]

In the end, it was the Boston aristocrat Henrietta Crosby, a member of the Massachusetts Horticultural Society and the New England Wildflower Preservation Society, who came firmly to the rescue and inspired some of the most lasting national impacts in the Humboldt redwoods. Crosby, the daughter of a notable Boston philanthropist, delivered a crucial rallying cry for the threatened forests of Northern California in the early 1920s during a brief time as president of The Garden Club of America.[175]

Writing in the national club's *Bulletin*, she also made one of the earliest known pleas to member clubs throughout the nation to contribute funds to the Save the Redwoods League.[176] Crosby's appeal marked the auspicious beginning of a decades-long partnership between the club and the league that ultimately saved 5,000 acres of redwoods in Humboldt Redwoods State Park. During the 1920s and early 1930s the old-growth redwoods of Northern California could claim no greater friend than The Garden Club of America.

The seed Crosby planted through the club's *Bulletin* especially motivated the Pacific Coast garden clubs that were increasingly establishing The Garden Club of America as a powerful national voice for conservation. As California Federation of Women's Club members voted in 1923 to buy their own grove, members of California garden clubs began writing their first letters on behalf of saving the redwoods to the national club's New York City headquarters.

Repeatedly then, they began to lobby their national leaders about opportunities to buy threatened groves in the forests of Northern California. The affluent garden club in Santa Barbara and Montecito, home to many prominent and wintering Eastern members, informally began raising its own funds for redwoods. The Pasadena Garden Club, home to famed conservationist Minerva Hoyt who later persuaded President Franklin D. Roosevelt to establish Joshua Tree National Park, similarly began to set aside funds to save the Northern California redwoods.

In the wealthy Chicago suburb of Lake Forest, Fanny Day Farwell, a Chicago merchant's wife and Conservation Chair of The Garden Club of America during the early 1920s, began to monitor and guide these first tentative fund-raising efforts among the West Coast garden clubs. Among her most important and lasting accomplishments, Farwell, a member of the Lake Forest Garden Club in Illinois, as well as the Garden Club of Santa Barbara and Montecito in California and the Wildflower Preservation Society of America, brought two key notables into the redwoods cause.

All through the remaining years of the 1920s Jean Howard McDuffie, wife of a wealthy San Francisco Bay Area real estate developer and conservationist, and like Farwell, a member of the Garden Club of Santa Barbara and Montecito, assumed a pivotal leadership role in The Garden Club of America's redwoods campaign. Alongside her stood the second of

Farwell's influential recruitments, Helen Thorne, wealthy in her own right and wife of a rich Eastern businessman. Thorne wielded her authority on behalf of the redwoods deep into the 1930s as a member of garden clubs on both coasts, the Millbrook Garden Club in New York and the Garden Club of Santa Barbara and Montecito.

Farwell, until her death in November 1926, slowly built the case for garden clubs nationally to save the redwoods and kept the cause alive with her writings. She also encouraged garden club campaigns in California to assist with creation of a state park system that would soon save thousands more acres of the state's greatest redwood forests.[177]

A powerful new force was awakening nationally. It was a force of garden club members who would soon push the movement to save the redwoods past a tipping point and onto its greatest successes. For Laura Mahan in Eureka, help was coming from all directions, at last.

Maps and Illustrations

The numerous ancestor species of the redwoods thrived for millions of years across the middle and northern belts of Earth (highlighted in gray). Most species died out across eons of time as the redwoods retreated to a coastal shelf of California approximately 25 miles wide and 450 miles long. An estimated five percent of the California redwood range remains as virgin forest. Courtesy of the U.S. National Park Service, Division of Publications.

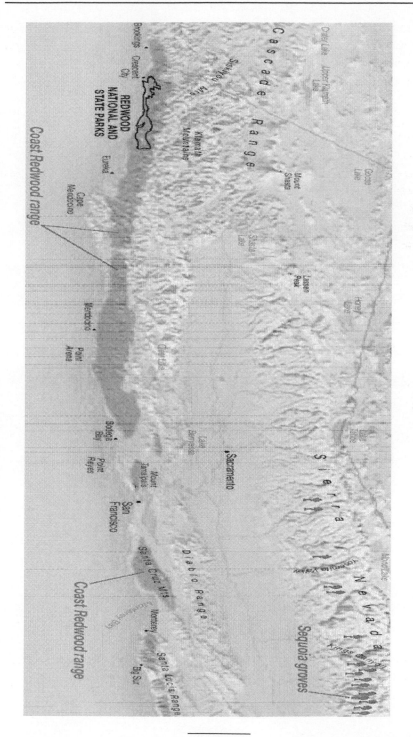

Humboldt County, California, named for the famed German naturalist and explorer Alexander von Humboldt, was home to 500,000 acres of the nation's largest old-growth redwood forests before lumber companies began cutting the trees for redwood lumber products during the second half of the 1800s. Photo courtesy of Humboldt County Planning and Building Department.

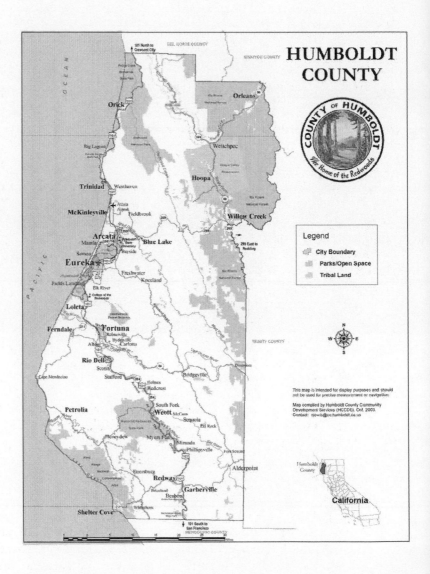

Our President Among the Redwoods

Helen M. Knight of San Francisco, president of the California Federation of Women's Clubs, posed inside Carson Woods near Fortuna during an August 1915 picnic with Humboldt County women's club members who aimed to make the forest a national park. The federation magazine, the *Clubwoman*, printed Knight's picture above the title: "Our President in the

Redwoods." Carson Woods was logged in the early 1920s. Photo courtesy of the California Federation of Women's Clubs.

Humboldt County redwoods activist Laura Perrott Mahan was in her early twenties at the time of this formal portrait in 1890. She was the daughter of prominent pioneers who came West in wagon trains and prospered in Humboldt County as ranchers and owners of timberland. Laura Perrott

Mahan was a rarity for women of her era and place, attending Mills College for women in Oakland, then studying art at the Mark Hopkins Institute in San Francisco. Photo courtesy of the Humboldt County Historical Society Archives.

In adulthood Laura Perrott Mahan was often in forests and clearings with her easel and paints capturing the extraordinary beauty of the redwoods. In 1919 she became president of the Humboldt County Women's Save the Redwoods League and served as the region's most visible, aggressive, and uncompromising leader of campaigns to preserve the best of the county's redwood forests. Before her death in 1937 she saw more than 30,000 acres of ancient forests preserved in the region's first government-run redwood parks. Photo courtesy of the Humboldt County Historical Society Archives.

A plaque erected in 1938 by the California State Park Commission marks the Mahan Grove, site of a profound act of civil disobedience in the early history of saving the redwoods. There in November 1924 Humboldt County redwood activists Laura and James Mahan discovered a Pacific Lumber Company logging crew felling trees in North Dyerville Flat near the town of Weott despite company assurances it would not log the area. Laura Perrott Mahan stood in the line of tree felling and forced the crew to stop while her husband drove to Eureka to obtain a court injunction. The forest was later saved for inclusion in Humboldt Redwoods State Park. Photo by the authors.

The 1919 photograph (next page) of four Humboldt County women and a touring car bearing a Save the Redwoods banner has become an iconic image of the early save the redwoods movement. The women, as determined by the Save the Redwoods League, are, from left to right, Lucretia Anna Huntington Monroe, Kate Harpst, Mary Anne Atkinson, and Ella Georgeson. All were members of the newly-formed Humboldt County Women's Save the Redwoods League and pillars of the Humboldt County establishment. The driver is Eureka chauffeur Frank Silence. The photograph by renowned Eureka redwoods photographer Emma Freeman originally appeared in *The Humboldt Standard* on September 6, 1919. Photo courtesy of The Humboldt County Historical Society Archives.

NEWTON B. DRURY
GROVE

HUMBOLDT REDWOODS STATE PARK

(Previous page) Newton B. Drury, right, an invaluable long-time secretary of the Save the Redwoods League, operated inside a whirlwind of fund-raising, negotiations, corporate and government relations, and often only steps ahead of the ax and saws seeking the same trees. He became the fourth leader of the National Park Service during the Administration of Franklin D. Roosevelt and headed the California State parks system during the 1950s. On June 15, 1968, he posed with former National Park Service Superintendent Dave Canfield during the dedication of the Newton B. Drury Grove in Humboldt Redwoods State Park. Photo Courtesy of the Save the Redwoods League.

The "Four Fireplaces" Hearthstone that anchors the ninety-acre California Federation of Women's Clubs Grove was designed by California architect Julia Morgan, designer of Hearst Castle and women's club buildings throughout California. The structure dedicated in 1933 is arguably one of Northern California's most significant architectural treasures. A sign marks the entrance to the federation grove. Photo by the authors.

(Next page) During the May 20, 1934, dedication ceremony for the 2,552-acre Garden Club of America Grove in Humboldt Redwoods State Park, Helen Thorne, right, Honorary Vice-President of The Garden Club of America, introduces keynote speaker Dr. Aurelia Reinhardt, left, president of Oakland's Mills College, to 150 attendees. The Garden Club of America eventually doubled the size of its grove and contributed $2 million to saving the redwoods in the decades after 1930. Photo courtesy of GCA Archives.

CHAPTER FOUR: SHOWDOWN IN THE FOREST, 1924–1925

"Every move the company makes, people run around and wave their hands, shouting, 'Save the Redwoods, Save the Redwoods,' and every time we go to work in another place we face an injunction."

— Donald MacDonald, Treasurer. Pacific Lumber Company. Feb. 12, 1925. *The Humboldt Times.*

For all the self-congratulations about a rising conservationist pulse in the redwood belt a single sobering statistic painted the truer picture. Midway into the great economic boom unfolding across America in 1924 a tiny, almost infinitesimal fraction, fewer than one percent of the surviving old-growth redwood forests were safely in public hands.

Between the foggy canyons of Big Sur in Monterey County and the cool mists of Oregon approximately 1 million acres of redwoods remained uncut and in their original condition of the previous 20 million years. Conservationists had protected precisely 6,157 acres.

Eighty percent of California's publicly-owned redwood forests now existed in two state parks, Humboldt Redwoods with 2,425 acres and California Redwood Park in the Santa Cruz Mountains, with 2,500 acres. Muir Woods National Monument in Marin County protected 294 acres and Sonoma County's Armstrong Woods held 400 acres. Various other groves scattered throughout the redwood belt included 166 acres in Humboldt County's new Prairie Creek Redwoods State Park and 310 acres newly purchased by San Mateo County for $70,000 near the tiny coastal town of Pescadero fifty miles south of San Francisco. [178]

It was scarcely enough for a public with growing access to automobiles and highways within easy reach of California wilderness. Residents on the move during weekends and holidays found themselves constantly, in their great outdoors of Pacific forests and oceans, rebuffed by warning signs of "Private Property," "No Trespassing," and "Keep Out." The state's almost insignificant acreage of public old-growth redwoods for hiking and camping revealed only the immensity of efforts it would take to acquire many more times that much.

In early 1924 the best of the remaining redwoods was on the books of the Pacific Lumber Company in Scotia. And the company allowed no discussions about selling them for parks.

Pacific Lumber opened its doors on a new year with business thriving in an America that was thriving. Timber prices were high and land values were rising. Industry profits were some of the best in history.[179] The company had begun accommodating the era's new thinking in the wake of consulting forester David T. Mason's 1922 study on forest management practices.

Redwoods historian Darren Speece in 2010 chronicled the lumber company's transformative moves to advance its competitive position and reputation as a venerable, paternalistic employer and local business. "During the 1920s and 1930s," Speece wrote, "the company, unlike most of its competitors, experimented with selective harvesting techniques instead of clearcuts. In 1923, the Pacific Lumber Company hired some of the state's first private foresters and developed a tree nursery to aid second growth regeneration."

Speece described a company with every advantage for the coming showdown with its rivals for the redwoods, writing, "The culture of innovation and efficiency helped the firm develop into a formidable foe for redwood activists. The company was financially sound and earned the loyalty of workers and community because of its stability."[180]

So in the new year a confident Pacific Lumber Company worked again to outmaneuver local, state, and national conservationists targeting the richest and the best of its nearly 70,000 acres for park land. Once more it offered nearly 300 acres of South Dyerville Flat, this time not to the Save the Redwoods League which had rejected it in August 1922, but to the friendlier State Board of Forestry which administered Humboldt Redwoods State Park.

There would be one familiar condition. The board would formally declare that the gift satisfied the Pacific Lumber Company's obligations to redwoods preservation in Humboldt County. No more would the firm concern itself with offers it did not wish to consider.

The pro-industry forestry board responded as expected. It accepted the gift of South Dyerville Flat on February 4, 1924, and described it accurately as "by far the largest and most important forest donation which has ever been made to the State of California." Forestry board chairman Fred A. Ellenwood, with consent of the Save the Redwoods League, expressed the board's "thanks for and appreciation of their public-spirited liberality," and resolved that "the donors, in our opinion, amply fulfilled any obligation, moral or otherwise, the Pacific Lumber Company may have incurred to the public in respect to redwood forest preservation."[181]

Pacific Lumber had claimed the moral high ground.

Yet opponents again saw only a shrewd, strategic company move to block their vision of a great redwood park in the region.

In Eureka, Mahan and the Humboldt County Women's Save the Redwoods League belittled the company's proposed donation as "dangerous and destructive." The offer and its conditions, said Mahan, effectively set the stage for logging beloved North Dyerville Flat and ruined any likelihood of preserving the entirety of the Dyerville Flat forests for public use.

Mahan and her women's league colleagues pressed their case directly to Pacific Lumber Treasurer Donald MacDonald, who assured them the donation contained "no strings." It did not, he said, "close the door" for the company to consider offers for its land. It meant only that the company was under no moral obligation to concede more land for state or national parks.

The company earlier made the same assurances to the Save the Redwoods League. The league's board, in deciding whether to endorse the donation to the state, chose, rather uneasily according to letters at the time, to believe the company was acting in good faith.[182]

Mahan remained unappeased. The Humboldt County Women's Save the Redwoods League hurriedly canvassed a dozen county towns with a petition that asked the Humboldt County Board of Supervisors to buy North Dyerville Flat outright from Pacific Lumber for a redwood park and a scenic reserve. Nine days after the Board of Forestry accepted the company's offer of South Dyerville Flat, league members delivered the signatures to supervisors at their regular Tuesday board meeting in Eureka.

It was an impressive display of local sentiment. One after another women's league members described the widespread desire of residents to keep loggers out of the beautiful Dyerville Flat forests. *The Humboldt Standard* reported that petitions from the dairy community of Ferndale alone contained the name of "practically every freeholder (property owner) in the town."

The county's elected leaders knew the political climate favored saving the treasured Dyerville forest. That afternoon, in an action capturing the spirit of the times, they approved a formal resolution to begin negotiations with Pacific Lumber to buy its Dyerville Flat holdings:

> Whereas as showed by said written petitions it is evident that a large portion of the taxpayers of Humboldt County deem it necessary and essential that Dyerville Flat be acquired for public park purposes and Whereas we, as representatives of the people of Humboldt County, believe that it is necessary to acquire Dyerville Flat for public park purposes, now therefore, be it resolved that the Board of Supervisors of Humboldt County enter into negotiations with the Pacific Lumber Company for the purchase of Dyerville Flat, and if satisfactory arrangements can be made, that the Dyerville Flat be purchased for public park purposes by the County of Humboldt.[183]

The Pacific Lumber Company allowed the county's proposal to simmer. Weeks passed without a response. Then, in a surprise appearance before the county board in early April, Pacific Lumber's MacDonald offered a resounding "no" to negotiations.

MacDonald said the timber on the 250-acre North Dyerville property was critical to the company's fifty-year business plan and reminded the board there were already 3,000 acres of Humboldt County redwoods in state parks. If county residents wanted more, there were plenty of them north of Eureka, he said.

The next day's *Humboldt Times* reported the company's defiance:

> The company felt that it had done its full duty toward saving the redwoods with its recent gift of three hundred acres to the State of California. That gift had been made on the understanding that the company would not be further hindered in its enterprises and industries. The company did not want to sell the Dyerville Flat, he emphasized, no matter what money was offered for it.[184]

Mahan grumbled that the company's brush-off came "from the lips of the very same Donald MacDonald" who personally assured her its gift carried no such conditions. Writing the Save the Redwoods League's Drury in San Francisco, Mahan fretted over the influence of the lumber industry in Humboldt County and its power to sway public opinion. She asked Drury for a round of pro-redwoods publicity "to keep the sentiments and business foresight of our people in the right mood."[185]

As tensions mounted in Humboldt County, Save the Redwoods League Councilor William F. Badè gave a revealing speech in San Francisco about the league's financial activities in the redwoods. Addressing the Mutual Business Man's Club at the Palace Hotel in April, he provided a rare public accounting of donor funding that he said had so far saved 2,827 acres of Humboldt redwoods valued at $1 million.

The largest share, said Badè, was $500,000 in acreage bequeathed for public use by residents of Humboldt County, primarily pioneer-era women such as Zipporah Russ, Martha McClellan, and Sarah Jane Perrott. The remainder, he said, included $300,000 provided by the State of California, nearly $100,000 allocated by the Humboldt County Board of Supervisors and $90,000 from Save the Redwoods League donors. It was surprising, perhaps, given the league's national stature and vaunted ability to target large contributors through personal contacts and small donors through mass mailings, that its fund-raising to date accounted for the smallest share.

There would be much more coming, Badè assured the city's businessmen:

> The movement has really just begun. For while fourteen miles along the Redwood Highway have been preserved, there are several hundred miles, many of them heavily timbered, which should be preserved on either side of the highway for a sufficient distance to keep its beauty unmarred. Moreover, we look forward to the establishment of a national Redwood Park of at least twenty thousand acres.[186]

In Humboldt County, 20,000 acres seemed far-fetched given the immediate problems. Mahan, as president of the Humboldt County Women's Save the Redwoods League, spent the summer of 1924 fearing she couldn't get even a few hundred acres of Dyerville Flat. Everywhere in Humboldt County, she wrote Drury, people believed the fight to save Dyerville Flat was finished due to Pacific Lumber's refusal to sell or even name a price. She asked Drury, again unsuccessfully, to help her pressure Humboldt County supervisors to budget necessary funds to buy the Dyerville redwoods.

The Save the Redwoods League, for the moment, could offer little help.

The league still viewed Dyerville Flat as a local controversy, a fight that needlessly provoked Pacific Lumber and hurt chances to buy what league president Merriam called "the finest forest in the whole history of creation" at Bull Creek Flat. The league, recognizing that Pacific Lumber officials considered Bull Creek Flat and Dyerville Flat "the cream of their timberlands," asked Mahan to avoid unnecessary confrontation with the company, even as rumors began circulating that cutting was imminent in North Dyerville Flat. The Save the Redwoods League was unconvinced. It believed, in the words of historian Susan R. Schrepfer, "such rumors to be perennial in Eureka."[187]

And thus, the waiting game continued.

Monument to a Founder

In August 1924, 5,000 invitations went out to Save the Redwoods League members and public officials across America, requesting their attendance at ceremonies to dedicate a 194-acre memorial grove to Franklin K. Lane, the league's founding president and former Secretary of the Interior under President Woodrow Wilson.[188]

On Sunday afternoon, August 24, at the southern end of Humboldt Redwoods State Park near Phillipsville, several hundred people attended the grand affair devoted to a man who oversaw creation of the National Park Service, recruited Stephen T. Mather to run it, and added six national parks during his tenure in Washington.[189]

Lane had died three years earlier after a long political career as City Attorney of San Francisco, a Theodore Roosevelt appointee to the Interstate Commerce Commission, and a Wilson Administration Cabinet member.[190] But to most people attending the Lane Memorial Grove dedication he was familiar as that Californian of "national standing" chosen to lead Save the Redwoods League in August 1919 until illness required him to step down in February 1921.

In many ways, he had been an unusual choice, the nation's chief conservationist who believed in adjusting wilderness to the benefit of humans. He, indeed, controversially sanctioned the flooding of Yosemite National Park's incomparably beautiful Hetch Hetchy Valley to store water for the City of San Francisco.[191] Upon his death, Lane's ashes, as personally requested and befitting the first National Park Service director, had been taken "to the top of El Capitan peak in Yosemite Valley, California, and scattered to the winds."[192]

Ceremonies opened at two o'clock in the afternoon with the reading of a telegram from an old Lane friend, Gilbert Grosvenor, President of the National Geographic Society. Grosvenor, himself a lion of the redwoods conservation movement, expressed gratitude at the "splendid tribute" to Lane's memory within a redwood grove, and wrote: "Franklin K. Lane was for many years a trustee of this society, and will ever represent to us the highest type of American statesman and a gentleman of whom California may be justly proud."

Lane's successor as President of the Save the Redwoods League, John C. Merriam, who held the job until 1944, dedicated the redwood giants towering above, some of the largest, it was said, in the redwood belt, as an eternal memorial to his predecessor.

"Added to the dignity and nobility with which nature endowed them," he said of the wild trees, "there come now to these members of the forest the honor and responsibility of carrying into coming centuries an expression of the meaning and power of an outstanding human life. We have faith both in the trees and in the generations of men following us that what is established here today will continue through time in which as yet our vision fails to reach."

Merriam, a paleontologist by profession who had long probed the ancient origins of life on earth, continued his lofty ode to the redwoods of the Lane Grove, using the exalted language so commonly heard amid such indescribable loveliness:

> Combining beauty with majesty, they stand before us the most venerable of living things. Here they have waited for centuries, representing a race which counts its generations back through years before our understanding. Before our mountains were born, and in ages when the sea still strove to hold the land on which we are gathered, the ancestral forests from which our Redwoods have sprung spread across the world, clothing hills and valleys much as we find them here today. In this vast period, creation was giving to these trees a strength and dignity and grace expressed in form and feature such that when we see them now there is lighted in us the desire to mould our lives to match their standards. And so we know, that the habit of their living, fixed in past aeons, will continue, and the members of this grove, standing in solemn quietness, will serve that noble purpose for which they are chosen.[193]

The league had purchased the grove with help of many national supporters, but especially with the fund-raising of Lane's close friend Edward E. Ayer, a Chicago industrialist, lumberman, and Save the Redwoods League Councilor who served as Indian Commissioner in Lane's Department of the Interior. Ayer personally gave $2,500, topped only by one of the largest checks yet written by any American to save the redwoods, more than $13,000 from Lora J. Moore of Santa Barbara, California.

Moore was the widow of financier James Hobart Moore who had held controlling interests in U.S. Steel and Nabisco. After a subsequent marriage she was best known as Lora J. Knight, builder of the Vikingsholm mansion on Lake Tahoe's Emerald Bay.[194]

As ceremonies concluded with the State Board of Forestry formally accepting the grove, Lane's daughter, Nancy Lane Kauffman, unveiled a bronze plaque attached to a large rock. "To Franklin K. Lane, 1864-1921," it stated, "Well-Beloved Son of California. Creative statesman in a democracy.

This piece of the forest primeval is forever dedicated in affection and reverence."[195]

A Profound Act of Civil Disobedience

In the epic saga of acquiring the first redwood forests of Northern California, November 1924 proved an extraordinary turning point toward victory. A showdown between Mahan and a Pacific Lumber logging crew that month set the precedent for a similar, but more famous confrontation seventy-three years in the future, Julia Butterfly Hill's 738-day vigil atop a Headwaters Forest redwood also owned by the Pacific Lumber Company. A California State Park Commission monument to Mahan and her husband, James, positioned in 1938 on a scenic Dyerville Flat trail near the Avenue of the Giants, pays respects to that fateful autumn day when Laura Mahan, fifty-six years old, stood in the path of tree felling and refused to move.

Differing accounts detail what happened during a confrontation that has since taken on mythic significance. One fact is clear. Mahan's historic defiance marked the beginning of the end for Pacific Lumber's long-term business plan to log Dyerville Flat and Bull Creek Flat. Her mid-November discovery of Pacific Lumber crews secretly cutting redwoods in North Dyerville Flat turned public opinion resoundingly against the company. In turn, the Humboldt County Board of Supervisors voted unanimously to condemn valued Pacific Lumber property to assure the future of Dyerville Flat as a redwood park.

One vivid description in the California State Parks Archives comes from the February 6, 1953, *Ferndale Enterprise*, which recounted the story of Laura and James Mahan's actions for a new generation of readers:

> Enjoying the comfort of their home one night in November they received the disturbing message, 'The trees are being cut in Dyerville Flat.' They would see for themselves and the next morning started for Dyerville. Parking their car just inside the first fringe of the grove their ears caught the unmistakable sound of workmen not far ahead. Hurrying toward their objective near the east side of the forest they saw sharp sunshine where they knew only the semi-darkness of the deep redwoods had prevailed since time immemorial. Unbelievably, before them were the results of logging operations. Huge trees stretching flat through the clutching underbrush, the fragrance of undisturbed sorrel replaced by the acrid fumes of gasoline, the flash of a double-bitted axe arcing swiftly through the air. In another moment they reached the foreman of the crew. Excitedly, they demanded he stop his men from further work of destruction. The foreman had his

orders and intended to carry them out. They cajoled. But the work must go on. In desperation, Mrs. Mahan climbed to the flat surface of a freshly cut stump. There she stood and defied the men to proceed. Only then did the work cease for she stood in the path of certain death had work continued. Her husband hastened to Eureka and was granted a temporary restraining order.

Neither of Eureka's newspapers reported a personal confrontation and standoff between Laura Mahan and Pacific Lumber Company loggers. Historian Schrepfer also says nothing about a dramatic personal showdown in her telling of the story.

Schreper, writing in 1971, stated that tree cutting began quietly on November 10, 1924, with Drury learning about it on November 19 when he met a state Board of Forestry member on the street in San Francisco. Drury heard soon from State Forester Merritt Pratt that Pacific Lumber had alerted the board on November 12 that it had been cutting in Dyerville Flat for two days and found "no indication from the people of Humboldt County that they are going to make any objections."

The board shared this development with neither the Save the Redwoods League nor Humboldt County residents, proving, wrote Schrepfer, "its pro-industry stance."

When Drury heard from a park ranger at Humboldt Redwoods State Park that eighteen trees had been felled, Save the Redwoods League Chairman Joseph D. Grant telegrammed Pacific Lumber with a message of urgency: "On behalf of the citizens of the State of California, the Save the Redwoods League protests this action on the part of your company, and respectfully requests that these operations be deferred until opportunity has been afforded for a conference."[196]

The Mahans took their story to the Eureka newspapers which reported the Pacific Lumber logging with blazing front-page headlines. The breathless coverage of coming days reflected a prevailing sense within the community of being double-crossed by a company that was born locally, but was now a giant national lumber operation, headquartered in Maine, run from Detroit, and responsible primarily to its Eastern shareholders.

On November 25, two days before the Thanksgiving holiday, *The Humboldt Times* thundered, "Humboldt County in Fight With Lumber Company for Trees." Smaller headlines below that one roared: "Dyerville Flat Redwoods Fall. Quiet Destruction of Splendid Trees at Gateway Has Been in Progress Week. Supervisors to Act. Immediate Condemnation Suit Expected with Restraining Court Order Sought." A story written for the ages began:

The magnificent giant redwoods, ages old, of Dyerville Flat, the pride of Northern California and the hope of generations yet unborn, are today falling under the axes and saws of the Pacific Lumber Company. This statement is bound to come as a shock to the people of Humboldt County, as well as to those of the entire coast who know the beauty and commercial importance they represent. Yesterday the news which had been rumored a few days earlier was verified by Mr. and Mrs. J.P. Mahan, the latter as president of the Women's Save the Redwoods League of Humboldt County, who made the trip to the flats for purposes of investigation. Mr. and Mrs. Mahan found that cutting was in active progress south of the highway, and were told that the company was merely cutting out a right of way in preparation of logging operations on the Bull Creek Flats. However, about twenty-five magnificent trees are said to be already down, and the cutting is making rapid progress. A new gasoline-driven saw is in use and its work of devastation is said to fell the trees much faster than any other method of appliance ever used in the forests of Humboldt County.

The newspaper, plainly showing the preservationist leanings of its owners, urged citizens to show up that afternoon at the Board of Supervisors meeting and "Lend Your Support to the Supervisors to Save the Flats:"

The county supervisors are faced with a momentous decision at the special meeting called for this afternoon. They need the moral support of the people in this matter of dealing with the Dyerville Flat problem, far more than in the transaction of ordinary business. If you are interested in the future of Humboldt County, if you have in mind the welfare of your children, and their children who may be among the people of the future in this community, show your interest by being present at the supervisors meeting in the courthouse this afternoon.

The fevered coverage testified to a community sentiment strongly in favor of saving the forest instead of logging it. This outburst of pro-redwoods commentary stands as a complete contrast to forty years later when much of Eureka reared up against 1960s environmentalists and a federal government aiming to save redwoods, finally, in a Redwood National Park.

Public attitudes in Humboldt County toward the redwoods gradually shifted during the mass unemployment of the Great Depression. Residents and business associations began to worry more about losing timber jobs and taxes than saving forests for tourism, let alone for distant future generations. Conceded redwoods historian Schrepfer: "One park brought tourists; ten parks brought, in the eyes of these economic boosters, nothing but nine times more land off the tax rolls. This loss of support became an obstacle for the league during the late 1930s and increased thereafter, becoming by the 1960s open hostility."

That was not the case in November 1924. Five Humboldt County supervisors — Alexander Masson of Fortuna, Benjamin Flint of Ferndale, Rasmus Anderson of Arcata, Daniel Baldwin of Blue Lake, and George Cole of Freshwater — reacted immediately to the public outcry, convening a special session and resolving unanimously to buy 160 acres of North Dyerville Flat.

The board, backed by a court order forcing Pacific Lumber to stop cutting, instructed, in a move that can only be called extraordinary, the county's district attorney to begin condemnation proceedings for public park purposes.[197] District Attorney Arthur W. Hill told supervisors during the board session that the county had "a nice little nest egg" of $12,500 on hand from liquor and other fines, and state highway and liberty bonds. He said the Save the Redwood League had also agreed to contribute $50,000 to buy the flat. The county would raise the rest of the money.

The special board session attracted a large crowd that included a pair of national figures, Save the Redwoods League Secretary Drury and visiting national forestry expert Frederick Erskine Olmstead. Olmstead was then quietly preparing, with Mahan's help, a strategic acquisition plan for the Save the Redwoods League to buy 3,000 additional acres of redwoods in southern Humboldt County, including Pacific Lumber's North Dyerville Flat and Bull Creek Flat.

Mahan and a delegation of Humboldt County Women's Save the Redwoods League members, as well as Eureka Women's Club members, packed the crowded board chambers. Also filling the room were representatives of the American Legion, Rotary and Elks clubs, Humboldt State Teachers College in Arcata, and residents of Ferndale, Loleta, Trinidad, Blue Lake, Fortuna, Rohnerville, Garberville, and Carlotta.

"After the passing of the resolution a scene of great enthusiasm, cheers and congratulations ended the meeting," The *Times* reported. The newspaper's follow-up editorial titled simply, "Congratulations," praised the actions of county supervisors and the public opinion that swayed them. More dramatically, and telling of the public mood at the moment, it issued a harsh, angry denunciation of the leading contributor to its local economy and tax base:

> Apparently, the Pacific Lumber Company has been proceeding in its dealings with the people in the Dyerville Flat proposition on the supposition that this is still the middle of the dark age — the 'public be damned age' — and that simply because it was in legal possession of this property the people could not help themselves, but would be

forced to stand by and see their heritage as citizens swept without remorse or compunction from living forests into dividends via the sawmill. During the past few years the whole trend of thought and education among the people has been undergoing a steady, but marked change, and the present move is nothing but what could have been, and should have been expected by anyone who cared to see and interpret the signs. The time has come when no private interest is big enough or powerful enough to stand in conflict with the public right, and the present action of the people and the county supervisors is a clear reflection of that fact.[198]

Pacific Lumber, which presumably seethed over the public scolding and the county's action, responded defiantly as could be expected given the stakes. While it agreed to stop cutting in Dyerville Flat pending the outcome of the legal action against it, its attorney, former State Senator Hans Nelson of Eureka, informed the county that the company would sue to block its condemnation proceedings.

The Pacific Lumber Company, Nelson told Hill, believed that condemning corporate property for park purposes was almost certainly illegal and would ask the federal courts to prevent it from going forward. Days later the company filed a lawsuit in federal court in Sacramento and won a temporary halt to the county's condemnation plans. Nelson now repeated to Hill the familiar company position: The Pacific Lumber Company would not sell its Dyerville holdings and "direct negotiations could be considered out of the question."[199]

The tension would continue through the Christmas and New Year's holidays.

Yet as this turbulent, dramatic year, 1924, in the history of saving the redwoods came to an end there was much to celebrate. Money and land was pouring into the save-the-redwoods movement. The Humboldt County Board of Supervisors had recently budgeted $25,000 for unspecified redwood purchases in the future. The Del Norte County Board of Supervisors also allocated its first $5,000 to buy scenic stands on its share of the Redwood Highway.[200] And in the year's final days, fifty-seven more acres of redwoods east of the Redwood Highway near Weott came into public ownership as a memorial grove to New York lumberman William H. Sage.

He had died weeks earlier on October 23, 1924.

Sage was a second-generation timberman based in Albany and the 1922 donor of Sage Hall, home of the prestigious Yale Forestry School.[201] Born into a patrician Eastern family that had contributed $1.25 million to Cornell University, he was the youngest son of Susan Elizabeth Sage and Henry

W. Sage, the Albany lumber baron, Cornell trustee, and former New York State Assembly Member. The family's philanthropy included Cornell's Sage Library, Sage Hall for Women, the university's first female residence hall, and Sage Chapel, the burial place of Susan and Henry Sage.[202]

William H. Sage was known in timber industry circles for a daring makeover of the family business in 1893, selling off its Eastern lumber operations and buying new forests throughout the American South and West. Those purchases included a substantial stake in Humboldt County redwoods by the family's newly incorporated Sage Land and Improvement Company. The reinvented company, operating as a land broker instead of cutting and milling lumber, sold property to lumber companies, but also donated and sold land for memorial groves in Humboldt Redwoods and Prairie Creek Redwoods state parks. The Sage memorial grove was a gift from the company in memory of its founder.[203]

Simultaneously, at year's end, an even bigger gift of 156 acres created a Del Norte Coast Redwoods State Park grove in acknowledgment of Henry S. Graves, eminent American forester and director of the U.S. Forest Service from 1910 to 1920. Like Sage, Graves was a graduate of Yale and later the first director of the Yale Forestry School. The Graves grove, funded by George Frederick Schwarz, naturalist and heir to New York City's FAO Schwarz toy store, fronted several miles of the Pacific Ocean and Redwood Highway and soon expanded to 280 acres.[204]

Del Norte County now had a first protected grove on the Redwood Highway.

The movement was spreading north.

Preserve the Redwoods to Preserve Our Prosperity

As the new year began Pacific Lumber Company officials appeared before the Humboldt County Board of Supervisors at their regular Tuesday meeting, January 13, 1925, and there announced a nearly irresistible proposal in lieu of selling Dyerville Flat to the county.

For the third time in twenty-nine months the company offered to donate 300 acres of South Dyerville Flat for a mile-long park along the Redwood Highway.

This time the company offered the property directly to Humboldt County since the land hadn't yet transferred to the state. The company also sweetened its compromise, offering to sell sixty acres in North Dyerville Flat to preserve scenic redwood views on both sides of the Redwood Highway. The strip it proposed was approximately 300 feet wide on the east side of the road. On the west side, it encompassed everything between the roadway and the South Fork of the Eel River. Arbitration would determine the price and only one condition applied: Humboldt County would never again use its eminent domain powers to condemn Pacific Lumber Company holdings for park purposes. All future sales of Pacific Lumber Company land would be on the company's terms only.[205]

A company letter outlining the offer clearly signaled to the board and to the county's business and political elites who they were dealing with:

> Our company has for many years paid more taxes for the support of Humboldt County than anyone else. Our operations have always been and are now the greatest in volume, value and extent of any in the county. We employ more men, pay more wages and put into circulation in the county more money than any other industry. The relations between ourselves and our employees have ever been on the most friendly basis; so much so, indeed, that our methods of operation in that connection have been most favorably commented on in the press. We respectfully submit that these facts entitle our interests to every consideration and support by the county which is it possible for you to give.

The company also raised a bedrock American issue that resonates in politics today as in January 1925: the importance of property rights and those who would abuse them:

> We appreciate the love of the beautiful which actuates those who would prevent any of the redwood trees of this state from being cut or destroyed. But we believe that such aestheticism should not be allowed to be carried to the extent where it destroys the property rights of others and prevents the carrying on of ordinary business operations according to the law of the land.

It was an extraordinary corporate declaration of the rule of law in the United States. And opposition to the argument surfaced immediately, that same afternoon, from the Humboldt County Women's Save the Redwoods League. An unmoved Mahan, who attended the board meeting and heard the surprise offer, told reporters afterward, "It would simply look like a high fence. There would be none of the shaded effect so much desired in a redwood park. And, in fact, the entire park effect would be lost. We really need the entire flat for park purposes, and without that there will be no incentive to proceed at all. We regard the proposed strip as inadequate and it does not appeal to us."[206]

The Eureka Women's Club, Business Women's Club and Eureka Realty Board quickly agreed, passing resolutions urging county supervisors to reject the offer.[207]

But much of the county business establishment thought otherwise.

Wearying of the long fight with a difficult adversary, official endorsements of the offer as "reasonable" began to mount. Though Mahan urged the Eureka Chamber of Commerce to "send a resolution to the Board of Supervisors begging them not to accept the proposal," the chamber's board of directors soon declared the offer "eminently fair" and "worthy of favorable consideration."[208] The Federated Commercial Bodies, a countywide business group, also formally resolved that the company's offer was "fair and liberal and that it should be accepted by the Board of Supervisors in the interests of the people of the county." The Arcata Chamber of Commerce concurred with the Federated Commercial Bodies opinion and recommended that county supervisors accept the offer as "eminently fair" and "very liberal."[209]

The Pacific Lumber Company's message, accompanied by a humble corporate sentiment "that this entire controversy and the litigation connected therewith is most unpleasant to us," resonated in the county business community as a way for the region to have both its scenic highway views and a viable lumber industry. More, it would cost so much less than buying all 190 acres of the flat.

The Pacific Lumber Company had played well to this sense of balance, compromise, and prudent financial management, maintaining that "the use of a such strip could be obtained for a small portion of the amount necessary to buy the entire tract. Ever substantial benefit would be thus secured by your Body, and the taxpayers of the county would not be burdened with immense debts and bond issues."

The company, ominously, also informed county supervisors it would use its considerable political influence to oppose any bond debt to buy North Dyerville Flat.

A majority of taxpayers would surely feel the same way, it warned.

Company owners then painted a target on those it held responsible for stirring up trouble regarding the Dyerville forests, obliquely and without naming names, the women and their local save-the-redwoods league, those people who didn't intimately understand money and big business and thought with their hearts and emotions.

The company's letter added a blast of hyperbole regarding its critics. It stated that an expensive bond to buy the entirety of North Dyerville Flat would be done "just to satisfy extreme aestheticism on the part of nature lovers, who would object to our cutting our own trees, even for our own rights of way." And finally, it reminded the board, and once more local politicians and businessmen, that the State of California, through its State Board of Forestry, had formally resolved that the Pacific Lumber Company fulfilled its obligation to redwoods preservation in agreeing the previous year to accept 300 acres of South Dyerville Flat for park use.[210]

The county Board of Supervisors, which had long stood firm in its intentions to acquire the entire flat, now began to waffle under the public pressure that Pacific Lumber applied.

The board, with newly elected Gilbert Sutherland of Rohnerville having replaced departed Supervisor Alexander Masson of Fortuna, scheduled a February 11, 1925, vote on the company's offer, and looked increasingly likely to back off its hard line and accept. Drury, concerned, wrote to Save the Redwoods League President Merriam in Washington, D.C., stating, "A month ago all of the Supervisors were with us. I found, on making a trip up there the day before yesterday, that out of five only one is strongly of his original mind, and the rest are in various degrees of uncertainty."[211]

Mahan struck hard at the Eureka Chamber of Commerce, for twenty years a stalwart ally in campaigns to save a portion of the county's redwoods. She said the chamber's endorsement of Pacific Lumber's offer was a verdict of the board of directors that simply did not reflect the majority of opinion among the chamber's business owners.

A fellow women's league member who belonged to the Eureka Chamber of Commerce concurred with Mahan's argument. "The offer does not appeal to us at all," she said, "and we do not feel that the women members of the Chamber of Commerce are at all in accord with the sentiment. We must have the entire flat."

Mahan went to the newspapers with documents proving the board's new viewpoint differed greatly from that of a year earlier when the chamber called Dyerville Flat "Humboldt County's greatest asset" and declared that "it must be preserved." When the newspapers printed the assertions chamber officials began to backtrack, saying they had called the offer "eminently fair as a basis for negotiations." It was not a blanket endorsement, they said.

Popular opinion, nonetheless, said Mahan, held the impression that it was. The episode, publicly aired, proved an embarrassment to the chamber board as it tried to maneuver the delicate politics of the issue. It also reflected the sheer force of Mahan in the battle for Dyerville Flat.[212]

The newspapers then weighed in on their editorial pages, *The Humboldt Standard* most forcefully. The city's evening newspaper urged county supervisors to decline Pacific Lumber's offer for the astonishing reason that rejecting it would be "good business" for Humboldt County.

One sees here the quiet hand of Ella Georgeson, the newspaper's co-owner and editorial director. Georgeson was a veteran member of the Humboldt County Women's Save the Redwoods League who rode with Kate Harpst's barnstorming "Save the Redwoods" car in the late summer of 1919.

The newspaper pointed out that thousands of tourists had visited the Humboldt County redwoods during the summer of 1924, "particularly those along the highway in the vicinity of Dyerville." While The *Standard* agreed that Pacific Lumber had every right to log its Dyerville forests, it contended that "to permit the removal of the timber IS AN INSANE PIECE OF BUSINESS ON THE PART OF THE COUNTY." The newspaper's owners, themselves cornerstones of the local business establishment, held that while the company must receive a proper price for its property, Humboldt County had the greater responsibility to preserve "its greatest asset, the wonderful redwoods on the South Fork."

The *Standard*'s owners then spun out an entirely different vision of commerce for the county, rebutting Pacific Lumber's vision of logging redwoods as the bedrock of the economy:

> The people of Eureka and Humboldt County must realize that the present growth of the city and county is due largely to the tourist trade. They must realize that if Eureka is to become a great center it must depend to a great extent upon the money brought here each year by visitors coming over the Redwood Highway. One false step may so reduce this traffic that millions of dollars will be turned away. Dividends that would come in year after year over a period of many decades would go elsewhere. Let's make a purely commercial proposition out of the redwoods. Rally around the cry: 'Preserve the redwoods to preserve our prosperity' and pay for a money maker in order that it shall make money for us for years to come, and for our children's children.[213]

It would take decades, nearly a century, to reimagine the local economy in this light and begin reaping tourist-driven prosperity on such a commercial scale. Humboldt County and Eureka itself, as warned by The *Standard*, would first endure a long, slow economic decline after thoroughly devastating its resource base for short-term jobs and income.

But long before that, in February 1925, came a miracle.

One Million Dollars from the Rockefeller Fortune

In all the chronicles of early environmental showdowns now long forgotten in California, few rank with the spectacle inside a Humboldt

County courtroom on Wednesday, February 11, 1925, over the fate of redwoods owned by the Pacific Lumber Company.

One question hung over the room: Would the Board of Supervisors accept Pacific Lumber's 360 acres and conditions or outright condemn its Dyerville Flat forest as a final political act to end the long standoff?

The historic confrontation began with a "sensational communication" the previous day in which the Save the Redwoods League committed $750,000 to buy North Dyerville Flat, part of nearby Bull Creek Flat, and if necessary, the company's 300 acres of South Dyerville Flat. Drury made the surprise announcement at the Board of Supervisors' regular Tuesday session in the presence of Pacific Lumber Treasurer MacDonald and its attorney, Nelson.

It was stunning, almost beyond imagination at this final hour, "the pivot," stated The *Times*, "upon which the final decision will hinge."

The full power of the nation had arrived at last.

The Save the Redwoods league, backed by a secret gift of $1 million provided the previous November by Standard Oil heir and philanthropist John D. Rockefeller, Jr., offered to pay full value for the company's prized holdings and to minimize impacts to company logging operations elsewhere. The league agreed to friendly negotiations, the option of arbitration if necessary, and condemnation only as a last resort.

A formal letter from Drury, league president Merriam and chairman Joseph D. Grant urged the Board of Supervisors to accept its proposal to negotiate with Pacific Lumber and buy the forests intact. The letter promised a redwood park "which will make Humboldt County world famous and will attract a continuing stream of visitors who will bring into the county each year revenue many times greater than the value of the lumber that could be derived from the destruction of these trees."

"Felled redwoods pay but one dividend," wrote Drury, Merriam, and Grant. "A Humboldt Redwoods park pays increasing annual dividends forever."

County supervisors suddenly found a way out of their political predicament. With cash in hand they could safely reject the company's offer. Better, they had financial backing now for a condemnation move, if needed.[214]

At the same Tuesday meeting Mahan announced a second offer of national assistance, a telegram to the Board of Supervisors from Mary Belle King Sherman, president of the national General Federation of Women's Clubs. It promised support "in every practicable way" of the federation's 3 million members.

Mahan had escorted Sherman through Dyerville Flat and Bull Creek the previous summer alongside Cora Call Whitley, an Iowa writer and the national federation's conservation chair. Joining them was Elizabeth Lawton, a New York federation member and founder of the National Roadside Council, which advocated for beautiful highways and opposed the outdoor advertising and billboard industry. On a separate occasion Mahan and members of her Humboldt County Women's Save the Redwoods League similarly entertained Sherman's predecessor as president of the federation, Alice Ames Winter of Minneapolis, with a picnic lunch beneath the Bull Creek redwoods and a day touring nearby groves. Mahan's hospitality had thoroughly grounded the General Federation of Women's Clubs on the situation in Humboldt County.

"Please make certain that no misunderstanding exists concerning the strong desire of the General Federation of Women's Clubs to see the outstanding groves of the Eel River, including the Dyerville and Bull Creek Flat saved," Sherman's telegram declared. "It is clearly the opinion of the interested observers that these groves are one of America's great treasures. I hope that Humboldt County will do its utmost to preserve these groves intact. You may depend upon the general federation to help in every practicable way."[215]

The next day, Wednesday, inside the Department One courtroom of Judge George D. Murray, husband of Humboldt County Women's Save the Redwoods League stalwart Annie Zane Murray, the forces of conservation and corporate lumbering clashed from ten o'clock in the morning until three o'clock in the afternoon with only a break for lunch.

In *The Humboldt Times'* vivid, colorful account of the day, Pacific Lumber Company officials sat in a small group to the right of the courtroom while the district attorney's party sat on the left. Throughout the day, each side presented its case for the redwoods much like a jury trial with the Board of Supervisors being the deciding judges. Ninety percent of the audience favored saving Dyerville Flat, according to The *Times*, and cheered the arguments of its allies while maintaining "ominous silence" following the points offered by the lumber company.

District Attorney Arthur Hill played forcefully to a hometown audience, arguing that the county would take up any legal battle the Pacific Lumber Company aimed to bring against it. He scolded the national company for going to federal court in Sacramento in late 1924 to fight the sentiment of the Board of Supervisors and people of Humboldt County. Hill then described for county supervisors his recent 1,000-mile automobile trip, in which the only surviving old-growth forests he saw were those which he returned to in California:

There are no primeval forests in the United States except in California. The only primeval forests are on the Pacific Coast, and the best of these forests are in Humboldt County. Because others have sold theirs and are now repenting will you sell your birthright? It is too late for the Eastern states to save their forests. It is not too late for us.

Pacific Lumber Company Treasurer Donald MacDonald described for county supervisors his company's frustration with the endless activism directed toward its legitimate property holdings. "Every move the company makes, people run around and wave their hands, shouting, 'Save the Redwoods, Save the Redwoods,'" he said, "and every time we go to work in another place we face an injunction."

MacDonald also explained, in the words of The *Times*, which was clearly caught up in the moment, "how much the lumber company meant to Humboldt County, what it had done for the county, how large a payroll the company carried, a great deal about the possible effect of giving way to the Save the Redwoods League would have on the world in general. He told everybody everything about the lumber company, but nothing at all about the proposition to save the redwoods for Humboldt County, the state, the nation, and the world."

Eureka Attorney Lawrence Mahan, brother and business partner of Laura Mahan's husband, James, told county supervisors he had never seen Pacific Lumber attorney Nelson more afraid of a condemnation lawsuit. "Should this case go to condemnation proceedings there are enough red-blooded lawyers who will fight the case through the courts free and all the expense to the people will be ten-dollar or fifteen-dollar filing fees. What difference," he continued, "how the company gets its money, whether by logging or purchase price, so long as it realizes so much per tree? They won't be cheated. Now is the opportune time, with the money ready, buy the North Dyerville Flat, buy it now," he said to great applause.

MacDonald, under siege and greatly outnumbered, complained to the Board of Supervisors that his company "had never had a fair show" in these proceedings. He repeated a dozen times, according to the newspaper account, that the company's generous offer to donate 300 acres and sell another 60 acres had not even been recognized in the proceedings.

Attorney Irwin Quinn of the American Legion told the crowd that his family members had been taxpayers long before there were lumber interests in Humboldt County, and though he had many professional relationships and friends in the timber industry, he would not remain silent. It was a choice, he said, between private monopolies and the "people as a whole." He favored acquiring the entirety of Dyerville Flat for the future of the county.

Drury then stood. He challenged MacDonald to meet with the Save the Redwoods League and "settle this matter."

"No," answered MacDonald.

The question on the table, MacDonald said, was whether Humboldt County would accept or refuse the company's offer of South Dyerville Flat and the additional sixty acres. If county supervisors refused the company's offer the next step was to resolve once and for all whether the county had legal authority to condemn its property for park purposes.

Years of agitation between the company and those seeking its properties had frayed patience inside the court room. Tempers began to rise. Laura Mahan publicly and personally accused MacDonald of reneging on promises he'd made to her, essentially lying, she said, about selling Dyerville Flat if preservationists could raise the money.

Her husband, attorney James Mahan, then accused MacDonald of further deceit in his dealings with county residents who hoped to save Dyerville Flat. "You took machinery secretly into North Dyerville Flat and starting cutting so secretly it took us hours to find your camp," he said. The two men began approaching each other, *The Humboldt Times* reported, "MacDonald stiffening and straightening and Mahan shaking his fist."

This produced another moment of great drama which has become mythical in its retelling during decades since. As MacDonald and Mahan seemed about to come to blows, Drury jumped in. It was time to show the money. Drury, earlier in the day, had arranged for three San Francisco banks to send confirmation that the league, indeed, had $750,000 on hand to buy the Pacific Lumber Company properties.

Drury, in a 1972 oral interview with redwoods historians Amalia Fry and Susan R. Schrepfer, recalled the details of that dramatic occasion:

> "Well, it happened that Mr. Rockefeller had given us a million dollars. That was deposited in the Crocker National Bank in San Francisco. But we had never divulged the amount of his gift. So I hastily got on the long distance phone and called (my brother) Aubrey, and we arranged that he would go around and get three bankers in San Francisco: Mr. William H. Crocker, who was president of the bank where our money was deposited; Mr. Joseph D. Grant, then vice-president of the Redwoods League and the director of a half a dozen banks; and Mr. J. P. Sperry, who was quite prominent in financial affairs, and one of our most active people in the league. I went back into the meeting in the afternoon, hadn't heard anything from San Francisco. The hearings began; I got more and more anxious. Suddenly, there appeared and wove his way through the crowd a Western Union messenger. In those days they wore uniforms that were more prominent. He came

up to the front where I was sitting in the jury box and handed me a telegram which I silently read and folded and put into my pocket. A few minutes later, another messenger came in with another telegram. It happened three times, and each time I just glanced at it and put it away. I was in a prominent position where everybody could see what I was doing. Finally, when there was a pause, I asked the chairman of the Board of Supervisors if I could read these telegrams. By that time, everybody was very curious to know what they were. So I read them, and they all corroborated the fact that we had a sum of money in the neighborhood of seven hundred and fifty thousand dollars. As a matter of fact, we had a million. And you could have heard a pin drop."[216]

Shortly after hearing confirmation that the money was available the board voted to accept the league's proposal. The board also offered "its cooperation in bringing about a settlement of this question that will protect the public interest and be fair to the Pacific Lumber Company."[217]

The *Times* gleefully editorialized the next day that "Judge Murray's court room yesterday became for the first time in the history of the county, the known and avowed battle ground between the two great and ever warring powers, public benefit and private gain, and to the everlasting glory of Humboldt County, the public won."

Writing beneath the headline, "A Great Moral Victory," the newspaper editorialized:

"The aid that came to the people of Humboldt County from outside sources proves that the people of the nation have come to see and realize that they, as much as the people who live within the confines of the county or the state, are the owners of these splendid forests, and that it is no longer a local concern as to what becomes of the forests. They cannot be destroyed without every man, woman, and child, and those yet unborn, being the loser. To those who fought and won the good fight, and to those who aided, and they did materially aid, by lending their moral support by their presence and encouragement, the people of the nation, as well as the people of Humboldt County and of California, owe a debt of lasting gratitude."[218]

Ironically, after the February 11 meeting, a powerful winter storm washed out the railroad tracks to San Francisco and forced Drury to stay at a hotel in Scotia, the company town owned by Pacific Lumber. As he recalled in his oral interview forty-seven years later:

"I'll always remember how gracious the president of the Pacific Lumber Company was. We had to put up at their hotel, and they asked us over for dinner, and we had a wonderful dinner together. It was very greatly to their credit because they had taken quite a beating at the hearings beforehand, and much to our embarrassment, we had to be their guests immediately afterward. Mr. John H. Emmert, who was the president of the lumber company, was particularly friendly. So that partly as a result of our getting marooned there, we got together and they offered to resume negotiations, and we ultimately acquired the property and established the nucleus of what is now the Rockefeller Forest."[219]

It would take six years to finish the deal.

One Hundred Dollars Buys a Tree

All the while elsewhere, California Federation of Women's Clubs members wrapped up the fund-raising for their anticipated memorial grove along two miles of highway in Dyerville Flat. Two years of creative approaches under President Augusta Urquhart of Los Angeles culminated on May 20, 1925, when the federation, meeting in Santa Cruz, presented a check for $40,000 to State Forester Merritt B. Pratt during ceremonies at the city's convention hall.

Eight more years would pass before the federation received state matching funds and dedicated its ninety-acre grove on a beautiful stretch of Dyerville Flat forest fronting the South Fork of the Eel River. Federation members were near at last to fulfilling Clara Burdette's 1900 founding vision of preserving redwoods for "their matchless grandeur" and contribution to the vitality and wealth of California.[220]

A *Los Angeles Times* account of the presentation reported that the federation's Los Angeles District had contributed more than all other California districts combined. Special honor went to Eleanor Margaret Toll of Los Angeles, a Save the Redwoods League Councilor and head of the city's prominent Ebell Club, the federation's most prolific fund-raiser for the redwoods.[221]

The statewide federation had raised money every way possible, including countless individual donations of a dollar each. But one method, in particular, stood out. Over two years the federation's "One hundred dollars buys a tree" campaign raised thousands of dollars for redwood "honor trees" that celebrated fellow clubwomen, past members, and even celebrities.

The Woman's Club of Hollywood funded trees in celebration of 1920s screen legends Mary Pickford, "America's Sweetheart," and Douglas Fairbanks. The Santa Monica Bay Women's Club bought three trees to acknowledge the work of Adeline Lorbeer, a Santa Monica School Board member and federation conservation chair during its redwood grove fund-raising drive. The statewide federation paid tribute to Urquhart and Toll for leading its redwoods campaign. The Ebell Club honored federation founder Clara Burdette. Women in Santa Barbara made their donation in memory of the late Joyce Kilmer, author of the 1913 poem, "Trees." The Santa Paula Women's Club saluted World War I veterans and pioneers of Ventura County.[222]

Humboldt County women's clubs brought their own $1,300 to the redwood endowment during the federation's 1925 Santa Cruz convention. They had raised nearly half at a single event, a Friday evening Humboldt County Federation of Women's Clubs ball on May 15, 1925, at Eureka's Cinderella Dance Hall.

These Humboldt County women, living nearest the threatened redwoods and on the front lines of the struggle to save them, dedicated their honor trees to great musicians, to their parents, and to pioneer mothers, as well as beloved members of their clubs. Five gift trees resonated with especially poignant meanings, their recipients chosen by the county federation board while meeting at the Eureka Young Women's Christian Association hall a day after the Cinderella ball:

1. "Mrs. Laura Perrott Mahan — In behalf of the honor which we wish to pay her, for her interest and zeal in behalf of our majestic and beautiful redwoods.

2. Mrs. Annie Zane Murray — For the esteem in which we hold her in regard for her many favors and long years of service for our Federation and the causes of the Redwoods.

3. Mrs. Clara Shields — In consideration of our former co-worker and the veneration and love that we feel for her memory.

4. For the Pioneer Women of the Humboldt County Federation — Those early workers in our organization that blazed the trail for us, endured the hardships of pioneer work, and that placed the institution on a firm foundation.

5. To the Humboldt County Federation of Women's Clubs — Because we love our redwoods and are proud of them, and to show ourselves eager, willing and glad to have a share in this work.[223]

The tributes provided a fitting marker to an ending phase of the fight for the redwoods and the beginning of another. No longer would the Humboldt County Women's Save the Redwoods League be a principal actor, nor the Humboldt County Board of Supervisors or the Eureka Chamber of Commerce.

Now, national players would become dominant in the redwoods.

From the hindsight of a century, saving the magnificent neighboring stands of Dyerville Flat and Bull Creek Flat appears near miraculous, one of those rare occasions when a confluence of events fell into the right order for larger forces to carry them forward. In Humboldt County, the women's league stayed ever true to its vision for Dyerville Flat. The Board of Supervisors, local politicians all, stood firm in the face of their county's biggest corporate taxpayer. Collectively, they all bought time for larger national forces to assemble. They defended the incomparable beauty in their midst, protected the world's finest old-growth forest, and held off the saws until the Save the Redwoods League found the money that changed everything.

Historians decades later would express amazement at the mass power of them all. As a student at Humboldt State University in 1980 historian John J. Amodio wrote that their movement did much more than save Dyerville Flat. It proved that "a caring and committed constituency" could effectively protect natural areas at a time when it was generally not considered possible. It also "demonstrated that government will respond to such strong pressure, even if it requires taking action against a powerful economic interest."[224]

Save the Redwoods League founders had always said the redwoods of Humboldt County were a national heritage. With the heaviest of the local agitation successfully concluded, the campaign for the redwoods drifted now in that direction.

CHAPTER FIVE: OUTSIDE INFLUENCES, 1926–1930

> "When we realize that this marvelous tree is preserved here, alone upon all the surface of the earth, and that its habitat now is limited to a slender stretch of territory along the northern coast, it becomes clear that we possess a grave responsibility of preservation. Under our control, and in our day, it would be a shameful thing if the royal lineage of the redwood came to an eternal end."
>
> — *Del Norte Triplicate*, Crescent City, California. February 13, 1926.

In the spring of 1926, ninety-six members of The Garden Club of America, fresh from their annual convention in Santa Barbara, a city of 30,000 people still rebuilding from a shattering earthquake ten months before, paid a visit, one with far-reaching and immensely positive consequences, to the redwoods south of San Francisco Bay.

For several days the clubwomen had visited the great ornamental gardens of Santa Barbara and Montecito, including the extravagant Las Tejas estate of garden club member Helen Thorne. They had toured then the awe-inspiring Monterey Peninsula, splendid with California wild flowers, "*sheets* of them," as one club member recalled, "a swirl of pink or blue or yellow or purple or red, or a combination of all five."

Now they stood before the giant trees, many seeing the redwood species for the first time.

So immense were the trees, 300 feet high and more, that Henrietta Crosby of Boston, a member of the North Shore Garden Club of Massachusetts, and a one-time president of The Garden Club of America, said they "made the twisted Del Monte cypresses and stately oaks of Santa Barbara's ornamental gardens seem 'pigmies [*sic*] in comparison.'"[225]

The women, many of them Easterners who had ridden a train from New York City to Pasadena and then to Santa Barbara for the garden club's thirteenth national convention, were equally impressed. Yet what they encountered at the base of the giants appalled them.

"The trees were big and God had made them grow to great proportions of beauty and dignity," read an account printed in the club's May 1926 *Bulletin.* "And then man built hot-dog stands beneath them and tied names, 'General Grant,' and 'W.C.T.U.' [Women's Christian Temperance Union], etc., around their necks like collars, and tourists had pinned their visiting cards to the shaggy iron-clad bark until one felt like weeping. It was tragic, to commercialize in this cheap way one of the wonders of America."

The visit shocked the club into undertaking one of the biggest accomplishments in the Humboldt Redwoods during the 1920s and early 1930s. Within eight years of its historic visit to the redwood belt, The Garden Club of America would buy more than 2,500 acres of earth's most majestic redwoods and deed them to the State of California.

The *Bulletin*, in the wake of the 1926 excursion, recognized that the club's heart, and that of some of the most prominent women in American life, belonged now to the California redwoods. Its editors enthusiastically described for them the great preservationist movement underway in Humboldt and Del Norte counties:

> Fortunately, in the northern part of the state an organized effort has been made by the Save the Redwoods League to conserve and cherish such as are left of these marvelous redwoods. The Garden Club of America has a great opportunity to endorse as a whole organization what is being done and to encourage the individual clubs composing it to do what they can.

Such enthusiasm by a club dedicated to natural beauty, wild flowers, and plant life, as well as protection of national parks and wildlife, had been incubating through the earliest years of the 1920s. The young club's *Bulletin* steadily built a national consensus for conservation issues and mapped the way toward its members taking up the cause of the redwoods.

Before it became a medium for saving the redwoods, the publication repeatedly expressed support for the new national parks. As the 1920s opened the *Bulletin* warned of attempts by hydroelectricity companies and irrigators to tap protected rivers for power generation under the Federal Water Power Act. After the *Bulletin*'s December 1920 publication of "The Present Peril of the National Parks," a warning against the disastrous impacts of such proposals by American Civic Association President J. Horace

McFarland, the club's Council of Presidents requested that members write their Congressmen to amend the law, which Congress soon did.[226]

Months later the *Bulletin* credited club members and especially, Conservation Chair Fanny Day Farwell of Lake Forest, Illinois, for the success of National Park Service Director Stephen T. Mather's 1921 National Conference on State Parks in Des Moines, Iowa. The historic conference sparked the state parks movement in the United States and before it adjourned, adopted Farwell's proposal for a National Conservation Day.

Mather, recognizing The Garden Club of America's national audience and commitment to parks and conservation, soon contributed his own *Bulletin* article: "Our National Park and Monument System," in which he analyzed the wildlife, plant life, and wild flowers protected in nineteen national parks and twenty-four national monuments.[227]

The same year, Save the Redwoods League Councilor William F. Badè provided *Bulletin* readers one of the earliest introductions to the redwoods, penning a delightful narrative, "Garden Hints from the Redwoods." His November 1921 report spotlighted the profusion of colorful green ferns that grew at the base of the redwood giants:

> Not even in a tropical jungle could one hope to see a more glorious wealth and variety of ferns than that which carpets the floor of these redwood forests. An acre or two of these ferneries, even without the trees, would make the fame of any park. But here are twenty thousand acres of them and the trees — the most stupendous plant miracle of all — are [in] the very condition of their life by immeasurable ages of friendly association.[228]

Farwell followed up fifteen months later in the January 1923 *Bulletin* with a particularly powerful appeal to club members. She stated that a third of the original redwood forests, which she estimated at 1.5 million acres, were already gone. They all would be gone in 150 years, she speculated, without financial contributions to protect them.

Yet Farwell advised hope for members who knew little of California and had never seen the redwoods. She wrote that "in 1921-1922 one and a half million dollars had been used toward saving the redwoods through the Save the Redwoods League, and that the Humboldt State Redwood Park of three thousand acres had been established. This extended twelve miles, bordering the State Highway in the basin of the South Fork of the Eel River."[229]

Farwell, nearing the end of her life in late 1926, relinquished her redwoods campaign to two colleagues in California: Helen Thorne of the Millbrook, New York, Garden Club and the Garden Club of Santa Barbara and Montecito, and Jean Howard McDuffie of San Francisco, also a member of the Santa Barbara and Montecito club. Months after her death, Henrietta Crosby of Massachusetts, who succeeded Farwell as Conservation Chair, used the *Bulletin* to print a fresh plea on behalf of the redwoods from Henry S. Graves, dean of the Yale Forest School and a Save the Redwoods League Councilor.

Crosby introduced the article with her own appeal to save the forests, revealing the extent to which the Save the Redwoods League relied on others, particularly women's organizations, to attain its goals: "Knowing how often one skips an article when the word 'Conservation' comes in near vicinity I would beg all members of The Garden Club of America to make an exception and read this one from start to finish — and then to join the Save the Redwoods League to show that we stand for saving the oldest living trees in the world!"[230]

Graves assured his readers that powerful financial forces were at work to save the redwoods, including the State of California, Save the Redwoods League, and private contributors. But acquiring enough land to preserve original redwood forest conditions would require thousands of new acres, he warned. The best tracts, he stated, would soon be "lumbered off" unless saved.

"One of the most satisfactory forms of assistance is through gifts for specific groves that may vary in size from forty to several hundred acres in extent," wrote Graves, making a case for the league's memorial grove program. "Many groves have already been established in memory of friends or relatives of benefactors."

The seed was clearly planted.

The State Parks Movement Opens a Door

The Save the Redwoods League, meanwhile, faced a financial challenge in the Humboldt Redwoods beyond almost anything it could imagine. When the Pacific Lumber Company finally came around to the idea of selling its most prized timberland for public use rather than timber production it did so practically with a vengeance, bargaining hard and bargaining big.

In early 1926 the company proposed to sell all that the Humboldt County Women's Save the Redwoods League and Save the Redwoods League had asked for, and more. The Detroit-based timber corporation offered the entirety of its Bull Creek Flat and Dyerville Flat holdings near Weott, 12,000 acres of the planet's most supreme redwood forests, for a price anticipated to be somewhere between $5 million and $6 million.

The Save the Redwoods League had gotten what it wished for, and the price tag shocked the organization. Though the league had agreed during months of contentious preliminary discussions to consider buying 10,000 to 12,000 acres, it held, in the words of redwoods historian Susan R. Schrepfer, an "aversion to a transaction of such magnitude."

> "Pacific Lumber refused to negotiate on other terms," she wrote in a definitive 1971 account of the initial bargaining. "[League President] Merriam presented this proposal to the league council, estimating the cost in excess of four million dollars, and appointed a negotiating committee, with Henry S. Graves, retired chief of the United States Forest Service, as chairman."

Almost immediately, Graves contended with an estimate from Oregon forestry consultant David T. Mason (who had advised Humboldt County lumber companies in 1922 of public hostility to their clear-cutting operations) that the commercial value of the forests was likely no lower than $5.4 million and could be as high as $7.9 million.

While league officials initially refused to consider paying more than $5 million, Graves counseled that posterity could judge them harshly if their inflexibility provoked a collapse of negotiations.

"In the future we are going to be judged by the public on whether or not this tract has been saved," he said. "If we succeed, the people in the future are not going to ask how much the timber cost. If we fail, we are going to be blamed for not saving it regardless of cost." It was a remarkable comment that showed the stakes of the game suddenly thrust upon them.

Both parties agreed to a board of arbitration to determine a suitable price.

The three-member board consisted of Mason as chair, James W. Girard, manager of the Oregon-based Fred Herrick Lumber Company, and E.T. Clark, a Yale-educated professor of forestry and logging engineering at the University of Washington.

When the board, on August 11, 1926, returned its decision establishing the value at $5.6 million, the Save the Redwoods League found itself unwittingly trapped by years of redwoods rhetoric and a price it now believed it could not afford. Forty-five years afterward, Schrepfer explained:

> The men of the league had failed to achieve what they regarded as a satisfactory settlement; neither the size of the acreage to be purchased, the price, nor the terms of the option pleased them. Their failure was a result of an unwillingness to force the company — through publicity or threat of condemnation — to agree to other terms and of their inability to gather data with which to prove their case. The enormity of the acreage, the high market value, and the terms of the option each

added to the total cost, until the league found itself facing the problem of raising six million dollars, a sum far greater than it had anticipated.

Businessmen elsewhere told the league that the price, while high, was fair, considering the disruption to Pacific Lumber's business plans by those demanding its finest timber for government-run parks. Directors of the Save the Redwoods League, finding no way out, no alternative, voted to somehow try and raise $6 million.

The question for a fledgling land trust in the earliest days of conservation was how?

The answer soon became obvious. It would have to be something colossally bigger than winning $250,000 from the California Legislature and governor in 1900 and another $300,000 in 1921. This was something only a statewide bond could do.

But to pass a big enough bond, they would need to sell a compelling motivation, beyond redwoods alone. What they needed, they began to see, was a state park bond. If it took creating and financing an entire state park system to save the redwoods that's what the league would do.[231]

And so began a political strategy in which the save-the-redwoods movement intersected with the nation's budding new state parks movement.

A fresh-minted California State Parks Committee, headed by Save the Redwoods League Parks Committee Chairman Duncan McDuffie, a San Francisco Bay Area real estate developer, conservationist, and husband of The Garden Club of America Redwoods Committee member Jean Howard McDuffie, convened at the city's Palace Hotel on February 7, 1927. There it began to build support for the necessary state legislation.

McDuffie was celebrated for his 1920s "residential park" developments, notably Claremont and Northbrae in Berkeley and St. Francis Wood in San Francisco. A *San Francisco Chronicle* remembrance of his legacy in 2004 recalled attractive neighborhoods "whose curving, tree-lined 'parkways' followed the contours of the hills."[232]

In Sacramento, California lawmakers were already paving the way for a parks bond campaign. Legislators friendly to the league's agenda introduced Senate Bill 439 to create a State Park Commission that would oversee a new state park system. They also unveiled Senate Bill 440 to survey landscapes throughout California suitable for a new park system. A third in the series, Senate Bill 441, proposed to submit a $6-million-dollar state park bond to California voters in 1928.

The park bond would be the state's fourth if passed. Two earlier state bonds had financed highways and another financed the University of California.[233] The bill specified that each dollar provided by taxpayers would be matched by one dollar in private contributions. It would create a fund of $12 million to buy park land throughout California and help the Save the Redwoods League pay its massive bill for prized Pacific Lumber Company redwoods in Humboldt County.

Endorsements came quickly from groups that had long supported the state's redwoods campaigns, and which had backed similar unsuccessful bills in 1925 to create a park commission and survey appropriate park sites. The state park supporters included many familiar names in the ascendancy of the conservation movement: National Park Service Director Stephen T. Mather, the California Federation of Women's Clubs, Native Daughters of the Golden West, Native Sons of the Golden West, the Sierra Club, Sempervirens Club, Calaveras Grove Association, and the Point Lobos Association.

A rising tourist and travel industry represented by the California State Automobile Association and the Automobile Club of Southern California, also endorsed the 1927 legislative campaign, as did newspapers, landscape architects, and local advocates for specific parks and public beaches throughout California.

Lawmakers considered the bills at a time when many states throughout the nation were following the lead of the federal government and creating their own park systems. California State Parks Historian Joseph H. Engbeck, Jr., reported, in his definitive 1980 history of building the California State Park system, that a handful of states had already passed park bonds.

Voters in New York, the nation's most populated state, had passed $26.5 million in state park bonds during the fifteen years before California considered its first park bond. Chicago and Cook County, Illinois, had already issued a $17.5 million park bond and would soon consider another for $20 million. Pennsylvania voters at the time, were considering a park bond of $25 million.[234]

California's park bills passed unanimously in both houses of the legislature during the 1927 spring session. The state's new park-friendly governor, Republican Clement Young, signed all three bills on May 25, and soon named a five-member State Park Commission to begin planning a state park system. The Commission authorized California landscape architect William Law Olmstead, Jr., to conduct a statewide survey of potential park sites. Olmstead was the son of William Law Olmstead, designer seventy years earlier of New York City's Central Park.

All that remained was a November 1928 vote on the $6-million-dollar park bond that would pay for it all. Three organizations, McDuffie's new State Parks Council, the Save the Redwoods League and Newton B. Drury's advertising firm, took the lead to coordinate publicity and daily operations of their "saturation campaign."

The voter inundation strategy to pass Proposition 4, as it was called on the ballot, featured endless rounds of speeches, written materials for newspapers, newspaper editorial cartoons, and a new phenomenon of bumper and window stickers for automobiles. California affiliates of The Garden Club of America alone handed out 10,000 automobile stickers and 50,000 pamphlets urging a "Vote *Yes* on number four and carry the state for state parks."[235]

"In the last weeks of the campaign approximately one million leaflets were distributed by local chambers of commerce, utility companies, and other organizations," Engbeck wrote. He cited additional efforts by the Campfire Girls, Boy Scouts, California Federation of Women's Clubs, Hollywood actresses, the American Legion, auto clubs, the California Farm Bureau Federation, oil companies, and tourist and travel organizations.

Even the Pacific Lumber Company quietly supported the ballot measure, redwoods historian Schrepfer reported in 1971, "revealing perhaps a desire to sell Bull Creek."[236]

When Californians finally received their sample ballots in the days before the election they read a ballot argument that indirectly cited the mounting threats to the redwoods: "What is the use of spending millions on our splendid highway system if the roads lead us to the blackened stumps of what were once mighty forests, and along a shoreline fenced off from the public with signs: 'Private Property — Keep Out?'"[237]

Proposition 4 passed handily on November 6, 1928.

With 975,979 votes in favor and 346,998 votes in opposition, the nearly three-to-one margin of victory earned majority support in each of California's fifty-eight counties.[238] Laura Mahan reported at year's end to members of the Humboldt County Women's Save the Redwoods League that the margin of victory in Humboldt County was even stronger at five to one.

State residents, during the next nine decades, would pass nine more statewide park bonds totaling nearly $6 billion.[239] The state park system grew to an astonishing 80,000 acres by 1930 and reached nearly 700,000 acres in 1960. By 2010 it had peaked at 1.5 million acres, the largest state park system in the United States after the 3.3 million acres of Alaska.[240]

Protected inside were the great redwood forests of Bull Creek Flat and Dyerville Flat.

A Free Inheritance from Past Ages

During the final week of 1928 Franklin Law Olmstead, Jr., completed his statewide park survey which arguably stands among the most magnificent accomplishments in California history. Simultaneously practical and visionary, the report's eighty-three pages of analysis compiled after months of tromping around California's beautiful landscapes has created a network of state parks without equal and one frequently said to rival the national park system.

Without Olmstead's far-sighted recommendations for saving the redwoods, beaches, lakeshores, waterfalls, deserts, and mountains, California might still be a landscape of widespread private ownership of the greatest views and most wondrous natural settings.

"For much of the next 50 years in California, the Olmstead survey guided state park purchase and development decisions as state government allocated public bond proceeds, tidelands oil royalties and General Fund revenues," concluded the California Commission on State Government Organization and Economy eighty-five years later in an investigation of management issues within the state park system.[241]

At the time of the Olmstead survey, a decade of unprecedented prosperity and ever-rising stock prices, California's nearly 5 million residents owned 1.8 million automobiles.

Mindful of growing car travel and tourism, Olmstead focused particularly on locations of high recreational value for motorists making weekend trips or longer. He wrote to the new State Park Commission that he considered every variety of landscape and every kind of proposition. Those included "offers to sell land which the owners or agents think there might be a chance of unloading on the state, to well-considered projects of the utmost importance, put forward in a public-spirited way and with an excellent understanding of the needs of a state park system."

Olmstead, who had often hiked the Northern California redwoods with Eureka's Laura Mahan, banker Arthur E. Connick, or publisher Frederick W. Georgeson at his side, spoke highly of the state's forests in general and the redwoods, in particular.

"Undoubtedly the forests of California are among its most notable scenic assets. Outstanding among them and unique in all the world are its Redwood Forests with their characteristic undergrowth, and its groves of Big Trees," he wrote.

The analysis, repeating a message frequently used by the California Federation of Women's Clubs and others during nearly thirty years of redwoods activism, warned Californians that their forests were fast disappearing and called on them to act on behalf of future generations.

> "This generation has received, as a free inheritance from past ages, a hoard of forest wealth. Regarded as economical or exchangeable wealth, not carrying a normal rate of interest, it calls for liquidation; and it is being liquidated by lumbering operations just as fast as it can be pushed on to a somewhat glutted market. But if any of the future generations for thousands of years to come are to have opportunity of enjoying the spiritual values obtainable from such primeval forests, this generation must exercise the economic self-restraint necessary for passing on some portion of this inheritance, instead of 'cashing-in' on all of it."[242]

Olmstead identified four major redwood zones worth saving as state parks in Humboldt and Del Norte counties. In the decades since all have largely come to fruition, yet as historian Schrepfer noted in 1971 the four proposed parks represented less than three percent of the redwoods in both counties. It is worth repeating in Olmstead's own words, though clumsy and bureaucratic in portions, what he saw and how he envisioned the future of the redwoods in 1928:

> Completion Of Humboldt State Redwood Park. Redwood groves, mixed forest, and undergrowth of outstanding beauty and associated stream and valley landscapes along and near South Fork of Eel River, Eel River, and tributaries. Desirable to round out and complete as far as practicable the detached groves of the present State Park by control and protection of the scenic beauty of the region along the Redwood Highway in which these units have been established, and by extending it northward especially in the notable Bull Creek and Dyerville Flat region.
>
> Prairie Creek. Redwood Forest and creek lands and possibly coastal lands to round out the present Russ Grove and other State Park areas along Prairie Creek. Notable redwoods and undergrowth. General recreational potentialities. From junction of Prairie and Redwood Creeks northerly to Humboldt-Del Norte County Line.
>
> Del Norte Coast Park. Notable redwood, mixed forest, and coastal views. Undergrowth luxuriant. Botanical and geological interest. Hiking and picnics. Desirable for amplifying the limits of the present Graves Grove, and to preserve an unmarred approach to it from the north and south. About eight to fourteen miles south of Crescent City and extending from the Redwood Highway to the Pacific Ocean.

Mill Creek–Smith River Park. Notable stands of redwoods and heavy undergrowth. Excellent forest and river scenery. Camping, picnics, fishing. Botanically interesting. Desirable for preserving an unbroken forest picture through a region of outstanding worth. Extending from a point in Elk Valley, four miles northeast of Crescent City to the new bridge on the Smith River, and including several miles of river footage and Redwoods along the River and on Mill Creek."

Olmstead listed three more northern groves as outstanding candidates for state redwood parks, including 1,600 acres of the Van Duzen River Park near Carlotta in Humboldt County (now a county park), 800 acres of the Montgomery grove, and 480 acres of the Joshua Hendy grove in Mendocino County (both now state parks).

At the southern edge of the redwood belt and closer to population centers Olmstead identified large potential additions to California's first state park, California Redwood Park in the Santa Cruz Mountains, in 1928 renamed Big Basin Redwoods State Park. Among them, he cited 12,000 desirable acres of mixed redwood forests in Santa Cruz and San Mateo counties with "excellent streams and interesting small falls." Most were never acquired by the state and much now exists as second-growth forest.

Olmstead also singled out, as special and worthy of state park status, the Monterey County canyon redwoods of Big Sur and the Calaveras Big Trees Sequoia groves in the central Sierra Nevada. Both have become popular California state parks.[243]

The New Problem of Tourism

As Olmstead completed his work, state officials overseeing California's redwood parks faced a new problem in addition to the woodman's ax and saw: the growing number of cars and tourists who were coming into the forests. In 1928 the California Board of Forestry commissioned U.S. Forest Service plant pathologist Emilio P. Meinecke to assess and recommend solutions to damaged redwood root systems caused by hikers and campers.

Meinecke, based in San Francisco and an acting professor of plant pathology at Stanford University, had become an eminent figure in assessing the human footprint in the nation's newly-accessible wildlands. In 1926 National Park Service Director Stephen T. Mather asked him to measure the impacts of tourism on the Giant Sequoias of the Sierra Nevada.[244]

Now the Board of Forestry asked for a similar look at the Coast Redwoods.

Throughout 1928, Meinecke walked slowly through the state redwood parks of California, identifying what was already been lost and reporting unsettling findings:

> In every grove, the evidence of heavily concentrated travel is immediately discernable. Roads and broad lanes, paths and wide areas are completely bare of vegetation, while in other parts no change in the original condition has taken place. Even in midwinter the camp sites, the social centers around the camp fire, the preferred playgrounds of the children, can as readily be outlined as though they were populated with hundreds of visitors. The exquisite beauty of the Parks which to a large degree rests upon the contrast between the vividly green undergrowth and the red boles of the huge trees in the play of sunlight and shade is no longer preserved, and it is merely a question of time and increased travel when the still remaining vegetation will be destroyed. The former wealth of wild flowers has already disappeared.

It was harder to measure impacts on the trees. The decline of an ancient species such as the redwood might come slowly and be "not witnessed by this generation," Meinecke reported.

The findings suggested a dilemma faced decades later by freeway builders who expanded their systems to relieve congestion only to see the improvements attract more congestion. Where previously travelers had wandered in small numbers throughout the expanses of the redwood belt they now concentrated along the South Fork of the Eel River where the state held 3,000 acres of public parks.

"Not so long ago the ground in the groves was covered with a rich and charming vegetation. Today the ground is bare wherever the people congregate," Meinecke wrote. "The soil is compacted and travel early in the year quickly kills even those young seedlings which may come up in spite of altered conditions."

The concentration suggested a great need for more parks to disperse visitors. Yet new parks would attract still more visitors. It was an immense responsibility for a new generation of professionals with precious little experience in managing wilderness and visitors.

"If the redwoods were merely saved from the axe to fall victim to the slow, but fatal change in their living conditions brought about by tourist travel, the main purpose of creating the parks would certainly fail," warned the forest pathologist, underscoring that responsibility.

Meinecke suggested that camping "be absolutely banned from the main groups [of trees] and concentrated in the marginal areas which as a rule, are better suited to camping than the Redwoods themselves." He advised building the system of forest trails that exists today.

"Definite lanes and paths through the Redwoods must be provided, and the visitors must be trained to use these without trespassing," he stated. "As a rule they will wander on the beaten path and will not go outside, as long as the paths are well-defined and set off against their surroundings." Meinecke, above all, called for state park supervisors to somehow promote a reverence for nature among the thousands of visitors now entering the redwoods. "To turn the austere temples we have inherited from past ages into cheap amusement resorts would constitute a wrong committed against the best there is in the American people. The legitimate demands of those who desire to carry the pleasures of the city life into the country are best taken care of by the many summer resorts along the way. They are out of place in the Parks themselves." [245]

By all measurements, the state and national redwood parks have successfully adhered to Meinecke's vision. In a nation where all things private are generally considered superior to those in the public realm, the opposite is on display within government-owned redwood parks. While private redwood forests typically lure visitors with drive-through trees, trinkets, and carvings, the public redwood forests of California are more often quietly associated with awe, tranquility, reverence, and loftier experiences of the human spirit.

A Who's Who of the Social Register Fortunes

By 1928 redwood memorial groves dedicated to deceased husbands, fathers, and family members chosen by donors represented a third of the Save the Redwoods League's funding, Schrepfer wrote in a 1971 history of the redwoods preservation movement. Overall, the league was getting about half of its funding "in the form of large donations from the vast personal fortunes of the wealthy elite of America." Donors in California, New York, and Massachusetts accounted for the largest share. The league targeted the wealthy through its network of personal contacts while it simultaneously sought smaller contributions through mass mailings. [246]

Drury, when asked during a 1972 oral interview with Schrepfer if the league got more donations from New York and Boston than other parts of the United States, answered:

> "Yes, decidedly so. I haven't the up-to-date figures, but there was a time when, in total money, by far the preponderance of our contributions came from New York State; Mr. John J. Rockefeller, Jr., and Mr.

Edward S. Harkness, and the ladies of The Garden Club of America are the outstanding contributors. But even in the membership, there's a remarkable response from New York, and also from Massachusetts. The Midwest is not as responsive as the East Coast. Of course, the return in California is very satisfactory."[247]

Gifts from wealthy American women typically accounted for the largest and most significant memorial groves. Heirs to the business fortunes of late husbands and fathers and rich in their own right they wrote bountiful checks for individual memorial groves to honor them. State park bond funds matched the gifts, doubling the generosity of donors whose names often read like a who's who of the social register in San Francisco and the Eastern United States.

Generous gifts from the East tell a compelling background story of the great Gilded Age fortunes earned in railroads, mining, steel, and in financing the beginnings of industrial America. Gifts from the upper classes of California tell a history of young ambitious men who left homes throughout America for the goldfields in 1849 and 1850. Many became rich and socially prominent beyond their wildest imaginations from business, ranching, finance, and real estate.

Among the first substantial donations in the latter half of the 1920s was 100 acres of redwoods from Kate Felton Neilson of San Francisco, dedicated Sunday, June 12, 1927, in memory of her father, the late Gold Rush pioneer and U.S. Senator from California, Charles N. Felton. Senator Felton died in 1914 at the age of eighty-two. The new Felton grove sixty miles south of Eureka anchored a picturesque bend in the South Fork of the Eel River across the Redwood Highway from the Bolling Grove dedicated in 1921.

Felton was among those many adventurous pioneers who prospered in California after leaving his Buffalo, New York, home at age seventeen, riding a ship around South America's Cape Horn, and arriving in San Francisco in 1849.

As a San Francisco shopkeeper and later as a banker, he entered politics in his new state on the Pacific and rose to the top. He had been a Yuba County Sheriff, treasurer of the U.S. Mint in San Francisco, a two-term California legislator, member of the U.S. House of Representatives, and from 1891 to 1893, a United State Senator, appointed to fill the vacant seat of deceased Senator George Hearst, father of newspaper publisher William Randolph Hearst. After serving in the Senate, Felton became director of California's state prison system and later, president of the Southern Pacific Railroad.[248]

Stanford University President Ray Lyman Wilbur, presiding over dedication ceremonies for the Charles N. Felton Redwood Grove, told his large audience of fellow Californians, "No other state could provide the type of pioneer whom we are honoring."

Wilbur, a Save the Redwoods League Councilor, a future California State Park Commissioner, and from 1929 to 1933, the Hoover Administration's Secretary of the Interior, paid homage to Kate Felton Neilson as donor of the grove, then offered the customary lofty serenade to the redwoods themselves:

> We need to contemplate them in order to balance off the smoke and dust and grime of that industrial life which we call civilization. We need havens of rest such as this where we can join with the birds and flowers in appreciation and enjoyment of the natural beauties of the earth. Nothing that we can do in the way of planting can give us such trees as these. Planting may give generations far in the future some such trees, but we must keep what nature gave to California. Unfortunately, great as are these trees, resistant as they have been to all the normal enemies of tree life, they can fall before man and his mechanical contrivances. Throughout our history we have seen the great trees go down before the needs or apparent needs of man. We are just beginning to realize that we must, for the benefit of ourselves and others, have those things in nature which inspire human beings. We have just begun to realize that the greater values of life lie in some of our natural assets.

Wilbur also touted Neilsen's gift as an example of how humanity might yet spare many of the surrounding redwoods from the lumberman's ax and saw.

> With the help of generous donors and of the people of the state through the state park commission there is still a chance to save many hundreds of acres for the happiness of those who are to come after us... No cathedral is more inspiring than a redwood grove. Its influence is ennobling, stimulating and inspiring. I hope that those of us who have gathered here to honor a great man and to dedicate a grove for public use for all time will consider this but one in a series of steps to enlarge the redwood holdings of the public.[249]

In 1929 a new collection of memorial groves added another 543 acres to the public redwoods of California, while marking the final months of the prosperity that defined the 1920s. Among them was the landmark Stout Grove visited in 1928 by President Herbert Hoover and considered still, with its landmark Stout Tree, one of the most scenic Northern California redwood groves available to visitors.

Donors Clara Wales Stout of Chicago and her four daughters, Katherine, Calista, Eleanor, and Allison, contributed the scenic Del Norte County grove of forty-four acres to the State of California to prevent it from being logged and forever lost. They named it memory of a husband and father, Frank D. Stout, a former president of the Del Norte Lumber Company who had died in 1927 at age seventy-three, one of the ten richest men in Chicago.

Stout was a renowned Midwestern lumberman, a founder of the Knapp, Stout & Company conglomerate that owned three lumber mills in Wisconsin and was believed in the 1870s and 1880s to be the nation's largest manufacturer of finished lumber. Stout had earned additional fortunes in railroads, cattle, oil, banking, and finance, leaving an estate of more than $10 million, according to family records.[250] Donor Clara Stout, known as a generous philanthropist, lived most of her life in Chicago, but spent winters in Santa Barbara, California, where she mingled with other wealthy people involved in the cause of saving the redwoods.

The Stout Grove, with trees rising from an alluvial flat much like Bull Creek Flat in Humboldt County, became the first dedicated grove within Jedediah Smith Redwoods State Park. State Park Commission Chairman William Colby, in a statement for the announcement, said:

> "In making this splendid gift to the state, the family of the late Frank D. Stout has assured the preservation of one of the most beautiful tracts of redwoods in California. In thus setting aside forever such groves as the one at Mill Creek, a twofold purpose is accomplished by the donors — that of perpetuating the memory of a loved one, and of preserving some of the finest and oldest living things for the inspiration of posterity for all time."[251]

Six weeks later, on June 1, 1929, State Forester Merritt B. Pratt, representing the California State Board of Forestry, dedicated a 265-acre memorial grove in Humboldt Redwoods State Park to the board's former deputy forester Solon H. Williams. Williams, the driving force for negotiations and acquisitions that brought more than 1,600 acres of redwood forests along the South Fork of the Eel River into the state park in 1922 and 1923, had resigned soon after his exhaustive undertaking on June 27, 1923, and died in October 1926.

Upon his death, the Board of Forestry, in the words of California forestry historian C. Raymond Clar, "formally expressed its regret at the loss of a man whose 'untiring efforts and zealous devotion' had made possible the acquisition of the northern redwood parks."

Today's millions of visitors who yearly drive Humboldt County's famed Avenue of the Giants owe much of their breathtaking experiences beneath the towering redwoods to Williams, who could easily be described as the father of one of earth's most scenic drives.

Also in 1929, Harriet "Hattie" Alexander of New York City, daughter of California railroad titan Charles Crocker, paid homage to her late husband, a prominent New York City attorney, railroad executive, financier, and art collector, with the donation of a ninety-four-acre Charles Beatty Alexander Memorial Grove in Humboldt Redwoods State Park.[252]

Charles B. Alexander had been a director of the Equitable Life Insurance Company, the Middletown & Union Railroad, Hocking Valley Railroad and several Eastern banks. He was a trustee of New Jersey's Princeton University and long-time member of the New York State Board of Regents, where he helped oversee the Empire State's system of public universities.[253]

Harriet Alexander was an especially prominent member of New York society, famed for her love of the opera and her large dinner parties and balls at two family mansions, including an opulent West Fifty-Eighth Street residence on the city's "Millionaire's Row." Alexander, who inherited with three brothers their father's $25-million railroad fortune in 1888, inherited another $10 million and several residences upon the death of her husband in 1927 at the age of seventy-seven.[254]

Alexander's redwood grove in memory of her late husband represented the newest contribution to the redwoods by descendants of Charles Crocker. Four decades after the death of the Central Pacific Railroad founder and construction manager on its share of America's transcontinental railroad, the family's generosity in the Northern California redwoods had become legend.

Harriet's Alexander's brother, William H. Crocker, recalled by California historian Kevin Starr in his 1985 book, *Inventing the Dream*, as "the leading personage, public or private of San Francisco" for more than fifty years, served on the Save the Redwoods League board of directors. William H. Crocker's wife, Ethel, provided $25,000 in 1923 to help maintain park acreage along the South Fork of the Eel River purchased by the 1921 Redwood Preservation Bill. In 1931, she contributed another $25,000 to help the State of California acquire 1,951 acres of the North Grove of Calaveras Big Trees State Park.[255]

Another wealthy matriarch at the apex of Eastern society, Justine Whittemore of Middlebury, Connecticut, bought 140 acres of redwoods at the southernmost edge of Humboldt Redwoods State Park in 1929 and designated it the Harris Whittemore Memorial Grove. The gift was in memory of her late husband, who, like Charles Alexander, had also died in 1927 at the age of sixty-three. The Whittemore redwoods, three miles north of Garberville and seventy-four miles south of Eureka, stand atop the quiet Western bank of the South Fork of the Eel River.

Harris Whittemore was a true son of the Gilded Age, inheriting the iron manufacturing, railroad investment, and real estate fortune made by his father, John Howard Whittemore of Naugatuck, Connecticut. While he upheld his father's business interests and served on the corporate boards of iron, railroad, and financial companies, Whittemore carved out his own reputation as a philanthropist and advocate for the forests and trees of his home state. As a citizen, and as a state forest and park commissioner, he personally reforested with his family fortune thousands of acres in heavily-logged Connecticut and remade them into public parks. Whittemore and his wife were also acclaimed for one of the nation's great private art collections. They owned more than 1,000 paintings, thirty alone by French Impressionist Claude Monet, and countless more by Edgar Degas, Mary Cassatt, and James Abbott McNeill Whistler. [256]

Five weeks before the American stock market crash of October 1929, on Sunday, September 21, Justine Whittemore, family members, and friends gathered alongside Laura Mahan, president of the Humboldt County Women's Save the Redwoods League, and San Francisco Save the Redwoods League officials to dedicate the grove.

League Speaker and Councilor William F. Badè used the occasion of "dignity and simplicity" to make a stirring comparison between the luxuriant California redwoods and the long-destroyed "forests of Palestine, where once-splendid stands of Lebanon Cedar are now scarred and ruined beyond redemption." Americans, he said, should not repeat in the California redwoods the great deforestation, for purposes of commerce and building materials, that had marred and defined the Mediterranean landscapes of Palestine for 2,000 years. The contrast between the cool, green and beautiful riverfront landscape before his audience and that of present-day desert Palestine, suggested, he said:

> "How important it is that we should guard our sacred forests in order that they may continue to maintain their beneficial relation to our lives. It behooves us who dedicate this grove today to remember that for a very large part of our American world, California has succeeded to the title of the Promised Land. The varieties of climate and scenery which Palestine compressed between the short range from sun-baked Jericho, thirteen hundred feet below sea level, to the snow-covered summits of Mount Hermon and the Lebanons, are spread out here on a more spacious scale and in still more picturesque varieties of grandeur. It behooves us who dedicate this grove today that, though these Sequoias are located in California, their preservation must not be local, but an all-American achievement. East and West, North and South are cooperating in saving these treasured wonders of the world from destruction."

Badè, in the flowery, classical-minded language of the era, acknowledged the eternal nature of the redwoods and compared them to the ancient grandeur of the Egyptian pyramids. He ended then with a salute to the man in whose name they had gathered:

> "We dedicate today this area of forest primeval, that henceforth its cathedral aisles may enshrine the name of one of Connecticut's worthiest sons. It was in far-away Naugatuck, amid the round-headed trees, daisied meadows and splashing brooks of New England, that Harris Whittemore laid the foundations of a life worthy to be remembered and perpetuated in this grove."

The redwoods got one last taste of American and global society before the Great Depression when British politician and writer Winston Churchill drove into Humboldt County on Sunday, September 8, 1929, while traveling south through, as he described it, "an aisle in a cathedral of trees."

Churchill, serving in the British Parliament and touring Canada and the United States for three months with his younger brother, nephew, and son, reached Eureka in the morning from Del Norte County's Crescent City, having stopped occasionally to marvel at the "solid wall of timber" fronting the Redwood Highway. In his later writings, he recalled how "men look like ants and motor cars look like beetles" against the panorama of towering redwoods.

At the Eureka Inn, Churchill visited *Humboldt Standard* Publisher Frederick W. Georgeson, pronouncing the morning drive "wholly delightful," the highlight, he said, of his trip along the Pacific Coast. Churchill and his party drove south then to the massive Bull Creek redwoods where they had lunch and a swim beneath the trees. One giant redwood prompted fifteen members of the party, which now included reporters and British naval officers, to join hands in a circle about the base, which Churchill estimated to be twenty feet thick.

Author Bradley P. Tolppanen, in his book, *Churchill in North America, 1929*, described Churchill's reflections on the overpowering sense of time the redwoods always evoke in visitors.

> Winston wrote in his *Daily Telegraph* article devoted to California's natural beauty that the trees were already old "when the smoke of sacrifice arose from the Pantheon and camelopards [giraffes] bounded in the Flavian amphitheater." He thought these trees may well survive, save for the efforts of the timber companies, until Macaulay's traveler from New Zealand stands 'upon a broken arch of London Bridge to sketch the ruins of St. Paul's.' The redwoods would grow, Winston concluded, as long as people allowed them to.[257]

The Garden Club of America Redwoods

A chance encounter over lunch in San Francisco in 1930 provided a catalyst nationally for The Garden Club of America to buy its own grove in the Humboldt redwoods. As the time came to make its stand, The Garden Club of America moved fast and with minimum drama. The goal would be set, and the money would come quickly from every club in the nation.

Years afterward, Myra Meyer of affluent Westchester County, New York, and a member of the Bedford, New York, Garden Club, recalled in a letter to Newton B. Drury of the Save the Redwoods League how a lunch date with league chairman Joseph Grant and his wife, Edith, propelled the club's Eastern leaders to act on an idea long embraced by the Pacific Coast clubs.

> I had returned with my husband from India, which for some years had been my home and went to New York to live, then came out to San Francisco and this special day was lunching with Mr. and Mrs. Joseph Grant. A guest next to me said, probably Mrs. [Ethel] Lansdale, "As you are going back to New York won't you do us a favor?" I said, "Certainly." She added, "You know how we Californians are keenly interested in saving the redwoods. Won't you bring buying a grove to the attention of The Garden Club of America. We want so much that they should do so." I assented readily, of course, tho' at that time I was only a member of the G.C.A. by belonging to a member club. However, the day following my return to New York I was at a luncheon where a guest next to me was the President of the G.C.A. Mrs. [Anne] Stewart. I broached the subject to her at once. She received it enthusiastically, said she was sure the club would be delighted with the idea.[258]

Anne Stewart of Philadelphia in 1929 had recently fulfilled her term as president of The Garden Club of America and was now a member of the board of directors. But she quickly carried the idea of a California redwood grove to the club's new president, Elizabeth Lockwood of New York City. Lockwood, too, warmed to the idea and agreed to bring it to the Council of Presidents and national membership when The Garden Club of America convened, just weeks ahead on July 7, 1930, for its week-long seventeenth Annual Meeting in Seattle.

Stewart wrote to Joseph D. Grant in San Francisco on May 26, 1930, explaining the appeal from Western garden clubs for a grove and asking for information about the league's program in the redwoods. She cited the rapid motion of the idea since his spring lunch with Meyer and offered encouraging news about the club's interest.

"I believe the idea will be popular," she told the league chairman. "Everyone knows of the necessity of protection for the trees, but it is difficult to rouse the Eastern mind to action about something so very far away." She added, "I must be ready to answer questions especially as to the size of groves available, the amount of money needed for one of moderate size, also if the amount raised will be matched from the state's bond issue funds, and where such a grove is likely to be situated."[259]

By the time of the club's Annual Meeting in Seattle, events had proved fast moving and extraordinary. On a convoy of westbound railcars from New York to Seattle dubbed "The Garden Club of America Special,"[260] nearly 100 members, including President Elizabeth Lockwood, Anne Stewart, Helen Thorne and Ethel Lansdale, had already raised $10,000 among themselves toward the purchase of a redwood grove.

In Seattle, the momentum accelerated. The Council of Presidents supported raising $25,000 to buy a grove. The national membership followed after lengthy discussion, offering the unanimous approval of 275 members representing ninety-one clubs in thirty-two states. Minutes of the convention proceedings note, "A wish was expressed that every member of The Garden Club of America should have some part, large or small, in the purchase of the Redwood Grove."[261]

Lockwood immediately appointed a Redwoods Committee to take control of the site selection, and by mid-July four members, Lucy Moffitt Lynch of Ridgeville, Connecticut; Alice Gertrude Williams of New York City; Sarah Fife of Middletown, Connecticut; and Olive Holbrook Palmer of Atherton, California (who would soon personally donate a redwood grove of 277 acres in memory of her late husband), were on the ground in Humboldt County. Drury rushed north to meet the delegation after writing to Louis Perske at the Eureka Garage, a chauffeur and rental car agency, imploring him to offer his best services to the garden club representatives:

> I want you to furnish a good closed car (not one of the old cars that you sometimes rent to me to drive myself but a fairly new and comfortable car) and a driver to meet a party at Grants Pass (Oregon), Tuesday morning, July 15th. The party will be headed by Mrs. John Lynch and will contain other members of The Garden Club of America who will be coming from Medford to Grants Pass by train. I have told them that your car and driver would be waiting for them Tuesday morning at the Redwood Inn, Grants Pass.[262]

The July 16, 1930, *Humboldt Standard*, published a picture of the visiting committee and reported an account of its trip into the redwoods in search of a grove site: "Members of the committee today were enthusiastic over

Humboldt County scenery, which in the words of Mrs. Fife surpassed the drives along the Riviera, or the coast highways of France, Italy or Spain. 'Their magnificence impress you beyond conception. They may be compared to no other phenomena,' Mrs. Lynch stated. Each were particularly impressed with the growth of Del Norte and Humboldt County forests to the rocky barrier of the coast line."

The committee members investigated thoroughly. Author William Seale, quoting from the December 1931 *Bulletin* in his 2012 history, *The Garden Club of America 100 Years of a Growing Legacy*, wrote: "The travelers' wise hosts had a tour plan. Their guests were taken on foot and by motor deep into the forest, where they walked among the great trees, pushed through lush green expanses of ferns and softened their steps in the deep, sweet mulch. At one point rain fell and mud deepened, yet the ladies moved on in wonder at everything they saw. At last they were guided to an area where the loggers were at work felling giant redwoods. The strangers awakened to see noble trees tremble and crash to the ground, thousands of years of growth cut into pieces for shipment to sawmills."

At month's end, July 28, 1930, The Garden Club of America issued a news release from its national headquarters in New York City, announcing that the club intended to buy a redwoods grove in California and there hold its 1935 Annual Convention:

> Following the unanimous vote of the Council of Presidents of The Garden Club of America at the convention of the organization at Seattle, July Seventh to Fifteenth, to purchase and present to the State of California an outstanding Redwood grove in the world-famous Redwood region of Humboldt County, a committee appointed by Mrs. William (Elizabeth) Lockwood of New York, grand president of the Garden Club, has just completed a tour of inspection over the Redwood Highway accompanied by an officer of the Save-the-Redwoods League, giving special attention to several groves in the vicinity of Bull Creek Flat, from which they will ultimately make a selection.

Ultimately, the club expanded its vision well beyond buying a moderate-sized grove and, with guidance from the Save the Redwoods League, settled on a large remote area known as Canoe Creek, 2,500 acres of lowland and hillside redwood forests west of the South Fork of the Eel River near Bull Creek Flat. Stewart, writing in the May 1931 *Bulletin*, provided members an elaborate description of their new redwood grove:

> Naturally placed in a well-protected basin, this magnificent forest floor is the jewel of our Grove held in a superb setting of gently rolling land

extending upward and back in a series of "flats" for two miles along Canoe Creek which flows unceasingly throughout the year, adding that touch of perfection which running water never fails to give. This protective basin affords shelter from devastating storms and acts as a screen to shut out cut-over land. The timber is varied, from magnificent trees which have really lived through the ages, to those of lesser height counting their years in mere hundreds, on to the young growth fringing the edges of the groves with light and airy foliage. Ferns and flowers in profusion add their beauty to a marvelous whole — the grandeur, dignity and silence of this grove is an unforgettable memory to those who have felt its inspiration. Your chairman makes this report with pride and enthusiasm. The saving of a unit of this primeval forest, like an army at its last stand, may inspire other organizations to acquire other units still to be had.

With treasurer Helen Thorne leading the fund-raising effort from Santa Barbara, the member clubs throughout America raised an astonishing $92,000, an amount made still more powerful by a $75,000 match from the State Park Commission, before the end of 1931.[263]

In all, it was an outstanding performance by a single organization during difficult times. Myra Meyer personally contributed $500 after her chance encounter in San Francisco helped propel the grove to reality. Her Bedford Garden Club in New York State donated more than $4,700.[264] Thorne, throughout the summer and autumn of 1930, barnstormed the Eastern clubs, riding in cars and trains to her "one-day stands" in Milton and Lenox, Massachusetts, and New York City in search of "thirty thousand dollars by the eleventh of November."[265] The Pasadena Garden Club contributed $1,500 after Thorne asked its members to get on with a "great national objective." Thorne also urged, through the *Bulletin*, for the "California clubs to 'mother' the redwood grove to be purchased."[266]

When the fund-raising effort concluded, every member affiliate of The Garden Club of America could boast of having contributed to saving a grove of primeval forest. Stewart, again in the *Bulletin* of May 1931, remarked, "We are happy to say that this gift comes from the entire membership, as every club contributed, in many cases subscribing one hundred per cent to the Fund — so eloquent of the spirit which animates the organization."

A mere dozen years had passed now since 1919 opened without an acre of Humboldt County's great redwoods yet in public ownership. Now the nation was rushing to the rescue and the State of California was soon to announce its own landmark success in the Humboldt redwoods. In the fight to save the redwoods, it was all, and at last, starting to come together.

CHAPTER SIX: CELEBRATING SUCCESS, 1931–1934

> "There was a garden on the other side of the world in which met the first garden club. The president was named Eve."
>
> — Dr. Aurelia Reinhardt, President, Mills College. May 20, 1934, dedication of The Garden Club of America Grove in Humboldt Redwoods State Park.

Then came the celebrations.

Years of fund-raising for the redwoods produced a sudden crescendo of memorable dedication ceremonies, even as the Great Depression tightened its grip on the United States. These jubilant events deep in the forest provided magnificent wilderness stages for participants to gather and reflect proudly on the achievements of their environmental crusade.

Throughout the early 1930s the sound of Christian hymns and poetry rang out within the great forests of Humboldt County. Financial contributors throughout California and the United States flocked to these celebrations, applauding their individual groves and the phenomenal acquisition of 30,000 acres of ancient forests for the first public redwood parks. Frequent arrivals of these prominent outsiders in rugged and remote Northern California, most traveling great distances by train and automobile, signaled how redwoods preservation had moved well beyond its local origins and into the realm of America's most affluent families.

With eloquent words and invocations, with songs, time capsules, and soulful moments of silence in the forests surrounding them, women foremost among the visitors, dedicated several new redwood groves funded by the Native Daughters of the Golden West, California Federation of Women's Clubs, and The Garden Club of America. Standing as equals alongside the Save the Redwoods League and the California State Park Commission they celebrated saving 13,000 acres of beautiful lowland forests at Dyerville Flat and Bull Creek for the new Humboldt Redwoods State Park. Affluent individual women saved hundreds more acres in memorial groves named for late husbands, parents, and pioneer ancestors who traveled to California by wagon train and prospered greatly. Other donors established a poignant redwood memorial forest of nearly 1,000 acres in memory of their deceased young children.

As they looked in all directions to the beautiful green mountains and forests, these early preservationists could see now the beginnings of a great redwood park system. Their collective accomplishment represented not only the culmination of years of fund-raising, but fulfillment of their noblest ideal of human civilization itself, in which the wonders of the world are not destroyed but passed intact to future generations.

On Mother's Day, May 10, 1931, 300 members and friends of the Native Daughters of the Golden West celebrated the first of these festive occasions, dedicating forty-six acres along the Redwood Highway as a memorial to the pioneers of California.

An organization founded by the first generation of California-born women in 1886 had raised nearly $7,000 matched by a new State Park Commission with proceeds from the 1928 state park bond for a beautiful half-mile stretch of forest along the banks of the South Fork of the Eel River.[267] Ceremonies opened with the raising of two flags, one each for the United States and California, above a large boulder marking the Native Daughters' contribution to the redwoods. Attached to the boulder a bronze plaque portrayed six oxen pulling a covered wagon across the mountain West and bore the names of local parlors (chapters) that conceived the memorial grove idea in 1926 and raised the funds within four years.[268]

Estelle Evans of San Francisco, president of the statewide organization, described the significance of choosing Mother's Day for the occasion in tribute to California's pioneer women, their mothers and grandmothers who endured every hardship on a wild and unruly frontier and helped build a new state on the Pacific. Evans, accompanied by Lily Peterson playing a piano inside the towering redwood grove, then sang the song, "Trees," a popular poem by the late Alfred Joyce Kilmer set to music after he died a soldier's death in World War I:

> I think that I shall never see
> A poem lovely as a tree.
> A tree whose hungry mouth is prest
> Against the earth's sweet flowing breast;

A tree that looks at God all day,
And lifts her leafy arms to pray;
A tree that may in Summer wear
A nest of robins in her hair;

Upon whose bosom snow has lain;
Who intimately lives with rain.
Poems are made by fools like me,
But only God can make a tree."[269]

The Native Daughters, long-time friends of the redwoods who had telegrammed California Governor Henry Gage in 1901 urging him to sign legislation to buy 2,500 acres of Santa Cruz Mountain redwoods, received special thanks from Save the Redwoods League Secretary Newton B. Drury. In brief remarks he told the Daughters, "An organization founded on the tradition of California history and pledged to the welfare of the state could show their love in no more adequate fashion than through such a project."[270]

Memorably closing the ceremony, Peterson sat again at her piano beneath the big trees and accompanied two tenor solos by Raymond Grinsell, a land development official and member of the Native Sons of the Golden West parlor in nearby Ferndale.[271] The scene of open-air singing characterized a time before television with radio still in its infancy. Three hundred people followed with a rendition of the state song, now largely forgotten with its poetic tributes to the state's missions, mountains, fertile valleys, and redwood forests, "I Love You, California."

I love your red-wood forests — love your fields of yellow grain.
I love your summer breezes and I love your winter rain.
I love you, land of flowers; land of honey, fruit, and wine.
I love you, California; you have won this heart of mine."[272]

The World's Greatest Redwood Forests Are Saved

Six weeks later on June 20, 1931, the Save the Redwoods League announced the greatest of the early successes in saving the Humboldt redwoods, a $3.3 million agreement with the Pacific Lumber Company for 9,369 acres of the most outstanding forests in California and arguably the world at Dyerville Flat and Bull Creek Flat. In all, the transaction with the Pacific Lumber Company and simultaneous broader deals with the Sage Land and Improvement Company and the Metropolitan Lumber Company brought overnight an astonishing 13,239 acres of ancient redwoods into permanent protection. The massive addition to Humboldt Redwoods State

Park contained 105,000 redwood trees with diameters greater than twenty inches.[273]

It had been a long time in coming. Twenty months after the stock market crash of October 1929 with the Great Depression in full swing, *The Humboldt Times* opened its Sunday, June 21, 1931, report with forty-seven words to describe the historic environmental occasion.

> The renowned Bull Creek and Dyerville Flat forests, acclaimed by world travelers the supreme development of California's giant Redwoods, and considered of the same national importance as Yosemite, Grand Canyon and other unique natural wonders, are assured of preservation as a part of California's State Park system.[274]

For residents of Humboldt County especially, the lowland forests of Dyerville Flat, so long defended and championed by the Humboldt County Women's Save the Redwoods League, had escaped at long last the ax of the woodman. Everything that had failed at Carson Woods had come to fruition in an entirely new and impressive landscape.

It nearly didn't happen.

Six months earlier Save the Redwoods League directors had become exasperated with the Pacific Lumber Company's perceived inflexibility during financial negotiations that had now stretched to six years. The California State Park Commission had taken over negotiations due to inability of the two sides to reach a deal. Finally, the league, exasperated, had voted to sue the company and seek condemnation of its Bull Creek and Dyerville holdings. Only the reliable and trusted Arthur E. Connick, president of First National Bank in Eureka, had the personal standing to break the deadlock. He did so bluntly, warning the Pacific Lumber Company and the California State Park Commission what women and others might do statewide and nationally, including starting a total redwood lumber boycott and bringing sustained disastrous publicity for the timber industry, if a condemnation battle broke out over these forests:

> "I know it is not right that such an attitude should arise or exist. But I am just as sure that it is apt to come about, and the logical result … is going to be the probability of organizations such as the California Federation of Women's Clubs and other organizations throughout California and the East fostering and developing a campaign against the use of redwood lumber. There will be pictured in national magazines such as the *Saturday Evening Post* the wanton devastation and destruction of these forests and trees by the ruthless lumbermen and the appeal to the public and users of lumber, to refuse to buy redwood."

The Pacific Lumber Company soon agreed on a price.[275]

With the swipe of a pen and signatures the acreage of Humboldt County redwoods saved since 1919 multiplied exponentially. Eighteen years after its 1913 picnic to assist planning efforts for a redwood national park at Carson Woods, the Humboldt County Women's Save the Redwoods League, standing alongside the Eureka Chamber of Commerce, Save the Redwoods League, and State Park Commission, beheld a great redwood park of four square miles, 16,000 acres of earth's most stunning landscapes with fifteen miles of river running through all of them.[276]

Major financing to buy the Pacific Lumber Company holdings had come from statewide and national women's associations and the taxpayers of California through the 1928 state park bond. But the biggest funder was oil money, in private checks from heirs of the Standard Oil Company. John D. Rockefeller, Jr., contributed $2 million and dedicated a forest grove in memory of his late mother, Laura Celestia Spelman Rockefeller. New York City philanthropist Edward Harkness, also among the richest men in America after inheriting his father's fortune earned from early investments in Standard Oil, contributed $500,000.[277]

It was not lost on Humboldt County residents that most of the money to save their redwoods came from outside. Local newspapers thanked those "who are not even residents of California" for "generosity in helping to conserve these 'world's finest forests' for all time."[278]

President Hoover's Secretary of the Interior Ray Lyman Wilbur, a former president of Stanford University, a Councilor for the Save the Redwoods League and founding member of the California State Park Commission, commended the league in a telegram:

> Nature was very kind to California. We have sometimes been a little rough in the way we have handled our natural beauties. Saving Bull Creek Flat for our children's children is a real triumph of the Save the Redwoods League. Hearty Congratulations.

League President Merriam also issued a statement. "This, with the other acquisitions of exceptional Redwood forest, guarantees to California and the nation the preservation of and enjoyment of the most remarkable tracts known." The acquisition, he said, "protects one of the unique features in the primitive life of America. This forest constitutes one of the greatest assets of California and of the United States, and will have increasing value as a spiritual influence in the life of the people of the state and of the nation."[279]

The Humboldt Times also spoke movingly under a headline, "An Eternal Asset for Humboldt County and California." In beautiful writing that spoke

of the eloquence of a local newspaper and its awareness of history and the
larger world, the newspaper editorialized:

> The trees many of which were living when Christ walked the earth,
> some of them when the mighty Alexander was laying waste the great
> Persian Empire, and a few of them even when the Babylonish kingdom
> was at its height, more than 2,600 years ago, make the state parks of
> which they form the interesting feature among the most interesting
> natural wonders of the world — containing as they do the oldest living
> things on the earth, representative as they are of a species of forests
> which properly flourished amid the steaming mists of the antediluvian
> world.

The *Times* editorial praised the officers of the Save the Redwoods League,
the Pacific Lumber Company, the State Park Commission, "and many public-
spirited citizens, among whom John D. Rockefeller, Jr., stands as the most
prominent." The *Times* also cited the role of women in the long struggle to
save the redwoods:

> Organizations such as The Garden Club of America, the California
> Federation of the Women's Clubs, Native Daughters of the Golden
> West, and others, are to be commended for their successful efforts to
> secure for the people of America for all time, this marvelous tract of
> prehistoric forest, as well as most accessible, delightfully attractive
> park.

The Eureka newspaper lastly thanked President Herbert Hoover, Wilbur,
and Merriam for "the glorious results which have just been announced, that
this unparalleled tract of redwoods approximately four miles square, has
been acquired for the permanent use of the people of the United States and
of those foreigners who will visit our shores."[280]

The Los Angeles Times published a congratulatory editorial the same
day, declaring that "forest lovers will be highly gratified," and praising
the contributions of State Park Commissioner Henry W. O'Melveny, a
hometown attorney, businessman, and naturalist. The *Times* also speculated
about what might have happened otherwise:

> The fine forest land conserved by the purchase would in the course of
> time have been all logged over, leaving little besides blackened stumps
> and second-growth redwoods. The significance of this splendid
> achievement is manifest to all who have witnessed or heard of the
> slaughter of the redwoods, giant trees grown only in California, which
> has been going on for many years, and would have halted only with
> the felling of the last of this titanic vegetation had not the park system
> been created and the big-tree regions been included in it. Bryant, who

never saw the Humboldt big trees, said: "The groves were God's first temples." Had he ever entered that stately tree cathedral, dim, lofty, high-pillared and peaceful, how his nature-loving heart would have rejoiced. It is a great boon to mankind that these trees have been saved and the thanks of the State and nation are due to those who saved them.[281]

On Sunday, September 13, 1931, 2,000 people celebrated the milestone environmental accomplishment beneath the giants of Bull Creek Flat, the new heart of Humboldt Redwoods State Park. National Park Service Director Horace Albright, Yosemite National Park Superintendent Colonel Charles Thomson, and Barton Everman, curator of the National Academy of Sciences, celebrated with them. The grand event, which included dedication of a "Founders Tree" to Save the Redwoods League founders John C. Merriam, Madison Grant, and Henry Fairfield Osborn, attracted scores of local and state elected officials. Also present were state park commissioners and several prominent lumbermen, including Stanwood Murphy, president of the Pacific Lumber Company of Detroit; Henry B. Hickey, principal partner of the Standish-Hickey Company of San Francisco; and W.J. Curry, a Humboldt County representative of Albany, New York-based Sage Land and Improvement Company. Save the Redwoods League Councilor Caroline Hunter of Santa Barbara and women representing the Humboldt County Women's Save the Redwoods League, California Federation of Women's Clubs, and Native Daughters of the Golden West also attended the dedication.

For all, Northern California provided an ideal September day in the grove with "the rays of the sun breaking through the tops and lending a beautiful subdued lighting effect that added to the solemnity and grandeur of the occasion." Merriam, in a keynote address, likened the beautiful setting to the Garden of Eden, representative of "forest which flourished over the whole world tens of millions of years ago." The league's president hailed its preservation as "continuation of the most splendid creative influence as we know them in the world of living things.

> "This grove is a thing of world interest, because it represents the finest type of forest composed of the most ancient and imposing trees. There are other forests with trees greater in diameter or with a greater mass. There are none in which the trees are more graceful or show these qualities combined with mass and age. Comparable to the cliffs of Yosemite, to the living geysers of Yellowstone and to the spectacular beauty of the Grand Canyon, these great trees stand silhouetted against the sky as the incomparable results of creation in the living

world, and as something which we inherit from a period before human history had its beginnings."[282]

The prominent role of women in saving the redwoods attracted generous credit during speeches from a bark-covered dais. Alongside tributes to the Save the Redwoods League founders, to Albright and former Congressman William Kent, personal accolades from State Park Commission Chairman William Colby went out to Laura Mahan, president of the Humboldt County Women's Save the Redwoods League, and her fellow stalwarts Annie Zane Murray of Eureka and the late Georgia Russ Williams of Ferndale. Colby also praised the state and national women's federations, and collectively, the many individual donors, predominately women, of memorial groves throughout the South Fork of the Eel River.

Master of Ceremonies Joseph D. Grant, chairman of the board of the Save the Redwoods League, added to the tributes: "Three organizations, the California Federation of Women's Clubs, The Garden Club of America, and the Native Daughters of the Golden West, have in recent months enabled us to add materially to the acreage of redwoods saved," he said. "Many have taken part in the acquisition of this forest that surrounds us. We have tried to give credit to all, and I only wish that I could mention here the many names of the generous men and women who have established memorial redwood groves."

Grant spoke prophetically to humanity's capacity to yet destroy hundreds of thousands of acres of old-growth redwoods still standing in 1931. As he spoke, lumber companies and the Roaring Twenties economy had already obliterated nearly ten percent of the 1 million remaining acres of old-growth California redwoods that had stood a decade earlier.[283]

"Some of these trees existed long before the advent of Christ," Grant said, pointing out that a man's average lifespan is seventy years. In that one man's lifetime, said Grant, "he and his fellows could destroy these, the product of between two and three thousand years of growth."[284]

The assessment would prove tragically accurate. As the league missed opportunities to save other large groves in decades ahead, the redwood lumber industry during the next seventy years obliterated all but five percent of California's original redwood belt.

Yet on a Sunday afternoon in September that was well in the future. In a grand, fitting conclusion to the ceremonies, the Humboldt Oratorio Chorus, under direction of Grace Rushing Henkel, performed a hymn, 200 years old that rivaled the majestic trees of Bull Creek Flat, Handel's "Hallelujah Chorus."

A simple dedication of the nearby Founders Tree followed at North Dyerville Flat, within a half mile of where Laura Mahan faced down Pacific Lumber Company crews in late 1924. No recorded mention was made of it. State Parks Commissioner Frederick Russell Burnham of Los Angeles recounted instead the origin and significance of the Save the Redwoods League in winning the giant trees for public use. State Park Commissioner Madie Brown of San Francisco then presented a hand-engrossed Commission resolution to Merriam, celebrating him and fellow Save the Redwoods League founders Osborn and Grant. The resolution attached their names in perpetuity to the world's tallest known redwood at the time, the 364-foot "Founder's Tree."

And then it was over, at last, the ten-year trial of local confrontation, the state political maneuvers, endless negotiations, and fund-raising. The greatest addition yet to California's new state park system was in public hands and safe. It was done and it was glorious, the "most wonderful redwood park in the world as a state park," as *The Humboldt Times* described it, "devoted to the pleasure of this and future generations."[285]

Silence in the Children's Forest

Only hours after the September 1931 dedication a wealthy Santa Barbara heiress and the Save the Redwoods League made still another extraordinary announcement, unveiling perhaps the most poignant and touching story of early redwoods preservation in California.

The "Children's Forest," a vast, outdoor memorial in the Humboldt redwoods, emerged as a touchstone for Caroline Hunter of Santa Barbara and friends throughout the nation grieving the premature deaths of their children. Collectively, they established a commemorative forest of 777 acres where parents of children who had died as infants, toddlers, or as teens, and friends who mourned the deaths of children dear to them, could memorialize them all.

In the early history of saving the redwoods the Children's Forest became an invaluable way for the league to solicit smaller contributions and use them to accumulate large acreages.

Hunter was the daughter of the late Anson Phelps Stokes, a prominent New York City banker, investor, and philanthropist who founded the New York Metropolitan Museum of Art. His family "had amassed several fortunes in banking, real estate, railroads, and mining during the last half of the Nineteenth Century," wrote Progressive Era historian Edward Allan Brawley in 2007. Upon his death, Hunter's father was one of the richest men in America.[286] Her grandfather, too, was financially and socially prominent; he helped establish the Republic of Liberia for freed American slaves to return to Africa.[287]

An early letter from Hunter to prospective donors explained the memorial concept:

> The plan is that those of us who have lost children, and who should care to join, could contribute a unit. The unit might stand as a contribution from one or more members of the family or from a group of the child's friends. Each unit would cost $1,250. This amount would be matched from Mr. Rockefeller's fund, set aside for saving the Redwoods, making $2,500, and this in turn matched by the State, making a total of $5,000. In other words, each original $1,250 would have a purchasing value of $5,000.

> The "Children's Forest" would become, similarly to the other Memorial Groves on the Redwood Highway, a part of the California State park system. The exact location has not yet been decided upon, probably near the "Bull Creek Flat" region, above Benbow on the Redwood Highway. It will be selected primarily as a grove which children would fancy, and in which one can fancy children; not too dense a grove, but one perhaps carpeted with oxalis and ferns, with shafts of sunlight, and maybe a playful stretch of river bank, and a little foot bridge leading to the farther side.

Hunter provided potential donors a few sentences of dedication she had written to grace the children's redwood grove. The words were heart-rending: "I leave to children inclusively, all and every flower of the fields and blossoms of the woods with the right to play among them freely, according to the customs of children. And, I devise to children the banks of the brooks and the golden sands beneath the waters thereof, and odors of the willows that dip therein, and the white clouds that float high over the giant trees."[288]

The Children's Forest, eventually located on the remote Western bank of the South Fork of the Eel River near Bull Creek Flat, exemplified how the nation's wealthiest women were increasingly the face of redwoods preservation in Northern California. Hunter, a leading force in preserving Point Lobos State Reserve on the Monterey Peninsula, a Save the Redwoods League Councilor, and wife of nationally-regarded poverty expert, author, and golf course designer Robert Hunter, stood among the influential women of California in the 1920s and 1930s who helped fuel much of the rising enthusiasm for state parks and the coast redwoods.[289]

Her daughter, Helen Louisa Hunter, had died in 1923, just shy of her thirteenth birthday. She was one of seven children named on the dedication plaque, their ages ranging from three weeks to sixteen years.[290] An intimate group of fifteen people, including the Hunters, would dedicate the Children's Forest grove on May 17, 1941, after rowing across the South Fork of the Eel River in small boats. An attendee later reported, "[It was] raining slightly when the dedication started, but just when the minister finished the dedication, the bright sun broke through, making a beautiful forest effect."[291]

Hunter's memorial grove to children, filled with silences and financed with contributions of families throughout the nation, grew to nearly 1,300 acres by 1943 and remains off the beaten track of tourists and hikers.[292] A plaque commemorating the purpose of the forest memorial still reads today: "Come to me, O ye children, for I hear you at your play."[293]

A Retrospective

By 1932, the Humboldt County Women's Save the Redwoods League was a shadow of its former self. It had largely expended its energies and given way to affluent outsiders who now saved the ancient trees. But the league's early heroics on behalf of the redwoods resurfaced brightly on Friday, January 15, 1932, in a breathtaking tribute to its members from women's editor Lillian Ross of *The Humboldt Standard*. Ross, in a lengthy retrospective titled, "Women's Save The Redwoods League Organized in 1919; Aided In Numerous Projects," offered a grand history of the women's league campaigns for a new generation of readers.

It was all there, the simple hopeful beginnings of 1913 in Carson Woods, the formation of the Humboldt County Women's Save the Redwoods League in 1919, and every subsequent defeat and success. The women's league at its height could count on help of 813 members, Ross recalled for readers, and provided ever afterward the bedrock support within Humboldt County for what had to be done. Those were great and better times, Ross recalled, in a county reeling now from the Great Depression and carrying on with half the jobs it had in 1928 and twenty-five percent of that year's payroll.[294]

Women's club members throughout the county surely read this remarkable summary of their campaigns and remembered the living and departed who stood with them in a cause that would prove ever more visionary and meaningful during generations to come.

Ross recounted the initial burst of enthusiasm during the summer of 1919 and donations of redwood acreage from Martha McClellan, Sarah Jane Perrott, and Zipporah Russ. She recalled 1921, when Laura Mahan and Eureka women lobbied the legislature and governor for $300,000 that saved nearly 2,000 acres of redwoods on the South Fork of the Eel River. She noted the growing interest of statewide and national women's groups in the redwoods and their financial contributions that followed. Ross particularly reminded her readers how the county women's league rallied and held the line when it was most important during 1924 and 1925 and saved the most beautiful of the county's redwood forests at Dyerville Flat.

"The determined battle between the officials of the Pacific Lumber Company and the Women's Save the Redwoods League before the Board of Supervisors in February 1925 is one of the most dramatic sessions in the history of the county," the women's editor wrote. "With attorneys on both sides, and their rapid-fire argument, the scene was one of ardent fight, often with touches of bitterness. Hundreds of citizens from all parts of the county were present at the hearing." Afterward, the Humboldt County Board of Supervisors had sided with the women's league, she wrote, and forced negotiations to save the magnificent stands of timber in Dyerville Flat for a park and posterity rather than for cutting and milling.

"The work is not over, but the hardest battles have been won by the glorious work of Mrs. J.P. (Laura) Mahan and the members of the Women's Save the Redwoods League," Ross wrote. In a treasure for future historians of the redwoods, Ross also listed each of the fifty-two individual groves and acreages saved so far in Humboldt and Del Norte counties. In all, Ross counted more than 19,000 acres of redwoods preserved in both counties in the eleven years since 1921, an accomplishment once considered all but impossible.

Within weeks the total climbed again, reaching 25,000 acres. A new gift of $500,000 from philanthropist Edward S. Harkness, matched by the California State Park Commission, added 6,000 acres overnight to Humboldt County's Prairie Creek Redwoods State Park miles fifty miles north of Eureka.[295] Years later, the league's Drury recalled with amusement how the league obtained last-minute funding from Harkness:

> Speaking of Mr. William H. Crocker and his help and influence, I might mention one episode which shows how close you are to success or failure in any enterprise. The great Prairie Creek Redwoods State Park was being planned. We had an opportunity to buy a million dollars' worth of property near Orick. It was offered to us at a price which is about one-thirteenth of what we are having to pay for redwood stumpage today. We didn't have the money. If we could have raised a half million dollars, we could get the other half million through matching by the state. Mr. Crocker was in New York, and one Friday he telephoned me saying that on Monday he was to be playing golf with Mr. Edward S. Harkness, a large contributor to Yale University and Harvard and a very fine benefactor of many enterprises.

Mr. Crocker thought that maybe if we had the right data to make the presentation to Mr. Harkness, we could get a half a million dollars from him. He said, "But I suppose you can't get anything to me by Monday morning." It just happened it was about that time that air mail across the continent had come to the fore as a means of communication that people hadn't previously used. Prior to that time, I don't think I'd ever sent anything airmail. I said, "Mr. Crocker, we can get something up today, put it in the air mail tomorrow, and you should get it by Sunday night," which he did. He played his golf game with Mr. Harkness, and we got the $500,000.[296]

Such monumental victories, which brought 30,000 acres of redwoods into public ownership by 1933, would often seem small and almost insignificant in coming years when weighed against a timber industry that logged nearly all the 2 million acres of California's old-growth redwoods.[297] But in their time those donors and club leaders acknowledged by Ross and Drury had given a seed-like notion of saving the great redwood forests what it needed most, the power to stand, and grow almost like a redwood itself.

To the Women of California

The next major celebration in the redwoods was especially momentous, materializing on a spring Sunday, April 30, 1933, when forty California Federation of Women's Club members gathered in afternoon rain to dedicate at last their ninety-acre grove in Dyerville Flat.[298] Ten years had passed since 1,000 federation members voted to buy a Humboldt County redwood grove during its "Conservation — The Hope of Civilization" convention in Eureka.

Across more than two decades no single organization had done more to sustain the idea of saving the redwoods of Humboldt County than the California Federation of Women's Clubs. From President Elizabeth A. Orr's first trip to the Humboldt redwoods in 1912 to visits afterward by every federation president, the women of California never faltered.

At four o'clock on a damp Sunday afternoon the federation's newest president, Annie Little Barry of San Francisco, led members into their beautiful new grove between the Redwood Highway and the South Fork of the Eel River. Four roaring fires blazed in a stone and wood hearthstone supported by four redwood columns that had been designed for the setting by the eminent California architect Julia Morgan. The hearthstone remains arguably remote Northern California's most significant architectural treasure. Morgan's design of Hearst Castle on the Central California coast had brought her fame. Years of designing women's club headquarters and Young Women's Christian Association centers throughout California, as well as several buildings at Mills College for women in Oakland, made her the federation's architect of choice.

Myra Nye, the long-time chronicler of the federation's drive to save the redwoods, praised Morgan's creation in the federation grove as "an altar dedicated to the glory of California womanhood and to the American home.

"On the stones of the hearthstone are engraved, 'Lo in the forest comes contentment and sweet peace in communion with nature,'" *The Los Angeles Times* writer told readers in Southern California who had raised the largest share of $45,000 for the federation grove. Describing the peaceful forest setting and the role of women in saving it, she noted, "On a fallen log of great circumference near the hearthstone, and nearer to the highway are inscribed these words: 'California Federation of Women's Clubs Grove, presented to the State of California, that these trees through the coming years shall still minister to the destiny of mankind.'"

The ceremony opened with stately classical music, a Haydn choral composition, "The Spacious Firmament on High," sung by the Humboldt Oratorical Chorus, "their voices ringing," in the words of *The Humboldt Times*, "impressively through the vaulted aisles of the beautiful outdoor Cathedral." Standing by and representing the equally unmatched commitment of Humboldt County women across twenty-five years of redwoods campaigns, was Laura Mahan, president of the Humboldt County Women's Save the Redwoods League. She was joined by former *Humboldt Standard* owner Ella Georgeson, now president of the Humboldt County Federation of Women's Clubs, and Eureka Women's Club President Elizabeth Hollinger.

Mahan, with less than four years to live, was pleased. She had written earlier, "The more I see of this grove the more wonderfully beautiful it seems." Morgan's hearthstone also delighted her. "The open fireplace is now completed and is a most imposing and beautiful structure and blends into the surroundings perfectly. As it looms up through the towering trees, its rugged and solid character fits well into this old and stately forest. Much more fitting than a lodge or any of the other buildings suggested which have long been under discussion could possibly be."[299]

In simple and brief ceremonies, the popular young Reverend Harold Morehouse of Garberville provided a Christian invocation while Claire Guiberson of Hanford, chair of the federation's Redwood Grove Committee, offered a poem. Augusta Urquhart of Los Angeles, chief fund-raiser from 1923 to 1925, described the redwood grove as the federation's greatest accomplishment to date. Secretary Drury expressed his thanks to members on behalf of the Save the Redwoods League.

Mahan and Guiberson placed then a small copper box and time capsule into a cornerstone anchoring the four fireplaces. Inside were newspaper and magazine articles about the redwoods campaign, women's club programs and names of every federation member who contributed to the grove. Mahan, sentimentally, also included a poem about the Humboldt redwoods, likely "Redwoods," written by her late friend and Women's League member from Ferndale, Georgia Russ Williams:[300]

> The low descending sun sends benediction down
> On gold-dust bars, that sift in widening rays
> Between brown-pillared trunks to rest upon
> Bowed ferns, and floor oxalis carpeted.
> Upward far, thy tunneled green converging
> Within a constringed space of wind-swept blue;
> Thy taper tips the fleeting clouds entrailing,
> Unstirred the depths in shadowed peace below.[301]

Ceremonies concluded with another moving Humboldt Oratorical Chorus rendition of the "Hallelujah Chorus" ringing through the forest grove. Nye described the dedication later as a fitting memorial to former federation president Minnie Rutherford Fitzgerald of Stockton and San Francisco, who presided over the federation's 1923 annual convention in Eureka where members toured Dyerville Flat and where they voted to save a grove of the old-growth giants. Fitzgerald had died in 1931 without seeing completion of the grove.[302]

Nye, who had attended the 1923 convention, recalled:

> "The last day in the grove, she spoke, in her unforgettable way, of what women might accomplish if they would but unite without pettiness or small personalities in the great work of buying the grove, a task that at the time seemed impossible. I think there was not a clubwoman who had the privilege of going on the pilgrimage last Sunday, who as she stood in the gloom of the shadows after a rainy day, did not recall Mrs. Fitzgerald the last time she ever presided in the sunshine."

For nearly 55,000 federation members the once-impossible task was now complete. Working alongside the Humboldt County Women's Save the Redwoods League, they had helped save Dyerville Flat from lumbering. And in their own federation grove, they had saved one of the most beautiful stands of redwoods in Dyerville Flat.

"When Mrs. Robert J. (Clara) Burdette organized the federation in Los Angeles in 1900 she urged as one of the tasks of California women the saving of the redwoods," wrote Nye in *The Los Angeles Times*. "Last

Sunday demonstrated that, in measure at least, the women had fulfilled her anticipation."[303]

Fortunes of the Gold Rush

New memorial groves added almost another 1,000 acres to public ownership during the early 1930s. Forests saved through the campaigns of Save the Redwoods League Councilor and Garden Club of America member-at-large Ethel Lansdale to memorialize family members in redwood groves had climbed to nearly 2,000 acres since 1926. State park bond funds matched the gifts, doubling the generosity of donors who, as in the late 1920s, were mostly San Francisco Bay Area residents, and typically heirs to Gold Rush or cattle ranch fortunes.

Among them, Olive Holbrook Palmer, a Garden Club of America member and owner of "a great estate in Atherton with handsome formal gardens," established the 277-acre Charles H. Holbrook Memorial Grove near Garberville in memory of her late father, a New Hampshire-born Gold Rush pioneer who had grown rich in the iron and metal business in San Francisco amid the bustle of a new Pacific state.[304]

Palmer, a San Francisco native and wife of wealthy San Francisco contractor Silas Palmer, was a famed philanthropist, a two-term president of the California Historical Society, and a Save the Redwoods League member and Councilor. As a devotee of formal gardens she held memberships in the Woodside-Atherton Garden Club and The Garden Club of America.[305]

Her father's death in 1925 at age ninety-four closed the remarkable chapter of a tradesman machine builder from New England who came to California by ship and a walk across the Isthmus of Panama to strike it rich. Holbrook steered the boards of many formative companies in the business of developing California, including the Market Street Railway, San Francisco & San Joaquin Valley Railroad, California Insurance Company, Pacific Lighting, and the Mutual Savings Bank and Union Trust Company of San Francisco.[306]

Jennie Blair, another member of San Francisco society, named the new ninety-acre Blair Memorial Grove in memory of her mother, Abigail; brother, William; and late father, Samuel Blair, a wealthy sea captain and Mendocino County redwood lumber company owner.[307] Bernice Boardman of San Francisco, heir to her late husband's business fortune, similarly dedicated the 135-acre Samuel H. Boardman Memorial Grove in Humboldt Redwoods State Park to the Gold Rush pioneer and commission merchant who had grown rich in a booming frontier state.[308]

In November 1934, *The Sausalito News* heralded the work of another wealthy San Franciscan, Emily Carolan, in rounding up prominent supporters for a special sixty-acre redwood memorial grove to the pioneers of San Francisco along the Avenue of the Giants near Miranda. The Pioneers Redwood Grove, the newspaper reported, "is to be a memorial to forebears of the donors who came to San Francisco in 1849, 1850 or earlier."[309]

Women accounted for most of the donors celebrating their fathers, the "49ers" who made the first fortunes in their new home on the Pacific Coast. The names of these Gold Rush pioneers, the young ambitious men who left homes throughout America to become rich and socially prominent, are often synonymous with the history of California's earliest days as a new American state.

Emily Carolan, Evelyn Carolan Timlow, and Genevieve Carolan Poett donated in honor of their father, the late James Carolan, who left New York in 1849 for Sacramento, where he opened a hardware store to serve the gold fields. Carolan accumulated a fortune in the hardware business and invested the profits in property, becoming, in the words of *The San Francisco Call*, "a wealthy clubman of Hillsborough and Burlingame."[310] Emily Carolan's brothers, Herbert and Edgar, also helped their sisters finance the redwood grove.

Genevieve Carolan Poett's husband, Henry Poett, contributed to the grove in memory of his own late father, Alfred Poett, a civil engineer who helped the new Central Pacific Railroad plan its route from Sacramento to Utah as the Western portion of the new Transcontinental Railroad. Alfred Poett, born in Chile of English parents, arrived in San Francisco in 1849 at age ten and trained as an engineer for several years in London before returning to California in 1863 to undertake major engineering projects throughout the state. *The Santa Barbara Morning Press* recognized him upon his death in 1909 as having played a principal role "in a majority of the important undertakings and improvements that have been planned and carried out in the course of this state's development during the past thirty-five or forty years."[311]

Four daughters, Emma, Nellie, Minnie, and Laura, of San Francisco pioneer, wealthy landowner, and rancher Crawford W. Clarke also provided money for the Northern California grove. Years earlier in 1915 their mother Philomen had similarly funded the decorative Clarke Gate entryway into Golden Gate Park as a tribute to her late husband.[312]

Isabel Julliard, likewise, furnished funds on behalf of her father, Charles Frederic Julliard, who had moved with his parents from France to Ohio, then left with his brother for the California gold fields. Julliard found his fortune in the Trinity County gold mines, then became a wine broker and founder of the Sebastopol Winery in Sonoma County.[313] Julliard's brother Augustus, a New York City textile manufacturer, is the name behind New York City's Julliard School, having endowed the school for the performing arts with $15 million in 1919.[314]

Among the nearly twenty donors to the Pioneers Redwood Grove, Mary Holbrook Knight of San Francisco made a second Holbrook family contribution in memory of her late father and businessman Charles Holbrook. Alice Griffith added to the fund to acknowledge her late father Millen Griffith who earned a fortune establishing a first early fleet of Red Star tugboats in San Francisco and pioneering use of the boats in the whaling and salmon canning industry in Alaska.[315] Edward Schmiedell gave in tribute to his late father, Henry Schmiedell, a native of Germany who left Lima, Peru, in 1849 for San Francisco and made a fortune investing in silver mines. He eventually helped found the San Francisco Stock Exchange.[316] Alice Larkin of Monterey helped fund the Pioneers Grove in memory of her late grandfather, Thomas Larkin, a wealthy businessman and United States Consul in Monterey to the Mexican government during the 1840s.[317]

Former San Francisco Mayor "Sunny Jim" Rolph, who led the city from 1911 to 1929, was also acknowledged by the Save the Redwoods League in 1931 with an eighty-five-acre redwood grove in Humboldt Redwoods State Park. Rolph had just been elected Governor of California and would guide the state through the worst of the Great Depression until his death of a stroke in 1934.[318]

Rolph's Progressive-Era legacy as mayor earned him the esteem of a redwood memorial grove. He presided over the city's greatest feats in the wake of the 1906 earthquake, a stately new Civic Center, the acclaimed 1915 Panama-Pacific International Exposition, the controversial Hetch-Hetchy project that delivered water from the Sierra Nevada, a public Municipal Railway, and millions more dollars in public works and landscaping projects that enhanced and beautified the city. Rolph's trademark nickname stemmed from his mission of making San Francisco feel good about itself while rebuilding and he performed brilliantly, wrote California historian Kevin Starr in his 1997 book about California, *The Dream Endures*:

> For a few wonderful years, Rolph's combination of personal charm and mayoral diplomacy perfectly fit the bill for San Francisco. During the exposition year of 1915, the ebullient mayor led innumerable groups in parade from Civic Center down to Van Ness Avenue to the fair, perfectly embodying the aspiring civility of the city he governed — a civility kept genial and robust by a certain Western flair, unpretentious and direct — as he greeted former Presidents Roosevelt and Taft,

Secretary of State William Jennings Bryan, composer Camille Saint-Saens, Marine Band Master John Phillips Sousa and other visiting dignitaries.[319]

In Berkeley, meanwhile, Eleanor Dungan and her brother, Dr. Garland A. Dungan of Eureka, delivered seventy acres of South Dyerville Flat redwoods in memory of their late parents, pioneer Humboldt County ranchers Garland and Mary Dungan who "accumulated a small fortune" in the cattle business near Ferndale.[320] Garland Dungan had traveled overland from Kentucky to California for gold and soon bought his first 160 acres of rangeland in a sparsely populated Humboldt County. He traveled again to Iowa in 1863 to marry, and returned to his ranch with a bride, Mary Jenkins Dungan, whom friends recalled as "a great lover of nature, particularly flowers, and a life-long lover of the great redwoods."[321]

Lastly, during this period, a notable Eastern fortune financed a sixty-acre grove dedicated in 1932 to the late Charles and Henrietta Fleischmann of Cincinnati, inventors and manufacturers of a standardized, reliable bread starter in 1868 that made their names synonymous with mass-produced bread and a revolution in American baking. Their son, Max C. Fleischmann of Santa Barbara, donated the grove in Humboldt Redwoods State Park near Weott after selling his parents' company to J.P. Morgan's Standard Brands in 1929 for $20 million in stock. Another Fleischmann son, Julius, served as mayor of Cincinnati from 1900 to 1905.[322]

Though most of the 1920s and 1930s memorial groves continued to be financed by women, it would take until 1935 for a woman to obtain a redwood memorial grove in her own name. The honor went to Katherine Phillips Edson of Los Angeles, a driving force for woman's voting rights in California and tougher milk sanitation laws on behalf of children. As the first California woman to head a major state government commission she also championed new labor protection and minimum wage laws for workers, including women and children.[323] The California League of Women Voters dedicated an eighty-acre redwood grove in her name, celebrating conservation as it saluted the impacts of powerful, individual women in bettering society.[324]

The Grandest of All Wonders

One last celebration closed the great foundational era of saving the redwoods. On a spring Sunday, May 20, 1934, donors dedicated one of the grandest of their enduring successes in the redwoods, the incomparable 2,552-acre Garden Club of America Grove. *The Humboldt Standard* welcomed club members as "old friends," writing with hometown gratitude that, "In preserving this magnificent grove for the ages, the Garden Club has rendered a notable service to contemporary civilization; a service that shall endure so long as the redwoods stand. It is a service, moreover, that will prompt increasing appreciation as generations pass in the future."[325]

A sunny afternoon graced a soul-stirring dedication brought to order with the call of a distant bugle deep in the forest.[326] The Garden Club of America members, Save the Redwoods League and State Park Commission dignitaries crossed the South Fork of the Eel River on a foot bridge and entered the vast timberland tract they had saved. An entourage of Humboldt County schoolteachers, parents, children, and long-time stalwarts such as Laura Mahan, joined them to pay respects and show appreciation. All were awed by sunlight falling "in golden shafts between the massive columns of the redwoods and glimpses of azure blue skies — and everywhere beautiful green ferns and luxuriously tangled growths of greenery and wild flowers."

A solemn Christian benediction by Garberville's Reverend Morehouse set a reverent tone in the splendid outdoor setting. A Garden Club of America founding member, Helen Thorne of Millbrook, New York, and Santa Barbara, California, long a force for protecting wild plants and banning unsightly billboards, welcomed 150 attendees from throughout the nation with a brief history of the garden club and its accomplishment in the redwoods.[327]

Later, Thorne, who had made all the dedication arrangements and sent invitations to each member of the national club, would remember "the light filtering through as in a great cathedral, a cathedral of greater majesty than any built by man ... It was one of those indescribably perfect days in May," she wrote. "The air warm and perfumed. A gentle breeze in the tops of the great trees gave out a sound which seemed a harmonious accompaniment to every word uttered and to each thought conveyed to the audience."[328]

Few supporters of the redwoods could boast of accomplishing so much in such a short time. Only four years earlier garden club founding member and one-time president Anne Stewart of Philadelphia and then-president Elizabeth Lockwood of East Hampton, New York, had pressed nearly 100 fellow members traveling on the "Garden Club of America Special," a convoy of westbound rail cars from the Eastern Seaboard to the club's annual convention, to save the redwoods in Northern California.[329] Garden club members had raised $92,000 to make this outstanding day possible and the State of California had matched $75,000 that the club paid for the grove.

Thorne, honorary vice-president of the club and a prolific fund-raiser for what now stands among the largest redwood groves in the California state park system, introduced attendees to The Garden Club of America's newest president, Sarah Bulkley of New York City and Ridgefield, Connecticut.[330]

After a standing ovation in the forest, Bulkley, granddaughter of an Ohio Civil War-era governor, and, with her husband, a controller of one of the nation's largest paper manufacturers, commended the "energy and vision" of Save the Redwoods League Chairman Joseph D. Grant for helping facilitate the garden club's work in the redwoods. She then formally presented the grove on behalf of The Garden Club of America and the California State Park Commission.

A milestone conservation speech followed Thorne's next introduction of Mills College President Dr. Aurelia Reinhardt, casting "a spell over the entire audience," as Thorne recalled afterward, and foreshadowing by thirty years the themes of modern environmentalism born in the 1960s. A local press still enthusiastic for wealthy outside forces saving magnificent local forests for posterity described an inspiring keynote address by Dr. Reinhardt, "standing like a solemn priestess in the center of the vast outdoor temple."

Reinhardt, an influential member of the California Federation of Women's Clubs and the national General Federation of Women's Clubs, faced her audience and spoke of generations to come, a theme so often evoked in women's efforts to save the redwoods, "that there should be one type of splendid giant preserved for the children of our time, and for the unknown generations of tomorrow and tomorrow and tomorrow."

The address described The Garden Club of America's redwood grove as the newest addition to the grand concept of America as a garden unto itself.

"Do you not see our continent from Atlantic to Pacific, from the lakes of the north to the Rio Grande on the south, become through woman's thought and service in part — a garden? A continental garden, grandly varied with the climes," she said, "musical with waters falling at Niagara and Yosemite, brinked with the thousand delicacies of arbutus and blue bonnet, with calacortus and lupine and rhododendron! Our nation's garden on whose Western borders lies the forest with its Sequoia columns, stately pillars of Gigantea and of Sempervirens."

Reinhardt, as quoted in *The Humboldt Times*, compared the stunning natural setting that The Garden Club of America had preserved with ancient sites throughout the world that for millennia had nourished human spirituality.

"Consider this grove of redwoods," she called out from a wooden stage beneath the big trees. "Can we not draw from its nobility a significance which younger members of the human family drew from their tree temples in other lands? It was among the shadows of primeval woods that the Druids worshipped their gods and sacrificed to them that which was most precious. The voice of Zeus spoke to the worshippers under the oaken shades at

Dodona in Epirus. The inspiration of Apollo came to the devotees who sought him where the palm trees waved at Delphi. It was the glory of an autumn tree from which came to another worshipper the voice of God in the land of Palestine."

Reinhardt voiced then a call for humanity to respect and protect the magnificent redwood forest temples which were so quickly disappearing from the shores of California:

> "In our redwood temple do not these fluted columns lift higher the vaults of heaven than the roof of the Greek Parthenon or Gothic cathedral? What words of dedication might we say on this auspicious day? Has not God himself dedicated these California slopes, planting them with his tree children, who ask of us only affection and preservation? Our dedication should be to an understanding of that great architect and builder whose master plan no human draftsman yet quite understands, whose magnificent landscapes no mortal apprentice has yet proved capable of preserving in their pristine loveliness."

The speech, a call to action that would have been at home in any environmental forum thirty or forty years in the future, asked finally, of its audience, and also of the larger world:

> "Shall we not dedicate ourselves to an understanding, to an appreciation of life-giving qualities of the earth — our mother — and to a consecration of ourselves never to abuse, never to destroy, never to make barren, the fertile fields of our planet, Earth? Rather shall we respect and preserve, saving for our children and our children's children the largesse of nature whose fruition man may destroy, but the secret of whose life is not yet in his childish hand."

As the applause ended, and as many of those attending wiped tears from their eyes, Helen Thorne again took to the stage with a breathtaking suggestion. A fitting answer to such noble sentiment, she said, was to sit for a time in collective silence and take in the hushed stillness of the forest itself. The gathering of The Garden Club of America members, then, "with bowed heads, heard, like the murmur of a thousand whispering lyres," The *Times* reported, "the quiet majesty of their accomplishment in the redwoods."[331]

So ended a great formative era in the history of saving the redwoods of California. The garden club had "completed one of its great undertakings," said Thorne, "one which reaches into the future for the benefits of untold generations to follow."

The majesty and the beauty of that Sunday afternoon in May would repeat itself endlessly in the future that Thorne envisioned, as millions each year from every continent on earth made their own pilgrimages into the grand stillness of the redwood forests. And if, in years beyond that afternoon, opportunities to build more grandly upon such noble foundations were often tragically missed, the work of saving the redwoods would continue to advance. In the end, all who worked across ninety years in the wake of Mahan and her Humboldt County Women's Save the Redwoods League, the Save the Redwoods League, and others of their kind, would manage to save five percent of the old-growth redwoods.

Yet there was scarcely a time, such a wonderful, golden time as theirs of the 1920s and 1930s when people throughout California and the nation came to hold a belief in saving wild trees and acted on it so magnificently. During their brief, shining moment in the redwoods they thought and spoke with a profound eloquence about the sanctity of the great primeval forests, and in their words and actions they gifted an ideal of civilization to the world.

AFTERWORD

In 1919, an aging Chicago lumberman who had grown rich supplying wooden railroad ties and telegraph poles to an expanding nation visited the owners of *The San Francisco Chronicle* to expose the "spectacle of devastation" in the redwoods of Northern California. When the owners advised him the state's redwoods would all inevitably be made into lumber, Edward E. Ayer argued they could certainly save at least five percent of them.

"If you would save five percent of the redwoods now standing, you would have several memorial groves and parks," he said. "They can be saved on each side of your main roads and seen and enjoyed by people as they drive through there."[332]

The old lumberman's words were prophetic.

In the eight decades following the events in this book, thousands of activists, donors, politicians, scientists, and tree sitters walked in the footsteps of the movement's pioneers and saved almost exactly five percent of the redwoods.

It might be said that the "save the redwoods" crusade started with low expectations and fulfilled them. Many opportunities were lost over the years due to human shortcomings and the hard realities of politics. Yet without those earliest expectations, all would have been lost. And in the end, much was gained. As Northern California historians Jerry and Gisela Rohde recalled in 1994, "It is easy to feel sadness or even anger at the greed and shortsightedness that destroyed so much of the ancient redwood forest, but it is easier still to walk through the great groves that remain, like those at Prairie Creek, or Mill Creek, or a hundred other places, and be filled with thankfulness for what has been saved."[333]

Americans since 1900 have saved 89,000 acres of old-growth redwood forests in Humboldt and Del Norte counties, and 24,000 acres elsewhere in the redwood belt of California. In all, they have protected approximately 345,000 acres of old-growth and second-growth redwoods in local, state, and national parks, forest reserves, and with easements preventing commercial lumbering activities and residential development. Twenty-two percent of the 1.6 million acres of redwood forests remaining in California are again safe for a centuries-long return to their original condition.[334]

It could have been more.

At almost every turn government and conservation forces fell short in the decades after the great celebrations of the early 1930s. Corporate lumber operations and market forces largely had their way in the forests. And conservationists, even with the best of intentions, sometimes got in their own way.

When the National Park Service under President Franklin D. Roosevelt proposed in 1937 to buy and protect 18,000 acres of Mill Creek redwoods in Del Norte County, the Save the Redwoods League, by then the dominant player in redwoods preservation, opposed the plan as an incursion onto the state park system's turf. The league, which disliked the National Park Service emphasis on recreation in its parks, disliked more the big-spending, big-government ideology of Roosevelt's New Deal, and acted accordingly to thwart its conservationist impulses in Northern California.[335] Not until 2002 did most of the Mill Creek redwoods join the state park system, and then at a substantially higher cost of $60 million for 25,000 acres.[336]

"Stubborn California provincialism," as historian John Raymond DeLong described it in 1968, similarly derailed a proposed Franklin Delano Roosevelt Memorial National Forest of 2.8 million acres in the northern redwood range. In 1946, and again in 1949, California Congresswoman Helen Gahagan Douglas introduced legislation authorizing $100 million to buy and protect redwood forests throughout four Northern California counties. The National Park Service, then headed by the league's Newton B. Drury, opposed the bill, objecting to U.S. Forest Service administration of the forest and its practices of allowing selected logging.

Simultaneously, the notion of a massive new national forest that would disrupt logging economies and deplete tax bases stirred up elected officials and chambers of commerce in Sonoma, Mendocino, Humboldt, and Del Norte counties, all opposing the bills as a "land grab." The California Legislature rushed to their defense with opposition on similar grounds.

One can only imagine how many hundreds of thousands of acres of redwood forest might still exist had this visionary congresswoman somehow prevailed against forces that opposed her. "The failure to establish a redwood national park in the 1930s or 1940s was tragic," historian Susan R. Schrepfer wrote in 1983. "The interwar decades were the last in which large, totally unlogged watersheds still existed."[337] By the end of World War II half of the original redwood forests of California had been logged and lumbered and the pace was quickening.[338]

Yet the acreage of protected redwoods still managed to grow with women often leading the way. Club and society women continued to buy memorial groves and initiate large acquisitions as they had in earlier years. Members of The Garden Club of America alone contributed $2 million to save the redwoods from 1930 onward. The club notably over the decades doubled the size of its original grove near the South Fork of the Eel River to more than 5,000 acres and later raised $400,000 to rebuild its trails and bridges.[339]

As World War II stretched onward the club expanded its efforts elsewhere throughout Humboldt and Del Norte counties. It raised $6,000 in 1942 for 222 acres to connect The Garden Club of America Grove to Caroline Hunter's Children's Forest. In 1943, the club bought fifteen acres to add an Arbor Day Grove to a memorial forest in Humboldt Redwoods State Park honoring Arbor Day founder and forest conservationist J. Sterling Morton of Nebraska. Again in 1945 the club campaigned for a National Tribute Grove in Jedediah Smith Redwoods State Park that eventually grew to 5,000 acres in a salute to 1.6 million Americans who served in the armed forces during World War II. The Garden Club of America's $52,000 contribution to the grove, alongside funding from the Daughters of the American Revolution and the Save the Redwoods League, spurred thousands of additional contributions nationally with the names of individual donors recorded in a "Golden Book" in the National Archives.[340]

The modern-day Save the Redwoods League counts now more than 1,000 such dedicated redwood groves in the California state park system.[341]

The end of World War II brought renewed demand for redwood lumber products and mirrored the sharp acceleration of redwood lumbering that had followed World War I a generation earlier. A time of maximum peril now unfolded for the redwoods of Humboldt and Del Norte counties as the 1950s economic boom produced a sudden, sustained tripling of redwood felling from prewar levels and a record annual cut in 1958.[342] The decade of explosive growth added 5 million people to California with all its related construction, and ended with only ten percent of the redwood belt's original 2 million acres still standing.

Nonetheless, during the 1950s, the Save the Redwoods League and State of California managed to largely finish what it had begun with the Redwoods

Preservation Bill in 1921. The league extended the original twelve miles of protected Redwood Highway landscapes to thirty-two miles on a newly renamed Avenue of the Giants Parkway dedicated by California Governor Edmund Gerald "Pat" Brown, Sr., on August 27, 1960. In all, Governor Brown pointed out in 1965, the Save the Redwoods League had raised $12 million to preserve the state's redwoods since its founding in 1918.[343]

Though the state also maintained a commitment to the redwoods with millions of dollars as it expanded its state park system with taxpayer contributions and royalties from oil drilling off the coast of California, the bulk of funding after the 1950s would come finally from the federal treasury. The near extermination of old-growth redwoods in Humboldt and Del Norte counties set the stage for significant waves of federal acquisitions in the 1960s, 1970s, and 1990s.

As the old 1920s campaigns for a redwood national park resumed in the 1960s, the local business and political establishments of Humboldt and Del Norte counties had become, in great contrast to earlier decades, utterly hostile to surrendering more of their land to the public domain. Yet the biggest expansion of protected redwood acreage in American history, one that would have surely thrilled Laura Mahan and other women activists of Humboldt County during their 1913 Carson Woods picnic, was about to begin.

On October 2, 1968, President Lyndon B. Johnson signed legislation to create Redwood National Park, approving $92 million initially, and ultimately $198 million, for 58,000 acres in Humboldt and Del Norte counties. The new national park boundaries included the three existing state parks north of Eureka, Prairie Creek Redwoods, Jedediah Smith, and Del Norte Coast Redwoods, and brought an additional 10,900 acres of old-growth forests, as well as 38,000 acres of previously logged forests, into public protection.[344]

A decade later on March 27, 1978, President Jimmy Carter signed Congressional legislation authorizing $359 million to enlarge Redwood National Park by another 48,000 acres.[345] Since 1994 the National Park Service and California State Parks system have jointly managed 113,000 acres, now known as Redwood National and State Parks.[346]

The last of the great public redwood acquisitions occurred in 1999 when the federal government and State of California paid $480 million to the Pacific Lumber Company for 7,500 acres of the Headwaters Forest in Humboldt County and 2,500 acres of nearby old-growth woodland. The government action followed a tumultuous decade-long battle for the redwoods that one prominent California newspaper described as "one of the most bitter environmental conflicts in California history, pitting blue-collar loggers against tree-sitters in dreadlocks and establishing Pacific Lumber owner Charles Hurwitz as the greatest eco-villain for U.S. environmental groups since the Exxon Valdez's Capt. Joseph Hazelwood."[347]

Across approximately twenty bitterly contentious years as the environmental movement became a powerful mainstream component of American life and politics, the federal government, with help from the State of California, spent $931 million to return more than 113,000 acres of Northern California redwoods to the public domain. By all measures, it was the capstone of a dramatic century spent accumulating, in small and large parcels, with enormous and small donations from Americans of all income levels and at all levels of society, the redwood giants that attract tourists throughout the world. Most know little of how they were saved or how close the entirety of the redwood range came to annihilation.

Today, in a new century of relative quiet in the remaining forests, the Save the Redwoods League continues to protect and restore much of the redwood belt to its original condition, and in 2018, celebrated its 100th birthday. The league's new 100-year vision for 2118 proposes to place 800,000 acres of California redwoods in permanent protection, an ambitious return of half the state's surviving redwood range to "old growth forest form and function."[348]

Encouragingly, league studies suggest that all these forests are likely to persist for the foreseeable future and adapt safely to a changing global climate.[349]

The California state parks system remains the largest protector of the ancient species, sheltering sixty percent of earth's last old-growth redwoods. It annually hosts millions of visitors foreseen by the redwood preservationists of the 1920s.[350]

The early twenty-year environmental drama described in this story is mostly forgotten. Most forgotten of all are the people, especially the women, who started it all.

The towering old giants they saved, however, still stand to tell their story.

Epilogue

Clara Burdette, who founded the California Federation of Women's Clubs in 1900 with a rallying cry to save the California redwoods, lived to the age of ninety-eight, dying January 6, 1954, in Pasadena. She was remembered for her role in the development of Huntington Memorial Hospital in Pasadena, as a founder of the Women's Legislative Council of California, and as a vigorous campaigner in the 1928 presidential campaign of Herbert Hoover.[351]

Kate Harpst of Eureka, owner of the Save-the-Redwoods car in which she and three other women barnstormed Humboldt County in the late summer of 1919 to rally support for redwoods preservation, died February 23, 1929, and was remembered in her obituary as a lover of flowers and beautiful gardens. Among the other riders in her car, Ella Georgeson, a former owner of *The Humboldt Standard* and long-time defender of the redwoods, died at her Eureka home on May 6, 1936. Mary Anne Atkinson died January 12, 1940, and was recalled for her considerable lumber industry wealth, generosity to local charities, and her annual Christmas holiday decorations. She is buried in Green Bay, Wisconsin. Lucretia Anne Huntington Monroe survived the longest of the foursome, dying February 10, 1948, in Mentone, San Bernardino County, California after a recent trip to Hawaii.[352]

Laura Olive Perrott Mahan, long-time president of the Humboldt County Women's Save the Redwoods League, died on February 6, 1937, in San Francisco at age sixty-nine after a long illness. Her husband James Mahan died in San Francisco ten days later, February 16, 1937, also after a long illness. A California State Park Commission plaque erected in 1938 at the Mahan Grove in the Dyerville Flat sector of Humboldt Redwoods State Park commemorates their work during the 1920s to save the Dyerville forest.

In her will Laura Mahan bequeathed 120 acres of redwoods to the State of California for park land. She is buried in the Perrott family plot at Table Bluff Cemetery near Loleta in Humboldt County.

The Humboldt Times, upon her death, reported, "It was largely through her personal attention and efforts that several of the large redwood parks have been added to the scenic wonders of this region." Save the Redwoods Chairman Joseph D. Grant and Secretary Newton B. Drury also recalled in a statement:

> Without the support of the people of Humboldt County, much that has been accomplished in saving the Redwoods would not have come about. Mrs. Mahan and her husband, James P. Mahan, from the beginning of the movement took a leading part. With a love of the Redwood forests that was her heritage as a member of a pioneer Humboldt family, Mrs. Mahan worked tirelessly to inspire others and secure their help in making her dreams a reality. Fortunately, she saw the fruition of her efforts. The value of her services to her own home community, and to her state, cannot be overestimated. These Redwood parks, now valued at millions of dollars, are a priceless possession of all our people, and their mighty trees through many centuries will stand as a memorial to those who helped to save them in all their dignity and beauty. In this cause Mrs. Mahan took an important part, and it will be gratefully remembered.[353]

Seventy years later in 2007 author Richard Preston, in *The Wild Trees*, reported that modern redwoods explorers Michael Taylor and Ron Hildebrant, in "finding redwoods of world-class height" in Humboldt Redwoods State Park, named one of their newly-discovered trees "Laura Mahan."[354]

Martha G. McLellan of Eureka, the nation's first donor of Humboldt County redwoods for public use in a national or state park, 160 acres in 1919 that later became part of The Garden Club of America Redwood Grove, died June 23, 1932, at age eighty-nine following an automobile accident near Miranda on the Redwood Highway.[355]

Annie Zane Murray, the long-time Humboldt County redwoods activist alongside Laura Mahan, lived to the age of 96. Her work with the redwoods was largely forgotten and went unreported in a June 8, 1960, newspaper story announcing her death the previous day. Though the newspaper story honored her as the founder of the Eureka Women's Club and a leader in the California Federation of Women's Clubs, the headline over her obituary remembered Murray for being "Born in Indian War Era."[356]

Augusta Wynkoop Urquhart, the California Federation of Women's Club president from 1923 to 1925 who steered the fund-raising campaign for the women's federation grove in Humboldt Redwoods State Park, died in Pasadena at age eighty-nine on January 13, 1960. An account of her death in *The Los Angeles Times* noted her many civic, social, and club accomplishments, including presiding at the first general Armistice Day celebration at the Hollywood Bowl in 1921 and her sixteen years as a member of the Los Angeles County Probation Committee, but reported nothing about her achievements in the redwoods.[357]

Caroline Phelps Stokes Hunter, founder of the Children's Forest in Humboldt Redwoods State Park, lived to the age of eighty-six, dying in San Francisco on July 6, 1964. Her obituary in *The New York Times* recalled her activity "in recent years in the Save the Redwoods movement in California, and in the movement to save the park area of Point Lobos, Monterey, California."[358]

Ethel Lansdale, the widowed military spouse who inspired donors to buy memorial redwood groves and helped bring The Garden Club of America into the redwoods campaigns, lived to the age of ninety-two. She died a multimillionaire in San Francisco on February 1, 1962, hours after the death of her live-in maid of thirty years. A joint funeral service for the two was held at St. Luke Episcopal Church in San Francisco.[359]

Aurelia Isabel Henry Reinhardt, who delivered a stirring environmental speech at the May 20, 1934, dedication of The Garden Club of America Grove, served as president of Mills College until 1943. She was a 1945 delegate to the founding meetings in San Francisco that established the United Nations. She died January 28, 1948, in Palo Alto, at the age of seventy.[360]

Helen Seymour Stafford Thorne, who led The Garden Club of America fund-raising campaign that contributed $92,000 for a redwood grove in Humboldt County during the Great Depression, lived to the age of eighty-six. She died November 10, 1952, and is buried in Millbrook, Dutchess County, New York. To this day, recalling the important role of Helen Thorne in The Garden Club of America history, the national club awards the Mrs. Oakleigh Thorne medal in recognition of outstanding achievement in garden design.[361]

Newton B. Drury, the long-time Save the Redwoods League secretary who led redwood acquisition efforts in Humboldt and Del Norte counties, became the fourth director of the National Park Service in 1940 during the Franklin D. Roosevelt Administration and served there until 1951. California Governor Earl Warren soon after appointed him Director of the California Division of Beaches and Parks. Drury oversaw a massive expansion of the state park system until his departure in 1959. Drury then returned to the Save the Redwoods League, where he resumed his work as Secretary until 1971, when he was elected president. He remained president until 1975, when he became the league's chairman of the board until his death, at age eighty-nine in Berkeley on December 14, 1978. The Newton B. Drury Scenic Parkway, a ten-mile drive through Prairie Creek Redwoods State Park, commemorates his redwoods legacy.[362]

John Raker, the Democratic U.S. House of Representatives member who carried the first congressional legislation to explore and seek national park status for Humboldt County redwoods, died while in office in 1926 and is buried in Susanville, California, near Lassen National Park. He is mostly remembered as the author of the controversial 1913 Raker Act, which dammed the Hetch Hetchy Valley in Yosemite National Park for a reservoir to store water for the City of San Francisco.[363]

The Pacific Lumber Company, the Scotia-based lumber giant that sold more than 9,000 acres of its Bull Creek Flat and Dyerville Flat holdings to the state park system in 1931, thrived for decades with selective cutting and sustained-yield practices while other redwood landowners continued to clear cut their forests. In 1985 Charles E. Hurwitz and his Houston-based Maxxam Group conducted a hostile takeover of Pacific Lumber and ignited years of protest by Earth First! and other environmental organizations as it doubled its logging to finance "junk bond" debts used to acquire the firm. In 1999 the federal government bought more than 7,000 acres of the company's Headwaters Forest holdings for $480 million. Pacific Lumber declared bankruptcy in 2007 and reestablished itself under new owners and with more sustainable cutting practices as the Humboldt Redwood Company.[364]

The Humboldt Times and *The Humboldt Standard* merged in 1967 to form *The Times-Standard* and continues to publish daily in Eureka. Its logo features a pair of redwood trees.

Henry Alexander Crabb, the San Joaquin County state legislator who in 1852 proposed putting the California redwoods off limits to logging and commercial development, failed to win re-election in 1854 and was killed on April 7, 1857, by a Mexican firing squad. The execution by Mexican troops followed an ill-fated expedition by Crabb and seventy other Americans to seize Mexican land in Sonora. A 2011 article in Crabb's hometown newspaper, *The Stockton Record*, suggested his execution was "cosmic retribution for his deplorable enacted state legislation," the Fugitive Slave Act of 1852, later upheld by the state Supreme Court, "which said slaves who escaped to California could be captured and returned to slavery."[365]

Acknowledgements

Our immediate thanks go to Algora Publishing for their professional guidance and recognition of the historic importance of this story. Our years of research efforts on the project were aided in part by the California State Library History Room, California State Archives, Bancroft Library, Humboldt State Library Special Collections, and California State Parks Archives.

We also extend our gratitude to the many organizations and individuals who helped with our research, sometimes locating the buried details of a long-forgotten story: the Save the Redwoods League; Pamela Ament, Vice President of the California Federation of Women's Clubs; Melissa Cronyn, Associate Manager of the Harpers Ferry Center Publications Office at the National Park Service; and in Humboldt County, Historian Jerry Rohde; Morgan Harvey, Research Assistant at the Humboldt County Historical Society; the Ferndale Museum, and Dr. Alexandra Service of the Fortuna Depot Museum.

A special thank you to the following Garden Club of America members for their time and investigative skills in retrieving details relevant to such an extraordinary story: Anne Myers, The Garden Club of America Archivist; Edie Loening, member of The Garden Club of America Archives Committee; Maggie Cruz, The Garden Club of America Archives Committee Staff Administrator; and Anne Butler, former Garden Club of America Staff Administrator.

Very important are the individuals who blazed a trail of research before us: John J. Amodio, Cameron Binkley, Shana Miriam Cohen, Susan R. Schrepfer, Elizabeth Roe Schlappi, Darren Speece, William S. Yaryan, and Laurence R. Warren. We also thank those people who showed interest in the project by reading and commenting on our earliest online posts about women who saved the redwoods: Vickie Gehri, Suzi Elizabeth Lawton, and Terri Burgett Lewis. And to Tom Bernardo, Yvonne Freve, and Tim Wasserman for reading early drafts and offering counsel.

Most importantly, we are grateful to our son Dillon, who throughout the entire process supported our efforts and encouraged us to complete this book.

Kevin Starr quote on pages 154-155 reproduced with permission of the Licensor, Oxford Publishing Limited, through PLSclear.

Bradley Tolppanen quote on page 131, *From Churchill in North America, 1929: A Three Month Tour of Canada and the United States* © 2014 Bradley P. Tolppanen by permission of McFarland & Company, Inc., Box 611, Jefferson NC 28640. www.mcfarlandbooks.com

Appendix A: Charter member clubs of the Humboldt County Federation of Women's Clubs[366]

On January 8, 1908, Annie Zane Murray of Eureka, prominent women's club activist and wife of a county superior court judge, hosted clubwomen throughout Humboldt County at her home to found the Humboldt County Federation of Women's Clubs. Following is a listing of the initial far-sighted clubs that pushed forward an agenda of saving the region's redwoods.

Arcata Woman's Club

Eureka Monday Club

Eureka Mother's Club

Eureka Wednesday Club

Ferndale Village Club

Fortuna Monday Club

Whanika Club of Blue Lake

Appendix B: Preserve an America Worth Fighting For

August 6, 1921, dedication address for the
Colonel Raynal C. Bolling Grove in Humboldt Redwoods State Park,
by Madison Grant, First Vice President, New York Zoological Society, and
Cofounder, Save The Redwoods League
(Courtesy of the Bancroft Library,
The University of California, Berkeley)[367]

"Preserve an America Worth Fighting For"

It is a peculiar privilege to be present on this occasion when for the
first time in the history of the country a memorial to a fallen soldier
has been selected from among the natural features of the land for
which he gave his life. Monuments of bronze, of marble, and of granite
strew the land, many of doubtful art value, but all of them symbolic
of the recognition of their countrymen for the heroes' sacrifice for
the common weal. It was a thought not merely happy, but one of
possibly far-reaching consequences, that inspired Dr. John Phillips of
Boston to select for his brother-in-law perhaps the most beautiful and
permanent memorial ever chosen for a soldier. The very air of these
groves is redolent with a suggestion of immortality, and the trees
themselves in their brave resistance to axe and fire symbolize better
than anything else I know the idea of immortality; and whoever it was
that conferred the name "sempervirens" upon these trees must have
had that very quality in mind. He must have seen how the tree, hacked
and burned and butchered, refused to die, and gave out of its base a
ringlet of shoots growing up ultimately into a magic circle around the
stump of their parent.

Colonel Raynal C. Bolling was the first American officer of high rank to make the supreme sacrifice in the World War, and the circumstances surrounding his death, the story of how he refused to surrender and fought against overwhelming odds in the shelter of a shell hole until his pistol was empty, form one of the dramatic chapters of military achievement. Colonel Bolling symbolizes many another officer of equal bravery who is perhaps less fortunate in the dramatic surroundings of his death. He further symbolizes the whole of that extraordinary army which was swept from civil life into the turmoil of a war which had already endured for several years. Side by side with the veterans of the old armies, these men showed the mettle that is in the American, and a grateful nation should and will cover the land with memorials to their fame, just as an older generation raised in every village square in the communities of the East a pathetic soldiers' monument, carving on the base the names of those who marched out of the little community leaving it impoverished of its best.

The American Legion, and those of us who desire to do honor to the men who fought, should carry on this idea of Dr. Phillips, and instead of spending vast sums of money in useless monuments, the example of this memorial should be followed. If every Redwood grove which is now left standing in California were dedicated to the memory of those splendid men that marched with a laugh to their fate on the Western front, the tribute would still be inadequate to the sacrifice they made. Those of us who could not enjoy the privilege of serving our country on the stricken field, can do no less than honor their memory to the full. We all mean to do this and it is only a question in the manner of the doing. The traditional method we know. How inadequate or grotesquely absurd it often is, our visitors from other lands only too often tell us, but no one can question the grandeur, the solemnity, and the unique value of these groves. They all belong to California. Why should not California honor its sons by their preservation? Not by some few trees here and there, but by the preservation of the larger groves at least. These men, in spite of so much that has been said about the ideals they fought for, went to battle in the simple faith of children and they died in the simple faith of children, for the one thing that is worth fighting for, for the one thing men die for without hesitation, and that is their country.

And what is their country? It is the inheritance that God gave us of forests and field, of river and stream, of mountain and plain. They did not give their lives for a field of blackened stumps, nor for a river drained dry in summer or a raging torrent in winter. They did not give their lives for a mountain-side torn open for the minerals and coal within it. They gave theirs for a country that had trees on the hillsides, that had fish in the streams, that had birds in the air, that had feather and fur in the forest. Let us therefore on this solemn occasion in dedicating this grove of Redwoods to the memory of Colonel Bolling resolve that we too shall continue the effort to preserve for those that come after us some portion of the heritage that was ours.

No more destructive animal has ever appeared on the face of the earth than the American backwoodsman with his ax and his rifle. Since the Civil War we have plundered half a continent. Nothing since Caesar devastated Gaul in a decade, has been accomplished in like time. In fifty years we have killed all the animals of the plain which in their millions had lived there for thousands of centuries. The buffalo has long since gone, except where protected. The herds of elk are dwindling fast, the antelope is all but gone, and your mighty California grizzly is utterly extinct, so that even a battered skull is a highly prized trophy for a museum. The small animals and birds are many of them gone. In many parts of the country, like the Red River Valley, the richest soil known to man has been exhausted in a generation. Our fish would have utterly disappeared from many streams if it were not for artificial restocking.

But bad as this slaughter of life has been, much of it can be restored if only we have a place of refuge for it when it is brought back. That place can be only the forest, and what have we done with our forests? Chopped them and wasted them, and burned them, and now almost the last of great stands of timber is here on the Pacific slope. We gather here in the center of the best of it. Probably nowhere on earth does there exist a forest to compare in continuous grandeur and unqualified beauty with the forest that stands along the Eel River and to the north. We have reason to believe that no finer forest ever did exist on earth during the millions of years since vegetable life first appeared. It is, therefore, not merely a privilege but it is a sacred duty for Americans to guard and to preserve what little is left of the heritage our fathers so cheerfully wasted. This is not a matter of sentimentalism. It is not a vague idealism. It is a reality. These trees are part of our national endowment, our national inheritance, of far more value to ourselves and to those who come after us than any of the works of man.

Those of you of the West who have been brought up in the midst of the great works of nature, are more impressed by the feeble structures of man, his buildings, his roads, his docks, and his railroads; more impressed, I say, than those of us in the East who live in the midst of these works of man and where the beauty that the Lord provided has been destroyed for so long its memory is becoming dim. Those of you who live on the Coast are fortunate to still have a portion of your birthright undestroyed, and it is just as much your duty to protect and preserve it, as it was the duty of Colonel Bolling and his fellow soldiers to fight for their homeland.

Colonel Bolling and his comrades gave their lives for their country. Let us dedicate ourselves in memory of them to keep and preserve a country worth fighting for.

Appendix C: The Garden Club of America's Redwood Grove

May 20, 1934, dedication address for
The Garden Club of America Grove in Humboldt Redwoods State Park,
by Dr. Aurelia Reinhardt, President of Mills College.
(Courtesy of The Eucalyptus Press, Mills College, Oakland, California).

"The Garden Club of America's Redwood Grove"

In this ineffable spot is it difficult to find words even for the proud task, Mrs. Thorne, of expressing some message dedicating to the people of California the magnificent gift of The Garden Club of America. Their gift through the Redwood League and your generous representative, together with the state government and those citizens particularly interested in the creation and preservation of parks, retains in perpetuity the incomparable beauty of a primeval, a Sequoia forest!

There is a phrase from out the Old Testament which comes to me first. It is that there were giants in those days. I was thinking when Mrs. Lynch framed her delightful account of the work that made possible this memorable day, that The Garden Club of America conspired that there should be one type of splendid giant preserved for the children of our time and for the unknown generations of tomorrow and tomorrow and tomorrow.

Or shall I put it this way? The significant name, The Garden Club of America's Redwood Grove reminds me of Walt Whitman. It has a kind of cadence like his lines that begin:

> "I hear America singing, the varied carols I hear —
> The wood-cutter's song, the ploughboys —
> The delicious singing of the mother — or of the girl —
> Singing with open mouths their strong melodious songs."

The Garden Club of America's Redwood Grove! Well, here you have come for this dedication, not unlike your ancestors of long ago, on other lands. In far-away centuries the Druids met, that in the presence of magnificent trees they might worship their unknown god and sacrifice to him that which was most precious. In Dodona in Epirus it was among the oaks that the worshipers of Zeus used to go to hear his Olympian commands. On the sunny slopes of Delphi the followers of Apollo went to worship him among the waving palms. On Horeb the shepherd of Jethro's sheep, in an autumn when the trees were blazing with color, heard coming from the crimson foliage the voice of one who said, *I am the God of thy father*. In how many lands have the groves been the most ancient temples! I am glad that I can speak of a woman poet at this point. She might have been a member of the American Garden Club. Elizabeth Barrett Browning, walking in the loveliness of nature she has praised in many ways, sang a song which begins:

> ". . . Nothing's small!
> No lily-muffled hum of a summer bee,
> But finds some coupling with the spinning stars;...
> No chaffinch here but implies a cherubim:
> . . . Earth's crammed with heaven,
> And every common bush afire with God."

The Garden Club of America's Redwood Grove! There was a garden on the other side of the world in which met the first garden club. The president was named Eve. She would have been introduced perhaps with less flattery than was this speaker by Mrs. Thorne, but out of Eve's life I bring a thought for the friends gathered under the Sequoia on this Sabbath afternoon in springtime. Are not Eve's daughters, when they are young, quite like her? Do they not pluck the fruit of the Tree of Life to smell and to taste it? Do they not root up the Mariposa lilies? Do they not pick many an exquisite mimulus and brodiaea for no other permanent purpose than to let them fade? Are we not all eager for the blossoms of today, heedless for the seed of tomorrow, destructive Eves? Do you not recall, as I do, that the symbol of the cherubim and the flaming sword in Genesis that drove from a garden forever those careless, lazy, undisciplined, destructive ancestors of ours? Do you not see in among those angelic cherubim, god-sent guardians of the terrestrial paradise, the same angels sent to avenge the watersheds destroyed in China, the same that have cursed our young land, wherever selfishness and greed have caused destructive erosion of the soil? It is not the same sort of proud indifference that has made Italy a land impoverished, a land almost without a tree? Like the angel of old with "flaming sword which turns every way" is the angel of vengeance living today. Exploitation will drive every child of the human family from our earthly Edens if we do not take thought in time. Every garden is a potential desert.

As a citizen of California, I am grateful to The Garden Club of America, that to save a forest and to commemorate their gift they meet today, coming from the gray Atlantic, from the lakes of the North, from Puget Sound and San Diego Bay, to renew their mutual fidelity to a noble cause in the beauty of these unrivalled monarchs of earth's forest folk. I am grateful that women have conceived the idea of our continent as a garden. From the Appalachians to the Olympics, from the Rio Grande and the pointed firs of Maine, to this state, so dear to some of us, where these redwoods raise higher the arch of heaven than the roof of Greek Parthenon or Gothic cathedral, a garden! A continental garden, grandly varied with the climes, musical with waters falling at Niagara and Yosemite, embroidered with the thousand delicacies of arbutus and bluebonnet, with calacortus and lupin and rhododendron! Our nation's garden on whose Western borders rises the forest with its Sequoia columns, stately pillars of gigantea and sempervirens!

The Garden Club of America's Redwood Grove! If you and I could carry from this morning a continental vision, would we not do more constructive work to preserve the native gifts of growing things throughout our country? As I listen this afternoon to stories how $150,000 was brought together to save many hundreds of acres of unspeakably beautiful forest, I dare to believe that henceforth no gift of nature will be unregarded in our land. As I passed the Children's Forest today and saw the oxalis and the ferns I said to myself, "This is a place where there will always be nymphs and oreads, fairies and brownies. They will live in magic greenery here on Kerr Creek to the end of time, and human children will journey thither to find America's fairyland."

How shall we thank those who are the doers and the donors of the Redwood League? Let us find some delightful way to canonize them!

St. Joseph, St. Steven, St. Arthur, St. Duncan and St. James of Sequoia! And double halos for St. Helen and St. Genevieve of the Silver Furs. Like heaven the modern world will be if we create such a roster of many new saints, young and old, sanctified by good works done in the Garden Club, in the Redwood League, in any and all conserving groups of people whose eyes have been opened to loveliness and who are teaching us to keep these things for our children and our children's children. I move the canonizing of these "heart remembered" names, all of which will be written in letters of gold when the history of the conservation of the forests in our country is inscribed for its citizens to read and understand.

A practical word must be added concerning the reasons for consciously organized conservation of the wealth of this continent of North America. *Conscious conservation is as important as discovery.* The last date we, as Americans, ought to remember is not 1492, when "Columbus sailed the ocean blue." Just as important is 1885 when New York legally created state forests. Today, thirty states in this union have set aside for preservation over five million acres of forests. Just as important is 1908, when that Roosevelt, whose first name means "the gift of God," and Theodore rightly believed it, began the Federal conservation movement which was to save from indiscriminate destruction priceless natural possessions in the name of the national government. The third date is 1911, when the United States act was passed by Congress which brought a hundred and sixty-five million acres into the national fold for the education, the recreation, and the joy of the non-forest owning, everyday, average, busy people. These three dates mean the discovery that citizens may through state and national government participate in the protection and enjoyment of the forests. Experience proves that they must participate if conservation is to become effective.

Citizens should read the Copeland Report to learn that the worst enemy to this forest heritage of the United States is not the lumber business as such. Even the indiscriminate harvesting of the fifteen thousand cubic feet that are cut every year, which is often unwise and sometimes barbarous is not the most stupid waste. This is rather the useless and horrible loss by fire, which is something like eight hundred and seventy million cubic feet, and the loss by insects and other vermin, which is almost a thousand million cubic feet. Care will prevent loss by fire, and scientific assault on insect life will prevent death to the grandest specimen of forest giants. These three sets of figures I am using with a purpose. Fire and insects destroy more forest than is used for all industrial purposes put together. Not only the recognition of beauty is promised in the principles of The Garden Club of America, but the recognition of planned safeguarding against destruction.

We destroy more timber than we use; we slaughter for fun bird life, which in turns permits the unresisted multiplication of insect pests. Insect life can be controlled better by birds than by any method man can devise. Nature has an equilibrium that man will do well to learn, and learning, use. To abuse Nature's equilibrium brings tragedy. The most deadly enemy of Sequoia grandeur is *animalculae*. Insect life, bird life, tree life, are bound together by Nature's laws that garden clubs must make part of their parliamentary bylaws.

The greatest voice that was ever lifted in our country to dedicate a holy place was his that said that people gathered respectfully, reverently, at Gettysburg could not dedicate that ground, for dedication had taken place long before in the deed that had sanctified that chosen spot. So our mountain slopes and canyons in California were dedicated to the Creator himself when he caused to be sown the seeds of these great trees. We are here to be dedicated to a timely and significant task. Our dedication should be to an understanding of that great Architect and Builder whose master plan no human draftsman yet wholly comprehends, whose magnificent landscapes no mortal apprentice has yet proved capable of preserving in their pristine loveliness, or of rebuilding when man has blasted them.

Shall we not dedicate ourselves to an understanding, to an appreciation of the life-giving qualities of the earth, our mother, and to a consecration of ourselves never to abuse, never to destroy, never to make barren, the fertile fields of our planet, Earth? Rather shall we respect and preserve, saving for our children and our children's children the largesse of nature whose fruition man may destroy, but the secret of whose life is not yet in his childish hand.

As we leave this sylvan Eden, let us contemplate in quiet the great Architect and his forest temples; let us study how we may become his humble draftsmen, his gardeners; let us so conduct ourselves that the angel of vengeance with the flaming sword shall not send the American people from the garden given them by the Creator himself. This is my message to the Garden Club on this May day.

Appendix D: Wild Flowers in The Garden Club of America Grove

"Wild Flowers in The Garden Club of America Grove"

A July 1939 *Bulletin* essay describing flora and fauna of The Garden Club of America Grove in Humboldt Redwoods State Park, by Ethel Lansdale, Member-at-Large, The Garden Club of America. (Courtesy of The Garden Club of America).

> When it was suggested that The Garden Club of America should interest itself in some special undertaking that would carry its name long after this generation had passed on, many ideas came up and eventually it was decided that nothing could be more in keeping than to buy a grove of California Redwood Trees that were fast being timbered — trees that had stood from one to three thousand years. Indeed, markings on the Giant Redwoods indicate their beginnings as fifty million years ago. These wonderful trees in our Grove would have been cut to the ground as many others in the surrounding groves have been, leaving dark charred trunks in open fields.
>
> So The Garden Club of America, through the generous support of its members, was able to buy a grove before it fell to the fate of many of those surrounding it; for once down, no science or money can replace these giants that have taken thousands of years to grow.
>
> We have all visualized the magnificent trees with their red bark and feathery boughs towering to the sky and feel very proud of what we have accomplished. But how many have stopped to think that by

saving the trees we were also saving the *flora*, too. For ours was really a "forest primeval," its depths unpenetrated, with no trails, so that the wild flowers and undergrowth had grown there undisturbed. Varieties too numerous to name, for we not only have the many that grow in the deep shade, but our land also goes up into the hills where there are quantities of flowers that love the bright sunshine.

As we enter the Grove on the foot-bridge over the river we are impressed with the soft green covering on the red needles. This is a carpet of oxalis (*O. oregana*) with its dainty pale pink flowers peering through the leaves. Mingled with the oxalis are little yellow violets (*Viola sempervirens* and *Viola glabella*) and white anemones (*A. quinouefolia*).

Conscious of a pungent odor, you have stepped on the trailing Yerba Buena (*Micromeria*) which grows over the ground and has tiny white flowers. San Francisco was originally called "Yerba Buena," named for this flower on account of the great quantities that grew on the hills where the city now stands.

Through this carpet of delicate green the trillium (*T. ovatum*), solomon's seal (*Smilacina*) and the lovely deep wine-colored clintonia are seen; for they all love the shade. Large patches of pink bleeding heart (*Dicentra formosa*) and the wild ginger (*Asarum*), whose heart-shaped leaves and spidery claret-colored flowers are found close to the ground.

Shrubs that grow a little higher up are the sala (*Gaultheria Shallon*) that has pink and white bell flowers shaped like lilly-of-the-valley; great quantities of wild lilac (*Ceanothus*); gooseberries (*Ribes speciosum*); rhododendron and dogwood; both varieties of the latter, one like the Eastern with large white flowers (*Cornus Nuttallii*) and the other that grows along the streams, the creek dogwood (*Cornus californica*), the stems of which take on a bright reddish-purple tint in the autumn. Also along the streams, growing in the moss, is the scarlet mimulus (*Mimulus cardinalis*); and here can also be found the little calypso orchid, that at one time grew in profusion, but can rarely now be found in this locality.

We must not forget the Western azalea (*Rhododendron occidentale*) which grows from fifteen to twenty feet high. Its blossoms are white and buff and are most fragrant and at their best from early June to the end of July.

186

The dainty flowers of the wood rose (*Gymnocarta*) are also to be seen, and it derives its name from the naked rose hip, as there is no calyx surrounding it.

Further up the bank are great patches of *Erythronium californicum*,small graceful clumps of white and cream-colored lilies with spotted grass leaves; and many varieties of iris, quite as delicate as orchids in their tints of lavender, white and yellow, are to be found on the hillside and in the half shade.

Among the lilies are the tiger lily (*Lilium pardalinum*), and when one is fortunate enough to find it, the redwood lily (*Lilium rubescens*), which rises from the ferns, a tall stalk of fragrant white blossoms turning pink, sometimes from twenty to forty flowers on the same stem filling the air with the most delicious perfume. One is often conscious of the fragrance long before the flower is seen.

I could go on to name many, many other varieties of flowers that grow in the shade under the redwood trees, but I want to leave a little space for those growing on the hillside.

The *Fritillaria lanceolata*, commonly called Mission Bells, are brown lilies mottled with purple and dull yellowish green; amongst them are scattered the tall spikes of the blue *Brodiaea capitala*; the brilliant Hounds Tongue (*Cynoglossum grande*); many varieties of lupin including the dwarf lupin (*Lupinus nannus*) and the blue and white lupin (*Lupinus bicolor*); cyclamen (*Dodecatheon*) commonly called the Shooting Star; besides numerous others.

Some beautiful ferns grow in the Redwoods, the better known being the Chain Fern (*Woodwardia radicans*), often growing to a height of six feet; Maidenhair Fern; Five-Finger Fern; and Golden Back, named on account of the yellow spores on the underside. If this fern is pressed against a dark material a perfect replica leaves its imprint.

Motors have made the countryside so accessible that many wild flowers have been picked and torn up by the roots by ruthless people who seem to know no better, and are fast disappearing from the fields and hillsides where formerly many varieties were to be found. It is only in guarded places such as The Garden Club of America Grove that they continue to increase. The grove can only be entered in summer by the footbridge, and there visitors are met by a custodian who sees that the few trails that have been made are used and flowers left undisturbed.

In winter it is impossible to enter the grove except by boat across the Eel River, for the water rises to such a height, in the winter months a permanent bridge is not feasible. In this way our grove is kept more or less free of the many motorists and campers who might otherwise tramp through it destroying much of the undergrowth. Last winter someone managed to enter the grove unseen and cut down the largest of three rare yew trees about fifty feet high. Yew wood is most valuable.

I feel in writing of the *flora* of the Redwoods that I have not mentioned a third of those to be found in the different seasons. But I do hope in the future that each member of the Garden Club will find it possible to visit the grove and thus realize more fully the feeling of pride in her share of the work that is being done, not only in saving the Redwoods, but in preserving the wild growth that, being left undisturbed, will go on increasing in its natural habitat.

ENDNOTES

Introduction: 160 Million Years and Counting

[1] Dewitt, John B. *California Redwood Parks and Preserves.* Save the Redwoods League. 1993, p. 4.

[2] Wallace, David Rains. *Redwood Official National and State Parks Handbook.* U.S Department of the Interior. National Park Service, Division of Publications. 1998, pp. 30,38-39.

[3] Norman, Steve. United States Forest Service. *Native American Redwood Ecology.* Web. December 4, 2018. ‹https://redwood.forestthreats.org/native.htm›

[4] Wallace, David Rains. *Redwood Official National and State Parks Handbook,* p. 72; and Beach, Patrick. *A Good Forest For Dying: The Tragic Death of a Young Man on the Front Lines of the Environmental Wars.* Knopf Doubleday Publishing Group. 2003, p. 26.

[5] Farmer, Jared. *Trees in Paradise.* Norton & Company, Inc. 1974, p. 7. And Pearsall, Clarence et al. *The Quest for Qual-A-Wa-Loo, A Collection of Diaries and Historical Notes.* Holmes Book Co. 1966, pp. 3,5,8.

[6] Farmer, Jared. *Trees in Paradise,* p. 8. And Dewitt, John. *California Redwood Parks and Preserves,* p. 7.

[7] *Jedediah Smith Redwoods State Park.* California Department Parks and Recreation. Web. December 4, 2018. ‹https://www.parks.ca.gov/pages/413/files/JedSmithRedwoodsSP_WebBrochure2014.pdf›; and Pearsall, Clarence et al. *The Quest for Qual-A-Wa-Loo, A Collection of Diaries and Historical Notes,* p. 26.

[8] Pearsall, Clarence et al. *The Quest for Qual-A-Wa-Loo, A Collection of Diaries and Historical Notes,* p. 41.

[9] Wallace, David Rains. *Redwood Official National and State Parks Handbook,* p. 73; and Beach, Patrick. *A Good Forest For Dying: The Tragic Death of a Young Man on the Front Lines of the Environmental Wars,* p. 27.

[10] Widick, Richard. *Trouble in the Forest, California's Redwood Timber Wars.* University of Minneapolis Press. 2009, pp. 160,161. And Farmer, Jared, *Trees in Paradise,* p. 35.

[11] Amodio, John J. *Save the Redwoods: 1919–1925 The Humboldt Redwood Movement.* Humboldt State University. 1980, p. 2.

[12] Farmer, Jared. *Trees in Paradise,* pp. 35-36. And Amodio, John J. *Save the Redwoods: 1919–1925 The Humboldt Redwood Movement,* pp. 3-4.

[13] Evarts, John, et al., editors. *Coast Redwood: A Natural and Cultural History.* Cachuma Press. 2000, p. 126. And Farmer, Jared. *Trees in Paradise,* p. 36.

[14] Farmer, Jared. *Trees in Paradise,* pp. 18,61,66,73.

[15] Seale, William. *The Garden Club of America 100 Years of a Growing Legacy.* Smithsonian Books. 2012, pp. 3-4.

Chapter One: The Loss of Carson Woods, 1913–1918

[16] "Coming Sunday to View Redwood Park. Special Committee Will Inspect Carson Timber Tract as Possible State Redwood Park." *The Humboldt Beacon.* May 13, 1910, Fortuna, California, p. 7.

[17] "Women's Clubs are for Redwood Park." *The Humboldt Standard.* September 29, 1913, Eureka, California, p. 6. (Humboldt County towns represented at the picnic included Eureka, Fortuna, Ferndale, Metropolitan, Arcata, Scotia, and Loleta).

[18] "Ferndale Notes." *USGenWeb Archives.* Part 10 of 27. From *The Ferndale Enterprise* and the Book of Deeds at the Humboldt County Court House. October 3, 1919, item.

[19] "Humboldt County Still Has 520,000 Acres of Standing Redwoods." *The Timberman.* January 1913, p. 38.

[20] Yaryan, William S. *Saving the Redwoods: The Ideology and Political Economy of Nature Preservation.* University of California, Santa Cruz. June 2002, p. 80.

[21] *Biography of Dr. John A. Lane.* Online Biographies. Humboldt County, California Biographies. Web. December 4, 2018. ‹http://www.onlinebiographies.info/ca/humb/lane-ja.htm›

[22] Evarts, John, et al., editors. *Coast Redwood: A Natural and Cultural History,* p. 124.

[23] "Redwood District." *The Timberman.* October 1913, p. 94; and "John Muir, Aged Naturalist, Dead." *The New York Times.* December 25, 1914. (Muir never made the trip to Humboldt County on behalf of the redwoods. He died of pneumonia on Christmas Eve 1914 in Los Angeles).

[24] Merchant, Carolyn. *Women of the Progressive Conservation Movement: 1900–1916.* Environmental Review: ER, Vol. 8, No. 1, Special Issue: Women and Environmental History. Spring, 1984, p. 59.

[25] "Uncle Joe' Tells Ladies to Go to ----! Mrs. Lovell White's Reply. Speaker Cannon the Victim of a Parody Rallying Women to Cause of the Big Trees." *The San Francisco Chronicle.* December 28, 1905, p. 14.

[26] Binkley, Cameron. *No Better Heritage than Living Trees: Women's Clubs and Early Conservation in Humboldt County.* The Western Historical Quarterly, Utah State University on behalf of the Western History Association. Volume 33, No. 2. Summer 2002, p. 183.

[27] *California Big Trees State Park.* California State Parks. Brochure, p. 3. Web. December 4, 2018. ‹http://www.parks.ca.gov/pages/551/files/CalaverasBigTreesFinalWebLayout101816.pdf› and *Crocker, Ethel.* San Mateo County Historical Association Online Collections Database. San Mateo County History Museum. Web. December 4, 2018 ‹https://historysmc.pastperfectonline.com/byperson?keyword=Crocker%2C+Ethel› (The state won control of the North Grove with $265,000 in state park bond funds and contributions from the Save the Redwoods League, Standard Oil Company heir

John D. Rockefeller, Jr., and Ethel Crocker, one of California's most powerful women for her philanthropy as the wife of William H. Crocker, son of the famed transcontinental railroad builder and California Gold Rush pioneer. More state funding in 1954 and another $1 million from Rockefeller enabled a $2.75 million purchase of the park's 2,151-acre South Grove).

[28] Yaryan, William S. *Saving the Redwoods: The Ideology and Political Economy of Nature Preservation*, p. 91. And Walker, Richard A. *The Country in the City: The Greening of the San Francisco Bay Area.* University of Washington Press. 1947, pp. 29-30.

[29] Evarts, John, et al., editors. *Coast Redwood A Natural and Cultural History*, p. 130.

[30] De Vries, Carolyn. *Grand and Ancient Forest. The Story of Andrew P. Hill and Big Basin Redwood State Park.* Valley Publishers. 1978, pp. 26,28,31. And *Our History.* The Sempervirens Fund. And Yaryan, William S. *Saving the Redwoods: The Ideology and Political Economy of Nature Preservation*, p. 172.

[31] Schlappi, Elizabeth Roe. *Saving the Redwoods.* University of California. July 10, 1959, p. 17.

[32] *People. Muir Woods National Monument California.* U.S. National Park Service. Mill Valley, California. Web. December 4, 2018. <https://www.nps.gov/muwo/learn/historyculture/people.htm/>

[33] Cohen, Shana Miriam. *American Garden Clubs and the Fight for Nature Preservation, 1890–1980.* University of California at Berkeley, 2005, p. 104.

[34] Seale, William. *The Garden Club of America 100 Years of a Growing Legacy*, p. 52

[35] Cohen, Shana Miriam. *American Garden Clubs and the Fight for Nature Preservation, 1890–1980*, p. 153.

[36] Clar, C. Raymond. *California Government and Forestry, from Spanish Days to 1927.* State of California, Department of Natural Resources, Division of Forestry. 1959, pp. 68-69.

[37] Binkley, Cameron. *No Better Heritage than Living Trees: Women's Clubs and Early Conservation in Humboldt County*, p. 182. And Marmor, Jason. *The Burdette House: Enduring Landmark of Clifton-by-the-Sea.* Redondo Beach Historical Society Newsletter. 1991. Web. December 4, 2018. <https://www.redondohistorical.org/?page_id=917>

[38] Merchant, Carolyn. *Women of the Progressive Conservation Movement: 1900–1916*, p. 59.

[39] Tyler, Ferdinand. *History of The General Federation of Women's Clubs and California Federation of Women's Clubs.* Web. December 4, 2018. <https://slideplayer.com/slide/7455882>

[40] Seale, William. *The Garden Club of America 100 Years of a Growing Legacy*, pp. 3-5, 50,52.

[41] Binkley, Cameron. *No Better Heritage than Living Trees: Women's Clubs and Early Conservation in Humboldt County*, pp. 185-186.

[42] "Carson Park Site Meets With Favor." *The Humboldt Standard.* October 20, 1913, p. 1.

[43] "Convention Humboldt County Federation." *The Clubwoman*. California Federation of Women's Clubs. October 1918, p. 8. And Binkley, Cameron. *No Better Heritage than Living Trees: Women's Clubs and Early Conservation in Humboldt County*, p. 188.

[44] *14th Census of the United States. State Compendium California*. U.S. Department of Commerce. Bureau of the Census. Washington Government Printing Office. 1924, p. 11.

[45] "Redwood Park Resolutions Adopted by Women's Clubs." *The Humboldt Standard*. October 20, 1913, p. 2.

[46] Hughes, Edan Milton. *Artists in California, 1786–1940. Third edition*. Crocker Art Museum. 2002, p. 716.

[47] *14th Census of the United States. State Compendium California*, p. 11.

[48] "Many Topics Are Handled by Club Women. Are Enthusiastic Over Redwood Park." *The Humboldt Times*. January 11, 1914, p. 6. (The vote appeared to reflect geographical divisions within the county. Nine women's clubs voted to endorse Carson Woods for a preferred redwood national park. Eight women's clubs voted not to name a site until later).

[49] Evarts, John, et al., editors. *Coast Redwood A Natural and Cultural History*, pp. 93,125.

[50] Binkley, Cameron. *No Better Heritage than Living Trees: Women's Clubs and Early Conservation in Humboldt County*, p. 188.

[51] Schrepfer, Susan R. *A Conservative Reform: Saving the Redwoods 1917–1940*. University of California, Riverside. August 1971, pp. 32-33; and Amodio, John J. *Save the Redwoods: 1919–1925*. The Humboldt County Redwood Movement, p. 7.

[52] Binkley, Cameron. *No Better Heritage than Living Trees: Women's Clubs and Early Conservation in Humboldt County*, p. 188.

[53] "School Children Petition Preservation of California's Redwoods." *The Journal of Education*. March 5, 1908, p. 278.

[54] Binkley, Cameron. *No Better Heritage than Living Trees: Women's Clubs and Early Conservation in Humboldt County*, p. 188. (Three years later in April 1911 the same school children invited now ex-president Roosevelt to visit Humboldt County while he was, at that moment, in San Francisco. Roosevelt declined due to a busy schedule but messaged his support for the local save-the-redwoods campaigns. "You know how heartily I approve of the movement for the preservation of the magnificent California redwood in your county; anything that can be done to conserve those trees I hope will be done," he wrote back. The April 3, 1911, *Humboldt Standard* in reporting on the response declared in a large headline at the top of its front page: "Ex-President Endorses Redwood Park").

[55] Widick, Richard. *Trouble in the Forest: California's Redwood Timber Wars*, p. 251.

[56] *Sixty-Second Congress, Second Session. Congressional Record. Volume 48, Part 4*. March 29, 1912. Page 4,068.

[57] "Will Ask for a Committee to Look at Park." *The Humboldt Times*. February 7, 1912, p. 3.

[58] Binkley, Cameron. *No Better Heritage than Living Trees: Women's Clubs and Early Conservation in Humboldt County*, p. 191.

[59] California Federation of Women's Clubs. *60 Year History*. 1961, p. 15. And *Sixty-Second Congress. Second Session*. Congressional Record. Volume 48. Part 6. May 18, 1912, p. 6,782.

[60] Binkley, Cameron. *No Better Heritage than Living Trees: Women's Clubs and Early Conservation in Humboldt County*, pp. 189,191.

[61] *Sixty-Third Congress, First Session*. Congressional Record. Volume 50, Part 1. April 7, 1913, p. 92.

[62] Binkley, Cameron. *No Better Heritage than Living Trees: Women's Clubs and Early Conservation in Humboldt County*, p. 191.

[63] Ross, Lillian. "Women's Save the Redwood League Organized in 1919; Aided in Numerous Projects." *The Humboldt Standard*. January 15, 1932, pp. 7,4.

[64] Schrepfer, Susan R. *A Conservative Reform: Saving the Redwoods 1917–1940*, pp. 57-58.

[65] *Sixty-Second Congress, Second Session*. Congressional Record. Volume 48, Part 4, March 29, 1912, p. 4,068, and *Sixty-Third Congress, First Session*. Congressional Record. Volume 50, Part 1, April 7, 1913, p. 92. (Congressman Raker's failure likely reveals more about the futility of his request than his influence within Congress. Raker, an early favorite of conservationists, passed legislation to establish Lassen Volcanic National Park in Northeastern California, and legislation, as well, to create a new National Park Service. Raker, however, is still best remembered for an act that went against the wishes of conservationist John Muir, the damming of Hetch Hetchy Valley in the Sierra Nevada to supply drinking water to the City of San Francisco).

[66] Knight, Helen M. "President's Letter." *The Clubwoman*. California Federation of Women's Clubs. October 1915, pp. 6-8.

[67] Brinkley, Douglas. *Rightful Heritage: Franklin D. Roosevelt and the Land of America*. 2016. Harper, p. 82.

[68] Royles, Anna L. "Forestry." *The Clubwoman*. September 1916, pp. 9-10.

[69] *History of Armstrong Redwoods State Natural Reserve*. California Department of Parks and Recreation. Web. December 4, 2018. ‹https://www.parks.ca.gov/?page_id=23367›

[70] Engbeck, Jr., Joseph H. *State Parks of California From 1864 to the Present*. Graphic Arts Publishing Co. 1980, pp. 41-42.

[71] Amodio, John J. *Save the Redwoods: 1919–1925 The Humboldt Redwood Movement*, p. 8. (Based on November 25, 1980, personal interview with John DeWitt, then executive secretary of the Save the Redwoods League).

[72] Schloss, Adella T. "Convention Humboldt County Federation." *The Clubwoman*. California Federation of Women's Clubs. October 1918, p. 8.

Chapter Two: First Encounters With Success, 1919–1921

[73] Coomber, Jeff. *Death in the Redwoods. The Effects of the Spanish Influenza on Humboldt County.* Humboldt State University. Charles P. Barnum History Award, 2012, First Prize, pp. 12,15,20, 22. Web. December 4, 2018. ‹http://humboldt-dspace.calstate.edu/handle/10211.3/131775›

[74] Amodio, John J. *Save the Redwoods: 1919–1925. The Humboldt County Redwood Movement*, p. 19.

[75] Rosenberg, Joseph et al. *The New Debate Over a Charitable Deduction for Nonitemizers.* The Urban Institute. October 2016. Web. December 4, 2018. ‹https://www.taxpolicycenter.org/sites/default/files/publication/135446/the-new-ebate-over-a-charitable-deduction-for-nonitemizers.pdf›

[76] Clar, C. Raymond. *California Government and Forestry, from Spanish Days to 1927,* p. 511.

[77] Cohen, Shana Miriam. *American Garden Clubs and the Fight for Nature Preservation, 1890–1980,* p. 105.

[78] Binkley, Cameron. *No Better Heritage than Living Trees: Women's Clubs and Early Conservation in Humboldt County,* pp. 197-198.

[79] Binkley, Cameron. *California Women and Politics, From The Gold Rush To The Great Depression.* University of Nebraska Press, Lincoln, Nebraska. 2011, p. 168.

[80] "Prominent Civic Leader Formerly Here Has Passed." *The Healdsburg Tribune.* February 10, 1926. And "Mrs. Aaron Schloss. Feminist Leader and Club Member Dies near Berkeley, Cal." *The New York Times.* January 1, 1930. And *Who's Who Among the Women of California.* California Civil League of Women Voters. 1922. Security Publishing Company, p. 117.

[81] Nye, Myra. "Urges Saving of Redwoods." *The Los Angeles Times.* April 28, 1921, p. 118.

[82] Irvine, Leigh H. *History of Humboldt County, California, With Biographical Sketches Of The Leading Men And Women Who Have Been Identified With The Growth And Development From The Early Days to The Present.* Historic Record Company, 1915, pp. 882-885. Web. December 4, 2018. ‹https://archive.org/details/historyofhumbol00irvi/page/n7›

[83] Amodio, John J. *Save the Redwoods: 1919–1925. The Humboldt County Redwood Movement*, p. 14.

[84] "Make Redwoods Troop Memorial Says Houston." *The San Francisco Chronicle.* July 20, 1919, p. F1.

[85] "Mather Says Redwoods To Be Saved By Fast Action" *The Humboldt Times.* August 9, 1919, pp. 1-2. And "Let's Save The Redwoods. We Can Do It." *The Humboldt Times.* August 10, 1919, p. 6.

[86] *Constitution.* League Minutes, Humboldt County Women's Save the Redwoods League. August 9, 1919. December 6, 1920. Humboldt State University Library,

Special Collections. Web. December 4, 2018. ‹http://library.humboldt.edu/humco/holdings/SaveRedAid.htm›

[87] Binkley, Cameron. *No Better Heritage than Living Trees: Women's Clubs and Early Conservation in Humboldt County*, p. 194.

[88] Amodio, John J. *Save the Redwoods: 1919–1925. The Humboldt County Redwood Movement*, p. 12.

[89] Putnam, Edna. Humboldt County Women's Save the Redwoods League. Meeting minutes. December 6, 1920.

[90] "Former Eureka Woman is Dead." *The Humboldt Times*. February 11, 1948.

[91] "Mrs. Kate L. Harpst Succumbs." *The Humboldt Times*. February 24, 1929.

[92] "Widely Known Matron is Mourned." *The Humboldt Standard*. January 12, 1940, pp. 1, 11.

[93] "Death Comes For Mrs. F. W. Georgeson." *The Humboldt Standard*. May 7, 1936, pp. 1,6. And "Mrs. F. Georgeson Passes On at the Family Home." *The Humboldt Times*. May 8, 1936.

[94] League Minutes. Humboldt County Women's Save the Redwoods League. December 6, 1919.

[95] Binkley, Cameron. *No Better Heritage than Living Trees: Women's Clubs and Early Conservation in Humboldt County*, p. 195.

[96] "Sarah Jane Perrott, Aged Pioneer Dies." *The Humboldt Standard*. February 27, 1937, p. 3.

[97] Perrott, John. "Pioneer Humboldt Perrott Family." *The Humboldt Historian*. Humboldt County Historical Society. Summer 2006, pp. 38-39.

[98] Hughes, Edan Milton. *Artists in California, 1786–1940*. Third edition Volume II L-Z, p. 716.

[99] "Popular Couple to Wed." *The Humboldt Times*. July 15, 1908, p. 2.

[100] Nye, Myra. "Redwood Fight Success Told." *The Los Angeles Times*. February 18, 1925, p. A1.

[101] Burns, Emily E., et al. Save the Redwoods League. *State of Redwoods Conservation Report*. 2018, pp. 14, 20. Web. December 4, 2018. ‹https://www.savetheredwoods.org/wp-content/uploads/State-of-Redwoods-Conservation-Report-Final-web.pdf›

[102] "Injuries Fatal to Mrs. Martha G. McClellan." *The Humboldt Times*. June 23, 1932, p. 3.

[103] Albright, Horace, with Frank J. Taylor. "How We Saved the Big Trees." *The Saturday Evening Post*. February 7, 1953. And Schlappi, Elizabeth Roe. *Saving the Redwoods*, p. 54. And Speece, Darren Frederick. *Defending Giants: The Battle Over Headwaters Forest and the Transformation of American Environmental Politics, 1850–1999*. University of Maryland, College Park. 2010, pp. 53-54.

[104] "Park Meeting Cheered By Announcements of Tangible Enthusiasm." *The Humboldt Standard*. September 6, 1919, p. 1.

[105] "Humboldt Women Aided Work for Redwood Park, Their Efforts Contributed to Success Thus Far." *The Humboldt Standard*. September 6, 1919, p. 2.

[106] DeLong, John Raymond. *The Ravaged Remnant: A History of the Logging and Preservation of the California Coast Redwood.* San Francisco State College. 1968, p. 98.

[107] Grant, Madison. First Vice President. New York Zoological Society. "Special Redwoods Number. Saving the Redwoods. An Account of the Movement During 1919 to Preserve the Redwoods of California." *Zoological Society Bulletin.* September 1919, pp. 91, 99, 107, 109-110, 112.

[108] Shankland, Robert. *Steve Mather of the National Parks.* Alfred A. Knopf. 1970, p. 197.

[109] Amodio, John J. *Save the Redwoods: 1919–1925. The Humboldt County Redwood Movement,* p. 20.

[110] Speece, Darren Frederick. *Defending Giants: The Battle Over Headwaters Forest and the Transformation of American Environmental Politics, 1850–1999,* p. 54.

[111] Osborn, Henry Fairfield. President. American Museum of Natural History. "Save The Redwoods. Sequoia–The Auld Lang Syne of Trees." *Natural History.* 1919, pp. 600-601, 612.

[112] Putnam, Edna Hildebrand. "The Oldest Living Thing In The World." *Travel.* August 1920, pp. 23-25,40.

[113] Clar, C. Raymond. *California Government and Forestry, from Spanish Days to 1927,* pp. 510-511.

[114] Kent, William. Letter to Save the Redwoods Secretary Newton B. Drury. December 27, 1921. Records of Save the Redwoods League. MSS 88/15/C. Bancroft Library. University of California, Berkeley.

[115] *Record of Members of the Assembly. 1849-2015.* And *Record of State Senators. 1849-2015.* California Secretary of State.

[116] Amodio, John J. *Save the Redwoods: 1919–1925. The Humboldt County Redwood Movement,* p. 20.

[117] Putnam, Edna. Secretary. Humboldt County Women's Save the Redwoods League. *Resume of 1921 Activities by the Women's Save the Redwoods League.* December 1921.

[118] Schrepfer, Susan R. *A Conservative Reform: Saving the Redwoods 1917–1940,* pp. 32-33. And Amodio, John J. *Save the Redwoods: 1919–1925. The Humboldt County Redwood Movement,* p. 101.

[119] California Federation of Women's Clubs. *60-Year History.* 1961, p. 23.

[120] Albright, Horace M. with Frank J. Taylor. "How We Saved the Big Trees." *The Saturday Evening Post.* February 7, 1953. And Schlappi, Elizabeth Roe. *Saving the Redwoods,* p. 128.

[121] Schrepfer, Susan R. *A Conservative Reform: Saving the Redwoods 1917–1940,* pp. 32-33. And Amodio, John J. *Save the Redwoods: 1919–1925. The Humboldt County Redwood Movement,* p. 101

[122] Widick, Richard. *Trouble in the Forest. California's Redwood Timber Wars,* p. 109. (The Pacific Lumber Co. obtained its first 10,000 acres of redwood forest land at $1.25 per acre through the Morrill Act of 1862, which provided states

30,000 acres per Congressional representative with the intent of the states selling the land to finance land-grant colleges and universities.) And Speece, Darren Frederick. *Defending Giants: The Battle Over Headwaters Forest and the Transformation of American Environmental Politics, 1850–1999*, p. 48.

[123] Amodio, John J. Executive Director. Northcoast Environmental Center. "A Voice In The Wilderness. Ru-Flo Harper Lee." *Econo-News*. April 1, 1976. Arcata, California. And "Known area writer dies unexpectedly." *The Times-Standard*. May 20, 1979, p. 3.

[124] *Final Calendar of Legislative Business*. Journal of the Assembly During the Forty-Fourth Session of the Legislature of California. 1921, pp. 84,1,873,1,899,1,938-1,939.

[125] "People Plead to Governor For Redwoods." *The San Francisco Chronicle*. April 6, 1921, p. 4.

[126] "Reports of the Secretaries." *The Clubwoman*. June 1921, pp. 6,8.

[127] Shankland, Robert. *Steve Mather of the National Parks*, p. 199.

[128] Clar, C. Raymond. *California Government and Forestry, from Spanish Days to 1927*, pp. 513. (Flora Stephens' role in convincing her husband to sign the bill is also noted on page 344 of Stephen Fox's *John Muir and His Legacy, The American Conservation Movement*. Fox asserts that the governor's wife, also a member of the General Federation of Women's clubs, "talked him into it.")

[129] Schrepfer, Susan R. *A Conservative Reform: Saving the Redwoods 1917–1940*, p. 114.

[130] The Historical Marker Project. *In Memory of Col. Raynal C. Bolling*. Web. December 4, 2018. ‹https://www.historicalmarkerproject.com/markers/HM17EP_in-memory-of-col-raynal-c-bolling_Washington-DC.html›

[131] Grant, Madison. *Preserve an America Worth Fighting For*. Save the Redwoods League. August 6, 1921.

[132] Seale, William. *The Garden Club of America 100 Years of a Growing Legacy*, p. 51.

[133] Weekly, Kent. "Lansdale, Philip Van Horne, LT." *Together We Served*. Web. December 4, 2018. ‹https://navy.togetherweserved.com/usn/servlet/tws.webapp.WebApp?cmd=ShadowBoxProfile&type=Person&ID=514001›

[134] Melendy, Howard Brett. *One Hundred Years of the Redwood Lumber Industry, 1850–1950*. Stanford University. 1952, pp. 110-114.

Chapter Three: The Ultimate Prize, 1922–1923

[135] Newton Drury, Parks and redwoods, 1919–1971, interview conducted by Amelia R. Fry and Susan Schrepfer, 1959–1970. Oral History Center, The Bancroft Library, University of California, Berkeley, 1972, Section 136.

[136] Nye, Myra. "Eureka to Get Next Meeting. Women's Clubs Select City For Convention." *The Los Angeles Times*. May 7, 1922, p. A13.

[137] Schlappi, Elizabeth Roe. *Saving the Redwoods*, p. 106.

[138] Clar, C. Raymond. *California Government and Forestry, from Spanish Days to 1927*, p. 513.

[139] Old-Growth Forest Network. *CA: Rockefeller Forest–Humboldt Redwoods State Park.* Web. December 4, 2018.
‹http://www.oldgrowthforest.net/rockefeller-forest--humboldt-redwoods-s›

[140] Clar, C. Raymond. *California Government and Forestry, from Spanish Days to 1927*, p. 513.

[141] Schlappi, Elizabeth Roe, *Saving the Redwoods*, 1959, p.56.

[142] Warren, Laurence R., *The Development Of The Memorial Grove System In Humboldt Redwoods State Park.* California State University Sacramento. 1966, p. 44.

[143] "Corporate Records." *The Harvard Graduates' Magazine.* Volume 29. 1921, p. 597.

[144] California Department of Parks and Recreation. *Standish-Hickey State Recreation Area.* Web. December 4, 2018. ‹*https://www.parks.ca.gov/?page_id=423*› And Teresa Shumaker. "Standish-Hickey State Recreation Area: An Ancestral Gift, Tie." *The Mendocino Beacon.* February 9, 2012, p. 1.

[145] Williams, Solon H. Deputy State Forester, State Board of Forestry. *Ninth Biennial Report of the State Board of Forestry of the State of California.* California State Printing Office. January 2, 1923, pp. 62-63.

[146] Newton Drury, Parks and redwoods, 1919–1971, interview conducted by Amelia R. Fry and Susan Schrepfer, 1959–1970, Section 137.

[147] Widick, Richard. *Trouble in the Forest. California's Redwood Timber Wars*, p. 207.

[148] Amodio, John J. *Save the Redwoods: 1919–1925. The Humboldt County Redwood Movement*, p. 14. And World Forestry Center. *David T. Mason 1883–1973.* Web. December 4, 2018. ‹https://www.worldforestry.org/wp-content/uploads/2016/03/MASON-DAVID-T.pdf›

[149] Hyde, Phillip and Francois Leydet. *The Last Redwoods. Photographs and Story of a Vanishing Scenic Resource.* The Sierra Club. 1963, p. 70. And Beidleman, Richard G. *Willis Linn Jepson–"The Botany Man."* The Jepson Herbarium. University of California at Berkeley. 2000. Web. December 4, 2018. ‹http://ucjeps.berkeley.edu/history/biog/jepson/jepson_the_botany_man.html›

[150] Amodio, John J. *Save the Redwoods: 1919–1925. The Humboldt County Redwood Movement*, pp. 13-14.

[151] Schrepfer, Susan R. *A Conservative Reform: Saving the Redwoods, 1917–1940*, pp. 133,135-138.

[152] "Tribute to L.A. Woman. Mrs. Carrie Bicknell Authority on Ornithology." *The Los Angeles Herald.*" October 29, 1921.

[153] Bicknell, Carrie F. "President of Los Angeles Audubon Society On Nature Study Trip Visits Eureka, Next year's Meeting Place of State Convention." *The Clubwoman.* October 1922, pp. 20-22.

[154] Schrepfer, Susan R. *The Fight to Save the Redwoods. A History of Environmental Reform 1917–1978.* University of Wisconsin Press. 1983, pp. 28-29.

[155] Schrepfer, Susan R. *A Conservative Reform: Saving the Redwoods, 1917–1940*, pp. 107-109,111.

[156] Eureka Women's Club. *History*. Eureka, California. Web. December 4, 2018. ‹https://www.eurekawomansclub.org/history›

[157] "Club Convention Opens. Enthusiastic Delegates Will Hold First Session This Morning, 9 O'Clock." *The Humboldt Times*. May 1, 1923, p. 6.

[158] Brands, H.W. *Reagan: The Life*. Doubleday, p. 16.

[159] Timerhoff, Emilie Mann. "California's Conservation Convention." *The Clubwoman*. June 1923, p. 9.

[160] "Fitzgerald, Mrs. W.A." *Who's Who Among the Women of California*. 1922.

[161] "Mrs. Urquhart, Ex-Head of Women's Clubs Dies." *The Los Angeles Times*. January 14, 1960, p. 26.

[162] Nye, Myra. "Clubs and Big Sticks." *The Los Angeles Times*. July 8, 1923, p. II6.

[163] "Memorial Grove Is Dedicated With Appropriate Ceremonies." *The Humboldt Standard*. September 3, 1923, p. 1-2.

[164] McKinney, John. "Preserving the Past in Ferndale." *The Los Angeles Times*. May 17, 1998.

[165] "Redwood Grove Given County by Mrs. Z. Russ." *The Humboldt Standard*. July 11, 1923. p. 2.

[166] Shepherd, Marvin. *A Scottish Syndicate in the Redwoods. Monopoly and Fraud in the California Redwoods, 1882–1892*. Georgie Press. 2015, pp. 101-161.

[167] "Hon. Joseph Russ." *The CAgenWeb Project. Humboldt County, California, Biographies*. Web. December 4, 2018. ‹http://www.onlinebiographies.info/ca/humb/russ-j.htm›

[168] Hunter, Judge G.W. *The Pioneers of Humboldt County*. Save the Redwoods League. Dedication of the Humboldt Pioneer Memorial Grove. September 2, 1923, p. 14.

[169] Badè, William Frederic. *An Ennobling Gift*. Save the Redwoods League. Dedication of the Humboldt Pioneer Memorial Grove. September 2, 1923, p. 7.

[170] Scott, Margaret. "Save Redwoods Movement Wins Strength. Nation Awakened to Necessity; Women of State Helping." *The Humboldt Standard* December 25, 1923, p. 4.

[171] Schrepfer, Susan R. *The Fight to Save the Redwoods. A History of Environmental Reform 1917–1978*, p. 111.

[172] Fox, Stephen. *John Muir and His Legacy: The American Conservation Movement*. Little, Brown and Company. 1981, pp. 342-343.

[173] Binkely, Cameron. *No Better Heritage than Living Trees: Women's Clubs and Early Conservation in Humboldt County*, p. 198.

[174] Mahan, Laura P. President. Humboldt County Women's Save the Redwoods League. *Summary of Activities*. 1923.

[175] Wolff, Geoffrey. *Black Sun: The Brief Transit and Violent Eclipse of Harry Crosby*. New York Review Books Classics. 2003, p. 15.

[176] Seale, William. *The Garden Club of America 100 Years of a Growing Legacy*, p. 52

[177] Cohen, Shana Miriam. *American Garden Clubs and the Fight for Nature Preservation, 1890–1980*, pp. 136-137.

Chapter Four: Showdown In The Forest, 1924–1925

[178] Wiley, Rease M. and J.L. "We are Saving the Redwoods." *The Arcata Union.* January 17, 1924. Arcata, California, pp. 1-2.

[179] DeLong, John Raymond. *"The Ravaged Remnant: A History of the Logging and Preservation of the California Coast Redwood,* p. 131.

[180] Speece, Darren Frederick. *Defending Giants: The Battle Over Headwaters Forest and the Transformation of American Environmental Politics, 1850–1999,* pp. 62-63.

[181] Wiley, Rease M. "Forestry Board Thanks Lumber Company." *The Arcata Union.* February 21, 1924, p. 8.

[182] Schrepfer, Susan R. *A Conservative Reform: Saving the Redwoods, 1917–1940,* pp. 142-143

[183] "Purchase of Redwoods Is Favored By Supervisors." *The Humboldt Standard.* February 14, 1924. (The 12 towns represented in the petition favoring the county's purchase of Dyerville Flat for a redwood park included Trinidad, Arcata, Blue Lake, Eureka, Loleta, Fortuna, Ferndale, Rohnerville, Carlotta, Hydesville, McKee's Mill, and Garberville).

[184] "Lumber Company Wishes to Retain Redwood Lands." *The Humboldt Times.* April 12, 1924.

[185] Schrepfer, Susan R. *A Conservative Reform: Saving the Redwoods, 1917–1940,* p. 145.

[186] Wiley, Rease M. "Redwoods Worth $1,000,000 Saved." *The Arcata Union.* April 24, 1924, p. 4.

[187] Schrepfer, Susan R. *A Conservative Reform: Saving the Redwoods, 1917–1940,* pp. 132, 140, 145-148.

[188] Wiley, Rease M. "Will Dedicate Another Grove." *The Arcata Union.* August 14, 1924, p. 7.

[189] Tourangeau, Dixie R. *Franklin K. Lane, Biographical Vignettes,* National Park Service: The First 75 Years, 2017, p. 1. Web. December 4, 2018. ‹https://www. nps.gov/parkhistory/online_books/sontag/lane.htm›

[190] Institute of Governmental Studies, University of California. *Franklin K. Lane.* 2009. Web. December 4, 2018. ‹https://igs.berkeley.edu/people/franklin-k-lane›

[191] Schrepfer, Susan R. *A Conservative Reform: Saving the Redwoods, 1917–1940,* pp. 70-74.

[192] "To Scatter Lane's Ashes; They Will Be Thrown From Peak—Body Cremated In Chicago." *The New York Times.* May 20, 1921.

[193] Merriam, John C. Save the Redwoods League. Dedication of the Franklin K. Lane Memorial Grove. August 24, 1924.

[194] McLaughlin, Mark. "Lora Knight's Wychwood: 100 Years at Tahoe. Part I." *Tahoe Weekly.* September 10, 2014.

[195] Wiley, Rease M. "Lane Grove Dedicated," *The Arcata Union*. Aug. 21, 1924, p. 2.

[196] Schrepfer, Susan R. *A Conservative Reform: Saving the Redwoods, 1917–1940*, pp. 152-154.

[197] Schrepfer, Susan R. *A Conservative Reform: Saving the Redwoods, 1917–1940*, p. 155.

[198] "Supervisors Order Suit to Condemn and Purchase Flat." And "Congratulations." *The Humboldt Times*. November 26, 1924, pp. 1, 4.

[199] "Firm Not Disposed to Agree to Sale." *The Humboldt Standard*. November 26, 1924, p. 1.

[200] Wiley, Rease M. "Humboldt and Del Norte Will Help Save the Redwoods." *The Arcata Union*. October 9, 1924, p. 6.

[201] "Yale Forestry School's New Home." *American Lumberman*. April 1, 1922, p. 59.

[202] "Death of Henry W. Sage." *The New York Times*. September 19, 1897, p. 13.

[203] Bergen, Tunis Garret, editor. *Genealogies of the State of New York: A Record of the Achievements*. *Volume 2*. Lewis Historical Publishing Co. 1915, p. 986.

[204] "Graves Redwood Grove Will Be Dedicated September 6." *The Healdsburg Tribune*. August 29, 1925, p. 3. And Schlappi, Elizabeth Roe. *Saving the Redwoods*, p. 82. And Simo, Melanie L. *Forest and Garden. Traces of Wilderness in a Modernizing Land. 1897–1949*. University of Virginia Press. 2003, p. 147.

[205] Amodio, John J. *Save the Redwoods: 1919–1925. The Humboldt County Redwood Movement*, pp. 26-27.

[206] "P.L. Co. Offers Portion of Dyerville Flats. Women Do Not Like Proposal." *The Humboldt Standard*. January 13, 1925, pp. 1,10.

[207] Mahan, Laura. *Report of the President, Women's Save the Redwoods League of Humboldt County for Year 1925*. December 1925.

[208] "Chamber of Commerce Would Take P.L. Offer." *The Humboldt Standard*. January 23, 1925, p. 1. And Mahan, Laura. President, Humboldt County Women's Save the Redwoods League. *Report of the President, Women's Save the Redwoods League of Humboldt County for Year 1925*.

[209] Wiley, Rease M. "Acceptance of Lumber Company's Offer Urged." *The Arcata Union*. January 29, 1925, p. 8.

[210] P.L. Co. Offers Portion of Dyerville Flats. Women Do Not Like Proposal." *The Humboldt Standard*. pp. 1, 10.

[211] Schrepfer, Susan R. *A Conservative Reform: Saving the Redwoods, 1917–1940*, p. 164.

[212] "Women Resent C. Of C. Redwood Resolution. Women's League Declares Members Of Chamber Not In Accord With Directors." *The Humboldt Standard*. January 27, 1925, p. 1.

[213] "Sentiment and Good Business." *The Humboldt Standard*. January 18, 1925, p. 4.

[214] "Vast Sum Held for Acquiring Redwoods. Dramatic Development Is Recorded in Negotiations With P.L. Co." *The Humboldt Standard*. February 10, 1925, p. 1.

[215] "Women of U.S. Urge Saving Of Big Trees. President of National Federation Says Membership Ready to Aid." *The Humboldt Standard*. February 10, 1925, p. 1.

[216] Newton Drury, Parks and redwoods, 1919–1971, interview conducted by Amelia R. Fry and Susan Schrepfer, 1959–1970, Section 141,142.

[217] "Resolution of League Body Approved by Supervisors." *The Humboldt Times.* February 12, 1925, p. 1.

[218] "A Great Moral Victory." *The Humboldt Times.* February 12, 1925, p. 4.

[219] Newton Drury, Parks and redwoods, 1919–1971, interview conducted by Amelia R. Fry and Susan Schrepfer, 1959–1970. Oral History Center, The Bancroft Library, University of California, Berkeley, 1972, Section 143.

[220] Binkley, Cameron. *"No Better Heritage than Living Trees:Women's Clubs and Early Conservation in Humboldt County,"* p. 182

[221] Nye, Myra. "Clubs Present Redwood Fund." *The Los Angeles Times.* May 21, 1925, p. A11.

[222] Nye, Myra "Busy Schedule for Convention. Federation Gathering This Month Outlined." *The Los Angeles Times.* May 10, 1925, p. D9.

[223] "Humboldt County Women's Clubs Raise $1,300 for State Memorial Park Fund." *The Humboldt Standard.* May 18, 1925, p. 2.

[224] Amodio, John J. *Save the Redwoods: 1919–1925. The Humboldt County Redwood Movement,* p. 33.

Chapter Five: Outside Influences, 1926–1930

[225] Cohen, Shana Miriam. *American Garden Clubs and the Fight for Nature Preservation, 1890–1980,* pp. 137-138.

[226] Webbink, P. "Federal Water Power Policy." *Editorial research reports 1929* (Vol. I). CQ Press. And McFarland, Horace J. "The Present Peril of the National Parks." *The Bulletin.* The Garden Club of America. December 20, 1921, pp. 60-61. And "Menace to National Parks." The *Bulletin,* p. 12. The Garden Club of America Archives.

[227] "National Conference on Parks." The *Bulletin.* The Garden Club of America. March 1921, pp. 24-25.

[228] Badè, William F. "Garden Hints from the Redwoods. The *Bulletin.* The Garden Club of America. November 1921, pp. 92-93.

[229] *The Redwoods.* General Minutes. The Garden Club of America. January 10, 1936, p. 1.

[230] Graves, Henry S. "The Redwood Forests — A Great National Heritage." *The Bulletin.* The Garden Club of America. September 1927, pp. 73-76.

[231] Schrepfer, Susan R. *A Conservative Reform: Saving the Redwoods, 1917–1940,* pp. 169,171,174-175,177-181.

[232] Weinstein, Dave. "Signature Style/Duncan McDuffie/Natural Neighborhoods. Visionary Developer Created Elegant Urban 'Residential Parks.'" *The San Francisco Chronicle.* February 7, 2004.

[233] Schrepfer, Susan R. *A Conservative Reform: Saving the Redwoods, 1917–1940*, p. 181.

[234] Engbeck, Jr., Joseph H. *State Parks of California, From 1864 To the Present*, pp. 48-50,53.

[235] Cohen, Shana Miriam. *American Garden Clubs and the Fight for Nature Preservation, 1890–1980*, p. 137.

[236] Schrepfer, Susan R. *A Conservative Reform: Saving the Redwoods, 1917–1940*, p. 182.

[237] "California Ballot Propositions." UC Hastings Law Library. California Ballot Measures Database.

[238] Engbeck, Jr., Joseph H. *State Parks of California, From 1864 To the Present*, p. 55. And Schrepfer, Susan R. *The Fight to Save the Redwoods. A History of Environmental Reform 1917–1978*, p. 33.

[239] California Commission on State Government Organization and Economy (The Little Hoover Commission). *Beyond Crisis: Recapturing Excellence in California's State Park System.* March 2013, p. 9. And Save the Redwoods League. *Election Results: #Yes on 68 Means Clean Water And Safe Parks For All.* Web. December 4, 2018. ‹https://www.savetheredwoods.org/blog/election-results-yeson68-means-clean-water-and-safe-parks-for-all›

[240] California Commission on State Government Organization and Economy (The Little Hoover Commission). *Beyond Crisis: Recapturing Excellence in California's State Park System*, pp. 1,11.

[241] California Commission on State Government Organization and Economy (The Little Hoover Commission). *Beyond Crisis: Recapturing Excellence in California's State Park System.* March 2013, p. 10.

[242] Olmstead, Jr., Frederick Law. *Report of the Director of the Survey to the California State Park Commission.* December 31, 1928, pp. 42-43.

[243] Olmstead Jr., Frederick Law. *Report of the Director of the Survey to the California State Park Commission.* December 31, 1928, pp. 63-64.

[244] The National Park Service. *Presenting Nature: The Historic Landscape Design of the National Park Service, 1916–1942. I.V. The Work of the Western Field Office. E.P. Meinecke and Campground Planning.* October 31, 2012. Web. December 4, 2018. ‹https://www.nps.gov/parkhistory/online_books/mcclelland/mcclelland4e.htm›

[245] Meinecke, Emilio P. Pathologist. U.S. Plant Bureau. *A Report Upon The Excessive Tourist Travel On the California Redwood Parks.* California State Printing Office. 1928, pp. 3,8,12-13.

[246] Schrepfer, Susan R. *A Conservative Reform: Saving the Redwoods, 1917–1940*, pp. 91-92,94. And Newton Drury, Parks and redwoods, 1919–1971, interview conducted by Amelia R. Fry and Susan Schrepfer, 1959–1970, Sections 120-123,137.

[247] Newton Drury, Parks and redwoods, 1919–1971, interview conducted by Amelia R. Fry and Susan Schrepfer, 1959–1970, Section 123.

248 "Felton, Charles Norton, (1832–1914)." *Biographical Directory of the United States Congress.*

249 Wilbur, Ray Lyman. President, Stanford University. *Address at the Dedication of the Charles N. Felton Redwood Grove as a Part of the California State Park System.* Save the Redwoods League files. MSS 88/15/C. Bancroft Library, University of California at Berkeley. June 12, 1927.

250 *Frank D. Stout Family Records, 1875–1944.* University of Wisconsin. University Library; Stout Library; Robert S. Swanson Library and Learning Center. Web. December 4, 2018. ‹https://beta.worldcat.org/archivegrid/data/618720318› And *Knapp, Stout And Company.* Encyclopedia Dubuque, Local History Network of the Iowa Historical Society, and Iowa Museum Association. Web. December 4, 2018. ‹http://www.encyclopediadubuque.org/index.php?title=KNAPP,_STOUT_AND_COMPANY›

251 "Finest Redwood Grove Given To State As Memorial Tract in Del Norte County Contains Biggest Trees." The *Healdsburg Enterprise and Tribune.* April 18, 1929, p. 4

252 Warren, Laurence R. *The Development of the Memorial Grove System in Humboldt Redwoods State Park,* p. 43.

253 The Frick Collection. *Alexander, Charles Beatty, 1849–1927.* The Frick Art Reference Library. Web. December 4, 2018. ‹http://research.frick.org/directoryweb/browserecord.php?-action=browse&-recid=7302›

254 "C.F. Crocker Dead. Vice President of the Southern Pacific Railway Expires in San Mateo, Cal." *The New York Times.* July 18, 1897.

255 Newton Drury, Parks and redwoods, 1919–1971, interview conducted by Amelia R. Fry and Susan Schrepfer, 1959–1970, Section 137. And *Crocker, Ethel.* San Mateo County Historical Association Online Collections Database. San Mateo County History Museum.

256 Smith, Ann Y. "The Whittemores of Connecticut: Pioneer Collectors of French Impressionism." *Antiques and Fine Arts Magazine.* March 16, 1931.

257 Tolppanen, Bradley P. *Churchill in North America, 1929.* McFarland & Company. 2014, pp. 136-139.

258 Meyer, Myra. Letter to Newton B. Drury. February 2, 1939. The Garden Club of America Archives.

259 Stewart, Anne T. Director, The Garden Club of America. Letter to Joseph D. Grant. May 26, 1930. The Garden Club of America Archives.

260 Battles, Marjorie Gibbon, and Catherine Colt Dickey. *Fifty Blooming Years. The Garden Club of America.* The Garden Club of America. 1963, p. 61.

261 *Garden Club of America Grove, Minutes from Board of Directors.* The Garden Club of America. 1919 through 1948.

262 Drury, Newton B. Secretary, Save the Redwoods League. Letter to Louis Perske. July 11, 1930.

263 Seale, William. *The Garden Club of America 100 Years of a Growing Legacy,* pp. 5-53.

[264] *Purchase of Grove of Redwood Trees in California.* Minutes. Council of Presidents. The Garden Club of America. July 1930.

[265] "Garden Club Aids in Raising Money for Purchase of Redwood Grove." *The Santa Barbara Morning Press.* September 2, 1930.

[266] "Garden Club To Buy Big Redwoods." *The Pasadena Star News.* February 2, 1931, p. 17.

Chapter Six: Celebrating Success, 1931–1934

[267] Warren, Laurence R. *The Development of the Memorial Grove System in Humboldt Redwoods State Park*, p. 20.

[268] "Native Daughters Dedicate Redwood Grove." *The Humboldt Standard.* May 11, 1931, p. 10.

[269] Kilmer, Alfred Joyce. *Trees.* The Poetry Foundation. Web. December 4, 2018. ⟨https://www.poetryfoundation.org/poetrymagazine/poems/12744/trees⟩

[270] Warren, Laurence R. *The Development of the Memorial Grove System in Humboldt Redwoods State Park*, p. 21.

[271] *Water companies and officials.* Appendix to Journals of Senate & Assembly California. Forty-Eighth Session. 1929, p. 597.

[272] Native Daughters Dedicate Redwood Grove." *The Humboldt Standard.* May 11, 1931, p. 10.

[273] "Tallest Tree in the World Will Be Christened." *The Los Angeles Times.* September 13, 1931, p. 11.

[274] "Giant Redwoods of Bull Creek, Dyerville Forests Escape Axe of Woodman." *The Humboldt Times.* June 21, 1931, p. 1.

[275] Schrepfer, Susan R. *A Conservative Reform: Saving the Redwoods, 1917–1940*, 1971, pp. 187-188.

[276] Wade, Kathleen Camilla. *History of California State Parks.* U.S. Works Progress Administration. 1937.

[277] "Big Redwoods Saved." *The Los Angeles Times.* June 24, 1931, p. A4. And *Philanthropy Hall of Fame: Edward Harkness.* The Philanthropy Roundtable. Web. December 4, 2018. ⟨https://www.philanthropyroundtable.org/almanac/people/hall-of-fame/detail/edward-harkness⟩

[278] "An Eternal Asset for Humboldt and California." The *Humboldt Times.* September 13, 1931, p. 4.

[279] "Giant Redwoods of Bull Creek, Dyerville Forests Escape Axe of Woodman." *The Humboldt Times.* June 21, 1931, p. 5.

[280] "An Eternal Asset for Humboldt and California." *The Humboldt Times.* September 13, 1931, p. 4.

[281] "Big Redwoods Saved." *The Los Angeles Times.* June 24, 1931, p. A4.

[282] "Hundreds of Humboldters Join with Park Officials in Dedication Ceremonies." *The Humboldt Times.* September 15, 1931, p. 1.

[283] Widick, Richard. *Trouble in the Forest. California's Redwood Timber Wars*, p. 214.

[284] Flaherty, Frank F. "Thousands See Bull Creek Redwood Park Dedication." *The Humboldt Standard.* September 14, 1931, pp. 1,15.

[285] "Hundreds of Humboldters Join with Park Officials in Dedication Ceremonies." *The Humboldt Times.* September 15, 1931, pp. 1, 3.

[286] "A.P. Stokes is dead at his City Home." *The New York Times.* June 29, 1913.

[287] Brawley, Edward Allan. *Speaking Out for America's Poor. The Life And Work of Robert Hunter.* Humanity Books. 2007, p. 11.

[288] Hunter, Caroline. Save the Redwoods League Collection. BANC MSS 88/15C. Bancroft Library, University of California at Berkeley.

[289] "Mrs. Robert Hunter, Conservationist, 86." *The New York Times.* July 8, 1964.

[290] Warren, Laurence R. *The Development of the Memorial Grove System in Humboldt Redwoods State Park,* p. 42.

[291] *Memo on Dedication of "Children's Forest"–May 17, 1941.* Save the Redwoods League Collection. BANC MSS 88/15C. Bancroft Library, University of California at Berkeley.

[292] Schlappi, Elizabeth Roe. *Saving the Redwoods,* pp. 60-61.

[293] Warren, Laurence R. *The Development of the Memorial Grove System in Humboldt Redwoods State Park,* p. 42.

[294] "Heavy Burden of Taxes to Hit Many." *The Humboldt Standard.* June 22, 1932, p. 1. (A lumber executive heading a Humboldt County Board of Supervisors committee on the local economy said he had never seen so many people unable to pay their taxes. Many feared the county might go bankrupt. In November 1932 the county voted for Franklin D. Roosevelt for president of the United States, the first time since 1860 it had supported a Democratic presidential candidate).

[295] Wiley, Rease M. "Gift Establishes Prairie Creek Park." *The Arcata Union.* March 11, 1932, p. 8. And *Philanthropy Hall of Fame: Edward Harkness.* The Philanthropy Roundtable.

[296] Newton Drury, Parks and redwoods, 1919–1971, interview conducted by Amelia R. Fry and Susan Schrepfer, 1959–1970, Sections 126-127.

[297] Schrepfer, Susan R. *A Conservative Reform: Saving the Redwoods, 1917–1940,* p. 268.

[298] "New Grove Dedicated." *The Humboldt Standard.* May 1, 1933, p. 5.

[299] Mahan, Laura. *Annual Report of the President. Women's Save the Redwoods League of Humboldt County For Year 1930.* And *Annual Report of the President. Women's Save the Redwoods League of Humboldt County For The Year 1932.*

[300] "Redwood Grove Dedicated by Clubwomen." *The Humboldt Times.* May 1, 1933, p. 7.

[301] Williams, Georgia Russ. *REDWOODS.* Dedication program for the Humboldt Pioneer Memorial Grove. Save the Redwoods League. September 2, 1923, p. 17.

[302] "Mrs. Minnie Rutherford Fitzgerald, wife of W.A. Fitzgerald, publisher of the Stockton Independent, died here today." *The Oakland Tribune.* September 25, 1931, p. 22.

[303] Nye, Myra. "Altar Rites Impressive in Redwoods. Hearthstone Marks Grove That Women Saved for State." *The Los Angeles Times.* May 7, 1933, p. B6. And "Grove Bought by Federation. Tract to Be Made Memorial To California Women." *The Los Angeles Times.* March 8, 1931, p. B17.

[304] "The San Francisco Garden Club's Vignettes of Early San Francisco Homes and Gardens." Horthhistoria, 1935. Web. December 4, 2018. ⟨http://www.horthistoria.com/articles/articles_articles/articles_articles_the_sf_garden_clubs_vignettes⟩

[305] Starr, Walter A. "In Memoriam. Olive Holbrook Palmer." *Calif Hist Q J. Calif. Hist Soc.*Volume 37, No. 2. June 1958, p. 181.

[306] Colbruno, Michael. "Charles Holbrook (1830–1925): Mayor's race bet became part of Nevada lore." *Lives of the Dead: Mountain View Cemetery in Oakland.* April 8, 2017. Web. December 4, 2018. ⟨http://mountainviewpeople.blogspot.com/2017/04/charles-holbrook-1830–1925-mayors-race.html⟩

[307] Mendocino Coast Model Railroad & Historical Society. *Glen Blair. Mendocino County Coastal Redwoods. How They Were Felled, Moved and Milled.* Web. December 4, 2018. ⟨https://www.mendorailhistory.org/1_towns/towns/glen_blair.htm⟩ And Kelly House Museum. *Samuel Blair-1829–1897.* Web. December 4, 2018. ⟨https://mendocinohistory.pastperfectonline.com/byperson?keyword=Blair%2C+Samuel%2C+1829+-+1897⟩

[308] N. Gray and Company. Funeral Record. San Francisco. July 19, 1923.

[309] "Select Redwood Memorial Grove in Honor of Pioneer San Franciscans." *The Sausalito News.* November 2, 1934, p. 7.

[310] "Wealthy Pioneer Taken by Death." *The San Francisco Call.* July 24, 1912, p. 1.

[311] "Alfred Poett's Life is Closed." *The Santa Barbara Morning Press.* January 5, 1909, p. 3.

[312] "Select Redwood Memorial Grove in Honor of Pioneer San Franciscans." *The Sausalito News.* November 2, 1934, p. 7.

[313] Gregory, Tom. *History of Sonoma County, California, With Biographical Sketches.* Historic Record Co. 1911, p. 317.

[314] "Augustus Julliard. Philanthropist, 1836–1919." *The Biography.com Website.* Web. December 4, 2018. ⟨https://www.biography.com/people/augustus-juilliard-21226433⟩

[315] "Scrapbooks on S.F.'s Capt. Millen Griffith." LiveAuctioneers.com. Web. December 4, 2018. ⟨https://www.liveauctioneers.com/item/5487769_1080-scrapbooks-on-sf-s-captain-millen-griffith⟩

[316] Scales, Gary. "The Schmidell Family." *This Week in Ross.* Ross, California. January 2017. Web. December 4, 2018. ⟨http://thisweekinross.com/the-schmiedell-family⟩

[317] "Thomas O. Larkin. 1802–1858." Monterey County Historical Society. Web. December 4, 2018. ⟨http://mchsmuseum.com/larkin_thomaso.html⟩

[318] Warren, Laurence R. *The Development of the Memorial Grove System in Humboldt Redwoods State Park,* p. 45.

[319] Starr, Kevin. *The Dream Endures California Enters the 1940s.* Oxford University Press. 1997, pp. 115-116.

[320] "The Very Sad Death of Garland A. Dungan." *The Santa Rosa Press Democrat.* "April 14, 1911, p. 1.

[321] "Dungan Grove To Honor Two Pioneers." *The Humboldt Standard.* September 14, 1931, p. 17.

[322] Schlappi, Elizabeth Roe. *Saving the Redwoods*, p. 61. And "This Day in Jewish History. 1871: Dashing Yeast Baron Who Would Reform Cincinnati's Police Is Born." *Haaretz.* June 8, 2016.

[323] Braitman, Jacqueline R. "A California Stateswoman. The Public Career of Katherine Philips Edson." *California History.* Volume 65. Number 2. June 1986, pp. 82-95.

[324] Warren, Laurence R. *The Development of the Memorial Grove System in Humboldt Redwoods State Park.* 1966, p. 43.

[325] "To Some Old Friends." *The Humboldt Standard.* May 19, 1934, p. 2.

[326] Seale, William. *The Garden Club of America. 100 Years of a Growing Legacy*, p. 158.

[327] "Garden Club of America Dedicates Beautiful Redwood Grove." *The Humboldt Times.* May 22, 1934, p. 6

[328] Thorne, Helen. "Dedication of the Garden Club of America Redwood Grove." *The Bulletin.* The Garden Club of America. July 1934.

[329] Seale, William. *The Garden Club of America. 100 Years of a Growing Legacy*, pp. 52-53.

[330] Battles, Marjorie Gibbon, and Catherine Colt Dickey. *Fifty Blooming Years. The Garden Club of America*, p. 61.

[331] "Garden Club of America Dedicates Beautiful Redwood Grove." *The Humboldt Times.* May 22, 1934, pp. 1,6.

Afterword

[332] Lockwood, Frank C. *The Life of Edward E. Ayer.* A.C. McClurg and Company. 1929, p. 241.

[333] Rohde, Jerry, and Gisela Rhode. *Redwood National and State Parks Tales, Trails and Auto Tours.* MountainHome Books. 1994, p. 24.

[334] Burns, Emily E., et al. Save the Redwoods League. *State of Redwoods Conservation Report.* 2018, pp. 14, 20.

[335] Schrepfer, Susan R. *A Conservative Reform: Saving the Redwoods, 1917–1940*, pp. 256,326,340,354.

[336] California State Parks. *Del Norte Coast Redwoods State Park.* Web. December 4, 2018. ‹https://www.savetheredwoods.org/wp-content/uploads/DelNorte CoastRedwoods_12142011_web.pdf› And "The Race to Save the Last Old-Growth Redwood Forests on Earth." *KCET.* September 12, 2018. Web. December 4, 2018. ‹https://www.kcet.org/shows/california-coastal-trail/the-race-to-save-the-last-old-growth-redwood-forests-on-earth›

[337] DeLong, John Raymond. "*The Ravaged Remnant: A History of the Logging and Preservation of the California Coast Redwood.* 1968, pp. 211-213. And Schrepfer, Susan R. *The Fight to Save the Redwoods. A History of Environmental Reform 1917–1978*, pp. 76-78.

[338] Widick, Richard. *Trouble in the Forest. California's Redwood Timber Wars*, p. 215.

[339] Save the Redwoods League. *Annual Report. Rising to the Occasion. Accomplishments You Helped Make Possible.* 2015, pp.14-15. Web. December 4, 2018. ‹http://www.savetheredwoods.org/wp-content/uploads/2015-annual-report.pdf›

[340] Warren, Laurence R., *The Development Of The Memorial Grove System In Humboldt Redwoods State Park*, pp. 17,29-31. And Battles, Marjorie Gibbon, and Catherine Colt Dickey. *Fifty Blooming Years. The Garden Club of America*, p. 61. And Hodder, Sam. Chief Executive Officer. Save the Redwoods League. *Memorial Redwood Groves Honor the Men and Women of America's Armed Forces.* May 26, 2014. Web. December 4, 2018. ‹https://www.savetheredwoods.org/blog/path/memorial-redwood-groves-honor-the-men-and-women-of-americas-armed-forces›

[341] Save the Redwoods League. *Dedicated Groves.* Web. December 4, 2018. ‹https://www.savetheredwoods.org/donate/dedicate-a-redwood-grove-or-tree/dedicated-groves›

[342] Schrepfer, Susan R. *The Fight to Save the Redwoods. A History of Environmental Reform 1917–1978*, p. 108.

[343] Save the Redwoods League. *Avenue of the Giants Parkway.* Web. December 4, 2018. ‹https://www.savetheredwoods.org/about-us/mission-history/avenue-of-the-giants-parkway› And Engbeck, Jr., Joseph H. *State Parks of California From 1864 to the Present*, p. 103.

[344] Bearss, Edward C. National Park Service. Division of History. Office of Archaeology and Historic Preservation. Redwood National Park. History Basic Data. September 1, 1969. Web. December 4, 2018. ‹https://www.nps.gov/parkhistory/online_books/redw› And Schrepfer, Susan R. *The Fight to Save the Redwoods. A History of Environmental Reform 1917–1978*, p. 158.

[345] "Redwood National Park Expansion Approved as President Signs Bill." *The New York Times.* March 28, 1978.

[346] California Commission on State Government Organization and Economy. *Beyond Crisis: Recapturing Excellence in California's State Park System.* March 2013, p. 37.

[347] "The Redwood Forests. Saved at a Price." *The Economist.* March 4, 1999. And Rogers, Paul. "A decade after Headwaters deal, truce comes to Northern California redwood country." *The San Jose Mercury News.* March 5, 2009. Web. December 4, 2018. ‹https://www.mercurynews.com/2009/03/05/a-decade-after-headwaters-deal-truce-comes-to-northern-california-redwood-country›

[348] Save the Redwoods League. *Centennial Vision for Redwoods Conservation.* 2018, p. 9. Web. December 4, 2018. ‹https://www.savetheredwoods.org/wp-content/uploads/Centennial-Vision-final-web.pdf›

[349] Burns, Emily E., et al. Save the Redwoods League. *State of Redwoods Conservation Report*. 2018, p. 29.

[350] Save the Redwoods League. *Parks*. Web. December 4, 2018. ‹https://www.savetheredwoods.org/what-we-do/our-work/partner/parks›

Epilogue

[351] "Dr. Clara Burdette, 98, Women's Leader, Dies." *The Los Angeles Times*. January 7, 1954, p.2.

[352] "Mrs. Kate L. Harpst Succumbs." *The Humboldt Times*. February 24, 1929. And "Death Comes for Mrs. F.W. Georgeson." *The Humboldt Standard*. May 7, 1936, p.1. And "Widely Known Matron is Mourned." *The Humboldt Standard*. January 12, 1940, p. 1. And "Former Eureka Woman is Dead." *The Humboldt Times*. February 11, 1948, p. 9.

[353] "Mrs. Jas. P. Mahan Succumbs in San Francisco." *The Humboldt Times*. February 7, 1937, p. 2. And "Friends Pay Last Tribute to Mrs. Mahan." *The Humboldt Standard*. February 10, 1937, p. 11. And "James P. Mahan, Prominent Eureka Attorney, Passes." *The Humboldt Times*, February 11, 1937, p. 1. And "Student Aid Fund Created By Mrs. Mahan." *The Humboldt Standard*. February 24, 1937.

[354] Preston, Richard. *The Tall Trees. A Story of Passion and Daring*. Random House, 2007, p. 87.

[355] "Injuries Fatal to Aged Woman." *The Humboldt Standard*. June 23, 1932, p. 7.

[356] "Mrs. Annie Zane Murray, Born in Indian War Era, Is Taken by Death." *The Humboldt Times*. June 8, 1960, p. 3.

[357] "Mrs. Urquhart, Ex-Head of Women's Clubs, Dies." *The Los Angeles Times*. January 14, 1960, p. 26.

[358] "Mrs. Robert Hunter, Conservationist, 86." *The New York Times*. July 8, 1964.

[359] "Mrs. Philip Lansdale Dies at 92." *The Daily Independent Journal*. San Rafael, California. February 2, 1962, p. 4.

[360] Find a Grave Memorial. *Aurelia Isabel Henry Reinhardt*.

[361] Find a Grave Memorial. *Helen Seymour Stafford Thorne*. And The Garden Club of America. *GCA Medals. Mrs. Oakleigh Thorne Medal*.

[362] Engbeck, Jr., Joseph H. *State Parks of California From 1864 to the Present.*, pp. 83-95; and "Newton Drury, Conservationist Who Led Redwood Drive, Dies." *The New York Times*. December 16, 1978.

[363] Biographical Directory of the United States Congress. *Raker, John Edward, 1863–1926*.

[364] Rogers, Paul. "A decade after Headwaters deal, truce comes to Northern California redwood country."

[365] "Henry A. Crabb, Filibuster and the San Diego Herald." *The Journal of San Diego History*. San Diego Historical Society Quarterly. Volume 19, Number 1. Winter 1973. And Fitzgerald, Michael. "Stockton's History of Slavery." *The Stockton*

Record. January 9, 1911. And Lapp, Rudolph M. "Negro Rights Activities in Gold Rush California." The Virtual Museum of The City of San Francisco.

Appendix A

[366] Binkely, Cameron. *No Better Heritage than Living Trees: Women's Clubs and Early Conservation in Humboldt County*, p. 188.

Appendix B

[367] Save the Redwoods League Records. BANC MSS 88/15 c. Carton 81, Folder 12. Courtesy of the Bancroft Library, The University of California, Berkeley.

Bibliography

Books

Barbour, Michael; Lyndon, Sandy; Borchert, Mark; Popper, Marjorie; Whitworth, Valerie; and Evarts, John. *Coast Redwood A Natural and Cultural History*. Cachuma Press, 2011.

Battles, Majorie and Dickey, Catherine Colt. *Fifty Blooming Years 1913-1963*. The Garden Club of America, 1963.

Beach, Patrick. *A Good Forest For Dying: The Tragic Death of a Young Man on the Front Lines of the Environmental Wars*. Knopf Doubleday Publishing Group, 2003.

Cherny, Robert W; Irwin, Mary Ann; Wilson, Ann Marie. (Editors) *California Woman and Politics. From the Gold Rush to the Great Depression*. University of Nebraska Press. 2011.

Clar, C. Raymond. *California Government and Forestry. From Spanish Days Until the Creation of the Department of Natural Resources in 1927*. Division of Forestry. California Department of Natural Resources, 1959.

Collier, Peter and Horowitz, David. *The Rockefellers: An American Dynasty*. Holt, Rinehart and Winston, 1976.

de Vries, Carolyn. *That Grand and Ancient Forest*. Valley Publishers, 1978

Dewitt, John B. *California Redwood Parks and Preserves*. Save the Redwoods League, 1993.

Dunning, Joan. *From the Redwood Forest. Ancient Trees and the Bottom Line: A Headwaters Journey*. Chelsea Green Publishing Co., 1998.

Engbeck, Jr., Joseph D. *State Parks of California from 1864 to the Present.* Graphic Arts Center Publishing Co., 1980.

Engbeck, Jr., Joseph D. *The Enduring Giants.* The California Department of Parks and Recreation, 1973.

Farmer, Jared. *Trees in Paradise.* W.W. Norton & Company, Inc., 1974.

Fox, Stephen. *John Muir and His Legacy. The American Conservation Movement.* Little, Brown and Co., 1981.

Harris, David. *The Last Stand: The War Between Wall Street and Main Street over California's Ancient Redwoods.* Sierra Club Books, 1996.

Hays, Samuel P. *Conservation and the Gospel of Efficiency. The Progressive Conservation Movement 1890-1920.* University of Pittsburgh Press, 1958.

Hill, Julia Butterfly. *The Legacy of Luna. The Story Of A Tree, A Woman, And The Struggle To Save The Redwoods.* HarperOne, 2001.

Hyde, Philip and Leydet, Francois. *The Last Redwoods.* The Sierra Club, 1963.

Ise, John. *Our National Park Policy: A Critical History.* John Hopkins Press, 1961.

Lillard, Richard G. *The Great Forest.* Alfred A. Knopf, 1947.

Musil, Robert K. *Rachel Carson and Her Sisters. Extraordinary Women Who Have Shaped America's Environment.* Rutgers University Press, 2014.

O'Hara, Susan J.P. and Service, Alex. *Mills of Humboldt County.* Arcadia Publishing, 2016.

O'Hara, Susan J.P.; Service, Alex; Fortuna Depot Museum. *Northwestern Pacific Railroad. Eureka to Willits. Images of Rail.* Arcadia Publishing, 2013.

Pearsall, Clarence; Murray, George; Tibbetts, A.C.; Neall, Harry. *The Quest for Qual-A-Wa-Loo, A Collection of Diaries and Historical Notes.* The Holmes Book Company, 1943.

Preston, Richard. *The Wild Trees: A Story of Passion and Daring.* Random House, 2008.

Puter, Steven and Stevens, Horace. *Looters of the Public Domain.* Portland Printing House, 1908.

Rhode, Jerry. *Both Sides of the Bluff. History of Humboldt County Places: I.* MountainHome Books, 2014.

Rhode, Jerry and Gisela. *Humboldt Redwoods State Park. The Complete Guide.* Miles & Miles, 1992.

Schrepfer, Susan R. *The Fight To Save The Redwoods.* The University of Wisconsin Press, 1983.

Seale, William. *The Garden Club of America 100 Years of a Growing Legacy.* Smithsonian Books, 2012.

Shankland, Robert. *Steve Mather of the National Parks.* Knopf, 1951.

Shepherd, Marvin. *A Scottish Syndicate in the Redwoods.* Georgie Press, 2015.

Starr, Kevin. *Endangered Dreams: The Great Depression in California.* Oxford University Press, 1996.

Starr, Kevin. *Inventing the Dream: California Through the Progressive Era.* Oxford University Press, 1985.

Tilden, Freeman. *The State Parks: Their Meaning in American Life.* Alfred A. Knopf, 1962.

Wallace, David Rains. *Redwood: Official National and State Parks Handbook.* U.S. Department of the Interior, National Park Service, Division of Publications, 1998.

Widick, Richard. *Trouble in the Forest: California's Redwood Timber Wars.* The University of Minnesota Press, 2009.

Williams, Michael. *Americans and Their Forests: A Historical Geography (Studies in Environment and History).* Cambridge University Press, 1992.

Academic Works and Papers

Amodio, John J. *Save the Redwoods: 1919-1925 The Humboldt County Redwood Movement.* Humboldt State University, 1980.

Cohen, Shana Miriam. *American Garden Clubs and the Fight for Nature Preservation 1890-1980.* University of California, Berkeley, 2005.

DeLong, John Raymond. *The Ravaged Remnant.* San Francisco State University, 1968.

Merchant, Carolyn. *Women of the Progressive Movement. 1910-1916.* University of California, Berkeley, 1984.

Schlappi, Eliazabeth Roe. *Saving the Redwoods.* University of California, Berkeley, 1958.

Shrepfer, Susan R. *A Conservative Reform: Saving the Redwoods, 1917 to 1940.* University of California, Riverside, 1971.

Speece, Darren Frederick. *Defending Giants. The Battle Over Headwaters Forest and the Transformation of American Environmental Politics, 1850-1999.* University of Maryland, College Park, 2010.

Warren, Laurence. *The Development of the Memorial Grove System in Humboldt Redwoods State Park.* Sacramento State College, 1966.

Yaryan, William S. *Saving The Redwoods: The Ideology And Political Economy Of Nature Preservation*. University of California, Santa Cruz, 2002.

Oral Histories

Newton Drury, Parks and redwoods, 1919-1971, interview conducted by Amelia R. Fry and Susan Schrepfer, 1959-1970. Oral History Center, The Bancroft Library, University of California, Berkeley, 1972.

Periodicals

Binkley, Cameron. "No Better Heritage than Living Trees: Women's Clubs and Early Conservation in Humboldt County." *The Western Historical Quarterly*, Utah State University on behalf of the Western History Association. Volume 33, No. 2., Summer 2002.

Fritz, Emanuel. "California Coast Redwood: (Sequoia Sempervirens) Extracts from books, pamphlets, reports, periodicals and newspapers in the libraries of the University of California," 1935.

Grant, Madison. "Saving the Redwoods." *The National Geographic Magazine*. National Geographic Society, June 1920.

Grant, Madison. "Special Redwoods Number. Saving the Redwoods. An Account of the Movement During 1919 to Preserve the Redwoods of California." *Zoological Society Bulletin*. New York Zoological Society, September 1919.

Osborn, Henry Fairfield. "Sequoia, the Auld Lang Syne of Trees." *Natural History*. American Museum of Natural History. Volume XIX. No. 6, 1919.

Perrott, John. "Pioneer Humboldt Perrott Family." (Part One). *Humboldt Historian*, Summer 2006.

Perrott, John. "Pioneer Humboldt Perrott Family." (Part Two). *Humboldt Historian*, Fall 2006.

Putnam, Edna Hildebrand. "The Oldest Living Thing in the World." *Travel*, August 1920.

The Arcata Union.

The Bulletin. The Garden Club of America.

The Clubwoman. California Federation of Women's Clubs.

The Humboldt Standard.

The Humboldt Times.

The Los Angeles Times.

The San Francisco Chronicle.

Government Documents

California Commission on State Government Organization and Economy. (Little Hoover Commission). *Beyond Crisis: Recapturing Excellence in California's State Park System*, March 2013.

Meinecke, E.P. *A Report Upon the Effect of Excessive Tourist Travel on the California Redwood Parks*. California State Printing Office, 1928.

Olmstead, Jr., Frederick Law. *Report of the Director of the Survey to the California State Park Commission*, December 31, 1928.

California Federation of Women's Clubs Documents

Gibson, Mary S. *A Record of Twenty-Five Years of the California Federation of Women's Clubs, 1900-1925*. California Federation of Women's Clubs, 1927.

60 Year History. California Federation of Women's Clubs, 1961.

Humboldt County Women's Save the Redwoods League Documents

Save the Redwoods League – Humboldt County Group Collection. Organizational materials (financial, correspondence, meeting notes) that show the range of community involvement and some of the activities undertaken during the time the group was active, 1919-1934. Humboldt State Library–Special Collections–Humboldt Room.

Save the Redwoods League Documents

Hodder, Sam. "A League of Their Own: The Women Who Started Saving the Redwoods." *Giant Thoughts*. March 16, 2016.

Save the Redwoods League. *Centennial Vision for Redwoods Conservation*, 2018.

Save the Redwoods League. *Rising to the Occasion. Accomplishments You Helped Make Possible*. Annual Report 2015.

Save the Redwoods League. *State of Redwoods Conservation Report*, 2018.

INDEX

A

Albright, Horace, 48, 143, 195, 196
Alexander, Charles Beatty, 129, 204
Alexander, Harriet, 129
American Legion, 52, 97, 106, 120, 176
American Museum of Natural History, 27, 44, 196
Amodio, John J., 37, 111, 171, 189, 192-198, 201, 202
Arbor Day, 163
Arbor Day Grove, 163
Arcata Chamber of Commerce, 101
Armstrong, Colonel James, 27
Armstrong, Lizzie, 27
Armstrong Woods, 27, 87
Assembly Bill 80, 48, 50
Assembly Bill 106, 66
Atkinson, Mary Anne, 38, 83, 167
Avenue of the Giants, 31, 40, 48, 57, 70, 94, 128, 153, 164, 209
Ayer, Edward E., 59, 93, 161, 208

B

Badè, William Frederic, 49, 73, 90, 91, 115, 130, 131, 199, 202
Baldwin, Daniel, 97
Baldwin & McKinnon, 58
Barry, Annie Little, 149
Bedford Garden Club, 135
Bicknell, Carrie F., 65, 198
Big Basin Redwoods State Park, 123

Big Sur, 87, 123
Binkley, Cameron, 19, 34, 38, 171, 190-195, 202
Blair, Abigail, 152
Blair, Jennie, 152
Blair, Samuel, 152
Blair, William, 61, 152
Boardman, Bernice, 152
Boardman, Samuel H., 152
Bodega y Quadra, Juan Francisco de la, 4
Bolling, Colonel Raynal C., 51, 59, 175
Boulder Creek Mountain Echo, 11
Brawley, Edward Allan, 145, 205
Brown, Edmund Gerald, "Pat", 164
Brown, Madie, 145
Bulkley, Sarah, 156
Bull Creek Flat, 28, 36, 43, 60, 63-65, 67, 91, 94, 97, 104, 105, 111, 116, 120, 128, 134, 139, 141, 143, 144, 146, 170
Bulletin, The, 114-116, 135, 202, 208
Burdette, Clara, 17, 25, 34, 109, 110, 151, 167, 209
Burnham, Frederick Russell, 145

C

Calaveras Big Trees, 13, 14, 22, 66, 123, 129
Calaveras Grove Association, 119
California Club, 13, 14, 66
California Commission on State Government Organization and Economy, 121, 203, 209
California Federation of Women's Clubs, 8, 9, 17, 18, 20, 24, 26-28, 34, 41, 49-51,

55, 56, 66, 67, 69, 70, 81, 85, 109, 119-121, 137, 140, 143, 144, 149, 150, 157, 167, 168, 171, 191, 193, 196

California League of Women Voters, 155

California Legislature, 118, 162

California Redwood Company Ltd., 72

California Redwood Park, 47, 87, 123

California State Automobile Association, 119

California State Board of Forestry, 53, 89, 128

California State Highway Commission, 41, 49, 52

California State Park Commission, 83, 94, 137, 140, 141, 148, 157, 167, 203

California State Park system, 119, 146, 156, 163, 203

Cannon, Joseph, 13

Canoe Creek, 134, 135

Carnegie Institution, 60

Carolan, Edgar, 153

Carolan, Emily, 153

Carolan, Herbert, 153

Carolan, James, 153

Carson, Mary Bell, 19

Carson Woods, 9, 10, 12, 13, 19, 20, 22, 25-30, 35, 36, 74, 81, 140, 141, 147, 164, 190, 192

Carter, Jimmy, 164

Cassatt, Mary, 130

Chapman, R.C., 58, 59

Churchill, Winston, 131

Clar, C. Raymond, 57, 128, 191, 194, 196-198

Clark, E.T., 117

Clarke, Crawford W., 153

Clarke, Emma, 153

Clarke, Laura, 153

Clarke, Minnie, 153

Clarke, Nellie, 153

Clarke, Philomen, 153

Clubwoman, The, 24, 26, 28, 56, 81, 191, 193, 197-199

Colby, William, 128, 144

Cole, George, 97

Connick, Arthur E., 50, 64, 121, 140

Copeland Report, 182

Crabb, Henry, 16

Crocker, Charles, 57, 129

Crocker, Ethel, 57, 190, 191, 204

Crocker, William H., 107, 129, 148, 191

Crosby, Henrietta, 75, 113, 116

Cummings, Frank, 48

Curry, W.J., 143

Cutler, Fletcher A., 47, 68

D

Daughters of the American Revolution, 163

Degas, Edgar, 130

Del Norte County Board of Supervisors, 98

DeLong, John Raymond, 162, 195, 200, 208

Devoy & Gillogly, 58

Dolbeer & Carson Company, 19

Don, David, 5

Douglas, Helen Gahagan, 162

Drury, Aubrey, 107

Drury, Newton B., 33, 47, 49, 56, 60, 75, 85, 90, 91, 95, 97, 102, 104, 107, 108, 119, 125, 132, 133, 139, 148-150, 162, 168-170, 196-198, 201-204, 206, 210

Dungan, Eleanor, 155, 207

Dungan, Garland, 155, 207

Dungan, Garland A., 133, 207

Dungan, Mary, 155, 207

Dyerville Flat, 36, 60, 62-65, 69, 70, 74, 83, 88-91, 94-99, 101-107, 109, 111, 116, 120, 122, 138-140, 145, 148, 149, 151, 155, 167, 170, 200, 201, 205

E

Ebell Club, 35, 109, 110

Edson, Katherine Phillips, 155, 208

Eel River, 28, 30, 31, 36, 40, 44, 48, 52, 57, 58, 60, 61, 63, 73, 100, 105, 109, 115, 122, 124, 126, 128, 129, 134, 138, 144, 146, 147, 149, 156, 163, 177, 187

Ellenwood, Fred A., 89

Emmert, John H., 109

Endlicke, Stephen, 5

Engbeck, Jr., Joseph H., 119, 193, 202, 203, 209, 210

Eureka Chamber of Commerce, 19, 22, 24, 35, 36, 47, 48, 55, 64, 68, 101, 102, 110, 141

Eureka Monday Club, 173

Eureka Realty Board, 101

Eureka Wednesday Club, 173

Eureka Women's Club, 19, 68, 97, 101, 150, 168, 198
Evans, Estelle, 138
Everman, Barton, 143
Exxon Valdez, 165

F

Fairbanks, Douglas, 109
Farwell, Fanny Day, 76, 115
Federal Act of 1853, 6
Federal Water Power Act, 114
Federated Commercial Bodies, 101
Felton, Charles N., 126, 203
Ferndale Enterprise, 94, 190
Ferndale Village Club, 10, 173
Fife, Sarah, 133
Fitzgerald, Minnie Rutherford, 151, 206
Fleischmann, Charles, 155
Fleischmann, Henrietta, 155
Fleischmann, Max C., 155
Flint, Benjamin, 97
Ford, Henry, 75
Franklin Delano Roosevelt Memorial National Forest, 162
Fraser, Gertrude, 40
Freeman, Emma, 43, 84
Fry, Amalia, 107

G

Gage, Henry, 14, 139
Garden Club of America, 8, 18, 40, 52, 74, 76, 85, 113-116, 118, 120, 126, 132-135, 137, 142, 144, 152, 155-158, 163, 168, 169, 171, 179-182, 185, 187, 189, 191, 197, 199, 202, 204, 208-210
General Federation of Women's Clubs, 17, 33, 69, 75, 104, 105, 157, 191, 197
Georgeson, Ella, 38, 83, 103, 150, 167
Georgeson, Frederick W., 24, 121, 131
Girard, James W., 117
Glen Blair Lumber Company, 61
Gombro, Frederick Bicknell, 65
Goodman, Ernestine Abercrombie, 18
Gould, Clara Hinton, 58
Gould, Frederick Saltonstall, 58
Graham, Jeanette, 40
Grant, Joseph D., 34, 64, 95, 104, 107, 132, 144, 157, 168

Grant, Madison, 27, 33, 36, 51, 52, 73, 143, 175, 196, 197
Graves, Henry, 35, 202
Great Depression, 96, 131, 137, 140, 147, 154, 169, 194
Griffith, Alice, 154
Griffith, Millen, 154, 207
Grinsell, Raymond, 139
Grosvenor, Gilbert, 92
Guiberson, Claire, 150

H

Hallelujah Chorus, 144, 151
Harding, Warren G., 69
Harper Lee, Ru-Flo, 31, 49, 197
Harpst, Kate, 38, 83, 103, 167
Hazelwood, Joseph, 165
Hearst Castle, 85, 149
Hearst, George, 126
Hearst, William Randolph, 66, 126
Heceta, Bruno de, 4
Henkel, Grace Rushing, 144
Hetch Hetchy, 92, 170, 193
Hickey, Edward Ritter, 59
Hickey, Emma, 59
Hickey, Henry B., 59, 143
Hill, Andrew P., 14, 191
Hill, Arthur W., 97
Holbrook, Charles H., 152
Holmes-Eureka Lumber Company, 30
Homestead Act, 6
House Joint Resolution 4, 24
House Joint Resolution 284, 23
Hoover, Herbert, 127, 142, 167
Hosford, Hester Eloise, 25
Houston, David, 35
Hoyt, Minerva, 76
Humboldt Beacon, 22, 30, 190
Humboldt County Board of Supervisors, 40, 44, 61, 89, 91, 94, 98, 99, 110, 148, 206
Humboldt County Women's Save the Redwoods League, 35, 38, 44, 46, 48-51, 60, 63, 64, 66-69, 82, 83, 89, 91, 97, 100, 103, 105, 110, 116, 120, 130, 140, 141, 143, 144, 147, 150, 151, 159, 167, 194-196, 199, 201
Humboldt Oratorio Chorus, 144
Humboldt Redwoods State Park, 40, 48, 52, 57, 65, 76, 83, 85, 88, 92, 95, 128, 129, 137-139, 143, 152, 154, 155, 163, 167-169,

175, 179, 185, 198, 204-208
Humboldt Standard, 12, 37, 38, 41, 71, 74, 84, 89, 102, 131, 133, 147, 150, 155, 167, 170, 190-193, 195, 199-202, 205-208, 210
Humboldt Times, 12, 21, 36, 67, 69, 87, 90, 95, 105, 107, 140, 141, 145, 150, 157, 168, 170, 192, 194, 195, 199-201, 205, 206, 208, 210
Hunter, Caroline, 143, 145, 163, 169, 205
Hunter, George W., 73
Hunter, Robert, 146, 205, 210
Hurwitz, Charles, 165

I

I Love You, California, 139

J

Jedediah Smith Redwoods State Park, 128, 163, 189
Jenkins, Mary, 155
Jepson, Willis Linn, 62, 198
Johnson, Lyndon B., 164
Joshua Hendy Grove, 123
Journal of Education, 22, 192
Julliard, Augustus, 207
Julliard, Charles Frederic, 153
Julliard, Isabel, 153

K

Kent, Elizabeth Thatcher, 15
Kent, William, 15, 33, 40, 58, 144, 196
Kilmer, Alfred Joyce, 138, 205
Knapp, Stout & Company, 128
Knight, Helen M., 25, 81, 193
Knight, Lora J., 93
Knight, Mary Holbrook, 154

L

Lane, Franklin K., 92, 93, 200
Lane, Vida, 11
Lansdale, Ethel, 52, 132, 133, 152, 169, 185
Lansdale, Philip, 53, 197, 210
Larkin, Alice, 154
Larkin, Thomas, 154
Law, Anna C., 35

Lawton, Elizabeth, 105, 172
Lea, Clarence, 36, 44
Lincoln, Abraham, 16
Little Hoover Commission, 203
Little River Redwood Company, 61
Lockwood, Elizabeth, 132-134, 156
Logan Estate, 58
Los Angeles Friday Club, 51
Los Angeles Times, 39, 69, 70, 75, 109, 142, 150, 152, 169, 194, 195, 197, 199, 202, 205, 206, 209, 210
Loveland, Mary, 10
Lynch, Lucy Moffitt, 133

M

MacDonald, Donald, 87, 89, 90, 106
Mahan, James, 83, 94, 107, 167
Mahan, Laura Perrott, 8, 20, 24, 25, 34, 37-40, 48-50, 55, 56, 59, 69, 70, 75, 77, 82, 83, 89-91, 94-97, 100-102, 104-107, 110, 120, 121, 130, 144, 145, 147, 148, 150, 151, 156, 159, 164, 167, 168, 199, 201, 206, 210
Mahan, Lawrence, 106
Marshall, James, 5
Martin, Elizabeth Price, 18
Mason, David T., 61, 88, 117, 198
Massachusetts Horticultural Society, 75
Masson, Alexander, 97, 102
Mather, Stephen T., 33, 40, 58, 66, 92, 115, 119, 123
McClellan, Hugh Webster, 40
McClellan, Martha, 40, 46, 59, 91, 147
McCrackin, Josephine Clifford, 14
McDuffie, Duncan, 118, 202
McDuffie, Jean Howard, 76, 115, 118
McFarland, J. Horace, 114, 202
McKinley, William, 13
Meinecke, Emilio P., 123, 203
Memorial Grove, 51-53, 58, 59, 69, 92, 98, 99, 109, 116, 128, 129, 138, 147, 152-155, 198-200, 204-208
Mendocino Lumber Company, 61
Merriam, John C., 27, 33, 60, 92, 143, 200
Meyer, Myra, 132, 135, 204
Mill Creek–Smith River Park, 123
Mills College, 20, 39, 82, 85, 137, 150, 157, 169, 179
Miller, William L., 48, 55, 68
Monet, Claude, 130

Monroe, Lucretia Anna Huntington, 38, 83
Montgomery Grove, 123
Moore, James Hobart, 93
Moore, Lora J., 93
Morehouse, Harold, 150
Morgan, Julia, 85, 149
Morris, George Pope, 11
Morton, J. Sterling, 163
Muir, John, 7, 13, 15, 24, 190, 193, 197, 199
Muir Woods National Monument, 15, 21, 87, 191
Murray, Annie Zane, 19, 37, 68, 105, 110, 144, 168, 173, 210
Murray, George D, 105
Murphy, Simon J., 63

N

National Archives, 163
National Geographic, 41, 92
National Roadside Council, 105
National Tribute Grove, 163
Native Daughters of the Golden West, 119, 137, 138, 142-144
Native Sons of the Golden West, 52, 74, 119, 139
Natural History, 27, 41, 44, 196
Neilson, Kate Felton, 126, 127
Nelson, Hans, 98
New England Wildflower Preservation Society, 75
New York Metropolitan Museum of Art, 145
New York Zoological Society, 27, 41, 175, 196
North Dyerville Flat, 69, 83, 89, 91, 94, 97, 99, 101, 104, 106, 107, 145
Northwestern Pacific Railroad, 30
Nye, Myra, 69, 150, 194, 195, 197, 199, 202, 206

O

Olmstead, Frederick Erskine, 97
Olmstead, William Law, 119
Olmstead, Jr., William Law, 119
O'Melveny, Henry W., 142
Orr, Eliza A., 24
Osborn, Henry Fairfield, 27, 33, 44, 143, 196

P

Pacific Lumber Company, 8, 20, 29, 49, 50, 60-64, 69, 83, 87-90, 94-102, 104-108, 116, 119, 120, 139-143, 145, 148, 164, 170
Palace Hotel, 36, 90, 118
Palmer, Olive Holbrook, 133, 152, 206
Palmquist, Peter, 43
Pasadena Star News, 204
Patrick, Nehemiah, 72
Perrott, Laura, 38, 82, 83, 110
Perrott, Luella, 39
Perrott, Sarah Jane, 40, 59, 91, 147, 195
Perrott, William, 39, 59
Pershing, John J., 44
Perske, Louis, 133, 204
Peterson, Lily, 138
Phillips, John C., 59
Pickford, Mary, 109
Pinchot, Gifford, 25
Poett, Genevieve Carolan, 153
Poett, Henry, 153
Point Lobos Association, 119
Portolá Gaspar de, 4
Prairie Creek Redwoods State Park, 47, 71, 87, 148, 170
Pratt, Merritt B., 109, 128
Preemption Act of 1841, 6
Progressive Era, 15, 26, 33, 68, 145
Proposition 4, 120
Putnam, Edna Hildebrand, 45, 196

Q

Quinn, Irwin, 106

R

Raker, John, 23, 170, 210
Reddington Report, 47
Redwood Highway, 31, 36, 45, 47, 49, 53, 56, 58-61, 63-65, 69, 91, 98, 99, 103, 122, 126, 131, 134, 138, 146, 149, 164, 168
Redwood National and State Parks, 8, 71, 125, 164, 208
Redwood National Park, 8, 10, 12, 13, 19, 20, 23, 25, 28, 29, 36, 37, 46-48, 50, 91, 96, 141, 163, 164, 192, 209
Redwood Preservation Bill, 56-58, 68, 129

Reinhardt, Aurelia, 85, 137, 157, 179
Richardson, Friend, 67, 69
Rockefeller, Jr., John D., 104, 141, 142, 191
Rockefeller, Laura Celestia Spelman, 141
Rohde, Gisela, 161
Rohde, Jerry, 171, 208
Rolph, James "Sunny Jim", 154
Roosevelt, Franklin D., 76, 85, 162, 169, 193, 206
Roosevelt, Theodore, 7, 13, 31, 92
Rosenshine, Albert A., 66
Ross, Lillian, 147, 193
Royles, Anna L., 9, 26, 193
Russ, Joseph, 71-73, 199
Russ Park, 71
Russ, Zipporah, 71-74, 91, 147
Ryan, Minnie, 20, 35

S

Sage, Henry W., 98, 201
Sage Land and Improvement Company, 99, 139, 143
Sage, Susan Elizabeth, 98
Sage, William H., 98, 99
San Francisco Call, 22, 153, 207
San Francisco Chronicle, 13, 14, 118, 161, 190, 194, 197, 202
San Jose Mercury News, 209
Santa Barbara Morning Press, 153, 204, 207
Santa Paula Women's Club, 110
Sausalito News, 153, 207
Save the Redwoods League, 8, 28, 29, 32-38, 40-42, 44-53, 57, 59-64, 66-69, 71-74, 76, 82, 83, 85, 88-93, 95-97, 100, 102-107, 109-111, 114-120, 125, 127, 129, 130, 132, 134, 137, 139-148, 150-152, 154, 156, 157, 159, 162-165, 167, 169, 171, 175, 189, 190, 193-197, 199-201, 203-206, 208, 209, 211
Schloss, Adella T., 28, 34, 193
Schmiedell, Edward, 154
Schmiedell, Henry, 154
Schrepfer, Susan R., 25, 63, 91, 107, 117, 163, 171, 192, 193, 196-203, 205, 206, 208, 209
Schurz, Carl, 17
Schwarz, George Frederick, 99
Scott, Margaret, 74, 199
Seale, William, 134, 189, 191, 197, 199, 204, 208

Sempervirens Club, 8, 14, 52, 119
Senate Bill 64, 48
Senate Bill 441, 118
Sequoyah, Chief, 5
Shaler, William, 3, 4
Shankland, Robert, 43, 196, 197
Sherman, Mary Belle King, 75, 104
Shields, Clara, 110
Sierra Club, 49, 52, 73, 119, 198
Silence, Frank, 37, 83
Smith, Jedediah Strong, 5
Smith, Sidney Mason, 53
South Dyerville Flat, 62, 88, 89, 99, 102, 104, 107, 155
South Fork of the Eel River, 28, 30, 31, 36, 40, 44, 48, 52, 57, 58, 60, 61, 63, 73, 100, 109, 115, 124, 126, 128, 129, 134, 138, 144, 146, 147, 149, 156, 163
Spacious Firmament on High, The, 150
Spanish Flu, 31, 59
Speece, Darren, 88, 171, 195, 196, 200
Sperry, J.P., 107
Sproul, Robert G., 24
Standish and Hickey, 58, 59
Stanford University, 14, 15, 20, 68, 123, 126, 141, 197, 203
Starr, Kevin, 129, 154, 207
State of California, 6, 42, 46, 47, 53, 63, 89-91, 95, 102, 114, 116, 128, 129, 134, 135, 150, 156, 163-165, 168, 191, 198, 205
Stephens, Flora, 51, 197
Stephens, William, 28, 41, 57
Stewart, Anne, 132, 133, 156, 204
Stockton Independent, 70, 206
Stoddard, Melinda, 58
Stokes, Anson Phelps, 145
Stout, Allison, 127
Stout, Calista, 127
Stout, Clara Wales, 127, 128
Stout, Eleanor, 127
Stout, Frank D., 128, 203
Stout, Katherine, 127
Strauss, Nathan, 75
Sutherland, Gilbert, 102

T

Thomson, Charles, 143
Timber and Stone Act, 6, 72
Timberman, The, 13, 28, 29, 31, 51, 190
Timlow, Evelyn Carolan, 153

Toll, Eleanor Margaret, 35, 109
Tolppanen, Bradley P., 131, 204
Travel magazine, 41, 45
Trees (poem), 110, 138

U

Union Lumber Company, 61
University of California, 24, 27, 47, 50, 62,
118, 175, 190-192, 196-198, 200, 202, 203,
205, 206, 211
Urquhart, Augusta, 70, 109, 150
U.S. Forest Service, 16, 22, 24, 25, 35, 47,
49, 53, 99, 123, 162
U.S. National Park Service, 77, 191

V

Vance Bottom, 40, 58
Vancouver, George, 4
Van Duzen River Park, 123
Van Duzer, Sarah Jane, 39

W

Wales, Calista, 127
Walter, Carrie Stevens, 14
Wells, Willard, 44
Whistler, James Abbott McNeill, 130
White, Lovell, 190
Whittemore, Harris, 129, 131
Whittemore, John Howard, 130
Whittemore, Justine, 129, 130
Wilbur, Ray Lyman, 126, 141, 203
Williams, Alice Gertrude, 133
Williams, Georgia Russ, 55, 144, 151, 206
Williams, Solon H., 56, 128, 198
Wilson, Woodrow, 24, 25, 92
Winter, Alice Ames, 75, 105
Woman's Club of Hollywood, 109
Woodridge, Edith, 22
Woodman, Spare That Tree, 11
Wright, T.M., 48

Y

Young, Clement, 119